T0319479

No Great Wall

HARVARD EAST ASIAN MONOGRAPHS 397

No Great Wall

*Trade, Tariffs, and Nationalism
in Republican China, 1927–1945*

Felix Boecking

Published by the Harvard University Asia Center
Distributed by Harvard University Press
Cambridge (Massachusetts) and London 2017

Printed in the United States of America

The Harvard University Asia Center publishes a monograph series and, in coordination with the Fairbank Center for Chinese Studies, the Korea Institute, the Reischauer Institute of Japanese Studies, and other faculties and institutes, administers research projects designed to further scholarly understanding of China, Japan, Vietnam, Korea, and other Asian countries. The Center also sponsors projects addressing multidisciplinary and regional issues in Asia.

Library of Congress Cataloging-in-Publication Data
Names: Boecking, Felix, 1981–
Title: No Great Wall : trade, tariffs, and nationalism in Republican China, 1927–1945 / Felix Boecking.
Other titles: Harvard East Asian monographs ; 397.
Description: Cambridge, Massachusetts : Published by the Harvard University Asia Center, 2017. | Series: Harvard East Asian monographs ; 397 |
Includes bibliographical references and index.
Identifiers: LCCN 2016001553 | ISBN 9780674970601 (hardcover : alk. paper)
Subjects: LCSH: China--Economic policy—1912–1949. |
China—Commerce—History—20th century. | Tariff—China—History—
20th century. | Zhongguo guo min dang. | Sino-Japanese War, 1937–1945—
Economic aspect—China.
Classification: LCC HC427.8 .B64 2016 | DDC 382/.9095109041—dc23 LC record
available at http://lccn.loc.gov/2016001553

Index by the author

♾ Printed on acid-free paper

Last figure below indicates year of this printing
21 20 19 18 17

For my parents, with love and gratitude

Contents

Maps, Tables, and Figures

Maps

Tables

Figures

Acknowledgments

Questions of trade, tariffs, and nationalism are as relevant in today's world as they were for Guomindang politicians during the period under discussion in this book. I started to think about these important questions at the University of Cambridge, and it gives me great pleasure to thank Hans van de Ven for his patient, thorough, and extensive support and guidance, without which I never could have done the work on which this book is based. Likewise, I thank Robert Bickers, Martin Daunton, Joseph P. McDermott, and Rana Mitter, whose comments on my work did so much to shape its direction.

I wrote this book while enjoying the benefits of the late Dr. An Wang's generosity, as an An Wang Postdoctoral Fellow at the Fairbank Center for Chinese Studies at Harvard University. Like others before me, I found the Fairbank Center to be a stimulating, welcoming, and supportive environment in which to work, and it is hard to find adequate words to express my gratitude for the opportunity I was given. I am especially grateful to the Fairbank Center's former director, William C. Kirby; former acting director, Mark C. Elliott; and former associate director, Lydia Chen, and all her colleagues, for making the Fairbank Center my academic home during the year of my fellowship. In addition, Henrietta Harrison, Elisabeth Köll, Michael Szonyi, and Ezra F. Vogel were all generous with their time and advice, and to them, too, I am deeply grateful.

My doctoral studies were made possible by a studentship funded by the Arts and Humanities Research Council, award APN 16,296, "The History of the Chinese Maritime Customs Service, 1854–1949," which it is my pleasure to acknowledge with gratitude. I also thank the Cambridge European Trust and the St. Catharine's College Graduate

Travel Fund for additional financial support of my research, and the Carnegie Trust for the Universities of Scotland, the Universities' China Committee in London, and the University of Edinburgh's Hayter Fund for subsequent research support. Huang Chengfeng and Robert Daly welcomed me back to the Hopkins-Nanjing Center for Chinese and American Studies as a doctoral student when I was conducting my research.

I am grateful to the directors and archivists of the Second Historical Archives of China, Nanjing; Shanghai Municipal Archives; Bundesarchiv, Department R, Berlin; Harvard University Archives, Cambridge, Massachusetts; Politisches Archiv des Auswärtigen Amtes, Berlin; The National Archives, Public Record Office, Kew; and to the librarians and staff of the Beijing University Library; the Chinese Department, Commonwealth Reading Room, and Munby Rare Books Room of the Cambridge University Library; Faculty of Asian and Middle Eastern Studies Library, University of Cambridge; Edinburgh University Library; Fung Library, Harvard-Yenching Library, Harvard Law School Library, Pusey Library, and Widener Library, Harvard University; Hoover Institution Archives, Stanford, California; Antiquarian Books Section, Nanjing Municipal Library; History Faculty Library, Nanjing University; Nanjing University Library; National Library of Scotland, Edinburgh; East Asian History of Science Library, Needham Research Institute, University of Cambridge; China Studies Library, Dickson Poon Center for China Studies, University of Oxford; and Shanghai Municipal Library.

I am also grateful to Robert Bickers, Donna Brunero, Jamie Carstairs, Federica Casalin, Chang Chih-yun, Chong Ja-Ian, Federica Ferlanti, Stephen Halsey, Patricia and Gerald Hayward, Jonathan Howlett, Jiang Ruiwen, Catherine Ladds, Nigel Lawford, Li Wenjie, Lian Xinhao, Marjory Lobban, Anne Reinhardt, Philip Thai, Shenxiao Tong, Aurora Tsai, Ts'ai Wei-pin, Hans van de Ven, Jim Williams, Wong Chunwai, Zhang Sheng (Nanjing University), and Zhang Sheng (Xiamen University), as well as to the European Commission Representation in the United Kingdom, for their assistance in obtaining rare materials, and I thank Patricia Hayward for her kind permission to quote from unpublished materials.

I thank the late Norman D. Apter, Ian Cooper, Rachel S. Core, Federica Ferlanti, Patrick Flack, Madeline Graham, Stephen Halsey,

Barak Kushner, Rachel Leow, Tabitha G. Mallory, Regina Sachers, and Joe Studwell for reading and commenting on one or more draft chapters of my dissertation. Marc Szepan cheerfully and thoroughly read through the entire book manuscript and provided invaluable advice.

In writing this book, I have greatly benefited over the years from conversations with and conference comments from Jennifer Altehenger, the late Norman D. Apter, Evelyn V. Boettcher, Martin Chick, Dai Yifeng, Martin Daunton, Devon M. Dear, Andrew S. Erickson, Federica Ferlanti, Patrick Flack, Luke Forsyth, Wendy Jiachen Fu, Marina Frasca-Spada, James Z. Gao, Karl Gerth, the late Christina Gilmartin, Madeline and David Graham, Stephen Halsey, Joshua B. Hill, Jonathan Howlett, Hu Mingfu, Miriam Kingsberg, Elisabeth Köll, Barak Kushner, Christopher Leighton, Greg Lewis, Lian Xinhao, Ma Jun, Tehyun Ma, Stephen R. McKinnon, Ian M. Miller, Rana Mitter, John Moffett, Stephen Morgan, Kenneth L. Pomeranz, Thomas G. Rawski, Elizabeth J. Remick, Ren Zhiyong, James Riedel, Robert S. Ross, Regina Sachers, Eric Schluessel, Monika Scholz, Florian Schui, Se Yan, Shen Xiaoyun, Julia C. Strauss, Marc Szepan, Edna Tow, Ts'ai Wei-pin, Rudolf Wagner, Wang Jingnian, Wang Yuru, Jim Williams, R. Bin Wong, Ying Qian, Lily Zhang, and Zhang Yinming. I am also very grateful to Parks M. Coble and a second, anonymous reviewer of my manuscript for their insightful and constructive comments.

In the course of conducting my research and writing this book, I enjoyed the hospitality of Hans-Henning Blomeyer-Bartenstein, Maria Day and the late Bob McLaughlin, Joshua Dominick, Stephen Halsey, Henrietta Harrison, Hu Mingfu, Jonathan E. Keller, Klaus Moehring, George Pasteur, and Karen and David Squire. Luke and Robert Forsyth generously provided IT assistance when it was most needed, and Rachel Core, David Dorson, and Hsu Kun saved my second research trip to China from a disastrous end. Madeline Graham and Marc di Tommasi kindly prepared the graphs, C. Scott Walker of the Harvard Map Collection of the Harvard College Library provided me with superb maps, and Anthony Lee designed a beautiful dust jacket. It is my pleasure to thank them all for their help.

Some of the material presented in this book has appeared in print before. I am grateful to the editors of *Modern Asian Studies* for permission to use material from "Unmaking the Chinese Nationalist State:

Administrative Reform among Fiscal Collapse, 1937–1945," *Modern Asian Studies* 45, no. 2 (2011); the editors of the *Harvard Asia Quarterly* for permission to use material from "The Bitterness of Fiscal Realism: Guomindang Tariff Policy, China's Trade in Imported Sugar, and Smuggling, 1928–1937," *Harvard Asia Quarterly* 13, no. 2 (Summer 2011); and the editors of *Frontiers of History in China* for permission to use material from my coauthored article with Monika Scholz, "Did the Nationalist Government Manipulate the Chinese Bond Market? A Quantitative Perspective on Short-term Price Fluctuations of Domestic Government Bonds, 1932–1934," *Frontiers of History in China* 10, no. 1 (2015). I thank the Ministry of Finance of the Republic of China for permission to use the calligraphy by Chiang Kai-shek that appears on the dust jacket, and the Historical Photographs of China Project for permission to use the photograph that forms the basis of the silhouette on the jacket. At the Harvard East Asia Monograph Series, I had the good fortune to work with Bob Graham, William Hammell, and Kristen Wanner, for whose patient encouragement I am immensely grateful. I am also very grateful to Julie Hagen for her meticulous editing of the manuscript.

Besides Harvard, two other universities played important roles in enabling me to complete this book. At my home institution, the University of Edinburgh, Sharon Adams, Martin Chick, Gayle Davis, David Greasley, Trevor Griffiths, and Stephen McDowall tirelessly (and sometimes ceaselessly) encouraged me to work on my manuscript. Ewen Cameron and Alvin Jackson kindly facilitated the prolonged absence of a junior colleague. I finished the doctoral dissertation on which this book is based while serving as a temporary lecturer in East Asian history at Newcastle University. I thank all my former colleagues there in the School of Historical Studies, particularly Jeremy Boulton, Keith Brewster, Martin Farr, David Saunders, and Naomi Standen, for providing a very supportive environment and for encouraging my completion of the dissertation.

Like many other young scholars, I remember the late Christina Gilmartin's interest in my work with gratitude. Claudia Ebrecht, Claus Ebrecht, and Bob McLaughlin did not live to see me finish the manuscript for this book but they always thought I had it in me to write it, even when I did not think so myself. It is likely that I could have written this book without my Massachusetts family, Maria Day and the late Bob McLaughlin, but I am glad I did not have to, and grateful for their warm welcome to New England. Norman D. Apter and I shared much of our archival work in Nanjing, and I mourn the fact that we will never be able to discuss the books arising from the work we conducted that winter. In Edinburgh and beyond, Jennifer Altehenger, Robert Bickers, Gayle Davis, Amanda Forsyth, Sebastian Gehrig, Madeline and David Graham, Naomi Haynes, Kristian Kerr, Stephen McDowall, Rana Mitter, Saeyoung Park, Rochna Poddar, Alexandra Rawe, and Marc Szepan helped me across the finish line.

Above all, I thank my parents, to whom I dedicate this book with love and gratitude.

Edinburgh, July 2016

Notes on the Text

I refer to the Chinese Maritime Customs Service (海關) by the abbreviated name Maritime Customs, to distinguish that institution from another agency, the Native Customs (常關), which collected tariffs on domestic trade. I use the terms Inspectorate General of Customs, inspector general of customs, commissioner of customs, custom house, and Customs Appraising Department as they were used at the time. In this book, they refer to the Maritime Customs Service unless specifically noted otherwise.

Throughout the book, the dollar sign ($) refers to Chinese dollars. United States currency is distinguished as US$.

Romanization

With the exception of the names of major historical figures for whom different romanizations have become established in the English language and individuals who chose a different romanization of their name when publishing in English, Pinyin romanization is used for Chinese names in this text.

Abbreviations

The following abbreviations are used for certain archival and government sources cited in the footnotes. Complete reference information can be found in the Bibliography.

BDFA   *British Documents on Foreign Affairs: Reports and Papers from the Foreign Office Confidential Print,* Part 2: *From the First to the Second World War,* ed. Barbara Trotter

DBFP   *Documents on British Foreign Policy, 1919–1939,* 2nd ser., vol. 8, ed. Rohan Butler and J. P. T. Bury

FO   Foreign Office: Political Departments: General Correspondence from 1906–1966, National Archives of the UK

FRUS   *Foreign Relations of the United States: Diplomatic Papers,* US Department of State

SHAC   Second Historical Archives of China, Nanjing (Inspectorate General of Maritime Customs Records)

SOAS   School of Oriental and African Studies, London (Sir Frederick Maze Papers)

No Great Wall

HARVARD EAST ASIAN MONOGRAPHS 397

Introduction

This book is about the tariff policy of the Chinese Nationalist government of Chiang Kai-shek. Tariffs were the single most important source of government revenue for the Nationalist government prior to the beginning of the Second Sino-Japanese War in 1937. When the Nationalists lost control of the eastern seaboard during the early stage of the war, they also lost control of this revenue source, with disastrous consequences for their finances. The Nationalist government's reliance on tariffs, which had proved such an asset to government finance before 1937, turned out to be a fault line at the heart of Nationalist governance. There was, however, another fault line: foreign influence. Having relied so heavily on tariffs to fund their regime, the Nationalists had no powerful defense against the Communists' claim that they had sold China out to the foreigners. Thus, this book is also about the dilemma of how a government can be nationalist when most of its revenue comes from tariffs on international trade.

Clearly, for the Nationalists, some accommodation had to be made: economic nationalism demanded infant-industry protection, and thus less foreign trade, but choking off foreign trade would be a disaster in revenue terms and could bring about the collapse of the government. Faced with this dilemma, the Guomindang, the ruling Chinese Nationalist Party, chose to compromise its commitment to economic nationalism in the interest of guaranteeing the medium political future with a stable stream of revenue. That compromise was feasible while the Guomindang controlled the eastern ports in China, where most tariff revenue originated. But when the Nationalists lost control of the eastern seaboard during the first few months of the Second Sino-Japanese War, they also lost control of their most important source of revenue at a time of burgeoning government expenditures to finance the war effort. To make up for the shortfall, the wartime Nationalist state resorted to older, more rapacious forms of taxation. As a result, it was politically discredited when the war came to an end in summer 1945, and its prewar accommodation of foreign trade seemed like yet another sellout. Nor was foreign trade the only policy anathema to doctrinaire nationalists that the prewar Nationalist state had accommodated. The Guomindang's political platform was based on restoring China to its former strength through a process of political and economic modernization. And yet for the majority of this period, the Guomindang relied on tariffs on China's international trade that were collected by a customs service dominated by foreigners.

Gaining control of tariff revenue was the first demonstrable achievement in the Guomindang's quest to become recognized as the legitimate government of the Republic of China by the foreign powers that, through bilateral treaties, had constrained China's sovereignty since the mid-nineteenth century. When the Guomindang ruled over the Republic of China from Nanjing during the period from 1927 to 1937, known as the Nanjing decade, tariffs provided as much as 40 percent of the central government's tax revenue, thus funding a large part of the Guomindang's political agenda. After the outbreak of the Second Sino-Japanese War, the Guomindang lost control over China's coastal regions, which produced 80 percent of tariff revenue, within the first nine months. The loss of this critical source of revenue propelled the Guomindang into adopting a harsh and unpopular deficit-driven fiscal policy. The Guomindang's resulting loss of political capital contributed to its defeat by the Communists in the Chinese Civil War of 1946–49 and helped bring an end to Guomindang governance on the Chinese mainland. Tariffs, thus, were essential to Guomindang governance.

To understand the policy choices of the Nationalist government, it is necessary to study tariffs as a part of Guomindang fiscal policy as well as the Nationalists' relationship with informal empire. I use the term "informal empire" to denote "an empire of trade and commerce and various degrees of informal political control," following Wm.

Roger Louis's definition.[1] With regard to China, this concept accounts for the fact that China remained "a non-partitioned, sovereign entity" even though "[the relationship] between Chinese society, economy and polity often demonstrates all the themes discernible in the processes of incorporation of African and Asian states into the European empires."[2] To analyze Guomindang tariff policy in isolation from informal empire would be to ignore a crucial policy choice that Nationalist leaders made in the late 1920s: to accommodate an informal imperial institution within the Nationalist polity in the interest of preserving and increasing government revenue and reassuring the foreign powers active in East Asia of the political reliability of the Guomindang. Having unsuccessfully attempted to declare tariff autonomy unilaterally in 1927, Nationalist politicians like Song Ziwen used tariffs as a source of increased government revenue within a policy framework of accommodating, but gradually diminishing, foreign influence in the administration of the customs service. When measured in terms of revenue, the success of this strategy was apparent from the central government's budget until, in 1937, the Nationalists lost control of those parts of China that were engaged in foreign trade and thus produced tariff revenue. Furthermore, it seems a reasonable assumption that, for this strategy to take effect, there must have been an elementary level of coordination between Nationalist fiscal and foreign policy. This point is underscored by the important part that successive ministers of finance played in determining foreign policy and negotiating with foreign powers.

In arguing for the success of Nationalist tariff policy from the point of increasing government revenue I also make the case for a more positive evaluation of Guomindang fiscal policy in general. A reappraisal of this crucial field of Nationalist policy making, on which all other aspects of Guomindang state building depended, offers a fresh perspective on the reasons for the eventual decline of Nationalist governance on the Chinese mainland. The decline of Nationalist governance in the war years and the attendant loss of political capital have to be seen within the context of fiscal and economic constraints that

1. Louis, "Introduction," p. 40.
2. Bickers, *Britain in China*, p. 8.

drove the transformation of the wartime state. Furthermore, prewar efforts to modernize not only the fiscal policy of the Nationalist state but also the government of the Republic of China, and to transform it into a technocratic regime, are best understood in the context of transnational interwar debates on the meaning of modern governance. In its modernizing quest, the Guomindang was looking not only to its neighbor Japan and to the liberal, constitutional modern states of Western Europe and North America but also to fascist and Soviet modernity.

Repositioning Nationalist tariff and fiscal policy within the exigencies of the prewar and wartime periods, and viewing the Nationalist government's modernization in its international context, adds another layer of interpretation to earlier works by scholars such as Lloyd E. Eastman and Parks M. Coble.[3] Both historians demonstrated the failure of the Nationalist modernization project. For Eastman, the Guomindang modernization project failed because of the nature of the Nationalist polity. Although the Guomindang undoubtedly included reformers who genuinely attempted to improve the condition of China during the prewar period, their efforts failed because the Nationalist party contained a greater or more influential number of authoritarian, militarist, corrupt, and incompetent officials. Also, many proposed reforms would have threatened the economic and political interests of those strata of society on which the Guomindang relied most for support. Coble added to the argument by pointing out that, especially in the early years of their governance, the Nationalists frequently violated their presumed class bias by extorting money from China's prosperous classes. Both Eastman and Coble discuss the issue of fiscal policy at length; however, neither of them had access to the archives of the Maritime Customs Service, held at the Second Historical Archives of China in Nanjing.

Those records, once opened to scholars, formed the basis of a new body of scholarship that has appeared in the past two decades, following earlier works such as those of Jean Aitchison and Donna Brunero, whose detailed analyses of the Maritime Customs as an institution had to be based on archival sources available outside the People's Republic

3. Eastman, *The Abortive Revolution*; Coble, *The Shanghai Capitalists*.

of China.[4] Within the new body of scholarship, the works of Hans van de Ven and Robert Bickers have been especially prominent. Van de Ven argues that, far from serving as the instrument of foreign oppression as it has traditionally been depicted in China the customs service acted as a conduit for bringing modernity into China and that its work shaped much of China's modern development. He also stresses the importance of tariffs as indirect forms of taxation for regimes lacking the political strength to enforce more intrusive, direct taxation, and the role of the Maritime Customs as a nationwide bureaucracy in a multi-state nation, preparing the ground for thinking "in larger than regional terms."[5] Bickers offers an interpretation of the Maritime Customs' work in China within a more general account of the contribution of foreigners to China's modern history.[6]

The same political changes that led to the opening of the Maritime Customs archives have also produced a flowering of historical scholarship in the People's Republic of China since the early 1980s. Some historians, like Chen Shiqi, had been studying the customs service before the reform period, and they now had the opportunity to make the fruits of their scholarship available to a wider audience.[7] Others, like Dai Yifeng and Lian Xinhao, made use of the opportunities afforded by the more liberal intellectual climate of the 1980s and 1990s to develop a research agenda that encouraged objective, empirically grounded analysis of a subject fraught with political complexity.[8]

The Maritime Customs records also furnished much of the archival material on which Emily Hill's study of the Guangdong sugar industry and its politics is founded. The chief importance of Hill's work for this volume is its emphasis on the contrast between national and regional economies, which is so important to understanding the efforts

4. Aitchison, "The Chinese Maritime Customs Service"; Brunero, *Britain's Imperial Cornerstone*.

5. Van de Ven, *Breaking with the Past*, pp. 3, 257.

6. Bickers, *The Scramble for China*. My intellectual debts to my two senior colleagues (and former supervisors) will be readily apparent to anyone reading this book.

7. Chen Shiqi, *Zhongguo jindai haiguanshi*.

8. Dai Yifeng, *Jindai Zhongguo haiguan yu Zhongguo caizheng*; Lian Xinhao, *Zhongguo haiguan yu duiwai maoyi*.

of the Nationalists to assert their trade regime.[9] Catherine Ladds and
Chihyun Chang used the Maritime Customs archives to produce detailed social and political histories of the service's foreign and domestic
staffs, respectively.[10] Chang echoes van de Ven's point about the importance of the customs service as a conduit for administrative modernity
and also stresses the delicate balance of loyalties and factionalism required among the Chinese and foreign staff of the Maritime Customs.[11]
Philip Thai's work on the Nationalist state's reaction to smuggling
explores the importance of the government's war on smuggling within
its state-building effort, stressing continuities with its successor regime
and similarities with other modernizing regimes, as well as the particular ways in which the Nationalist state's tariff policies encouraged the
very illicit trade it tried so hard to suppress.[12]

Taxation and the Modern State

In examining the literature on state making and fiscal policy in Republican China, it is helpful to consider how the literature on state making
and fiscal policy more generally has developed. This body of work is
based on the conceptual link between the emergence of the modern
state and the increase of its revenue-gathering powers. In the 1960s,
the economist John Hicks developed the concept of the administrative
revolution in governance in his *Theory of Economic History*: government expenditures have to be financed, and thus a strong government
needs reliable sources of revenue. According to Hicks, the amount of
political control that a set level of expenditures could generate increased sharply in the modern period as a result of organizational and
technological improvements; hence the term "administrative revolution."[13] Echoing Hicks's analysis, Gabriel Ardant and Rudolf Braun,
in their contributions to Charles Tilly's influential edited volume on

9. Hill, *Smokeless Sugar*, p. 230.
10. Ladds, "'In the Chinese Customs Service'"; Chang, *Government, Imperialism and Nationalism in China*.
11. Chang, *Government, Imperialism and Nationalism in China*, pp. 189–90.
12. Thai, "Smuggling, State-Building, and Political Economy," pp. 266–71.
13. Hicks, *A Theory of Economic History*, p. 99.

the rise of the modern nation state in Europe, drew attention to the link between taxation and state building in early modern Europe, arguing that the political capacities that characterize the modern state developed out of attempts to increase and regularize the collection of revenue.[14] The classic statement of this link came in John Brewer's study of the fiscal state building in Stuart and Hanoverian Britain.[15] Brewer argued that, because they required more government revenue to fund a succession of military campaigns, the seventeenth- and eighteenth-century British governments developed a revenue-gathering bureaucracy that formed the nucleus of Britain's modern state: an approach that was rational, efficient, and honest. Hence, war created fiscal pressure, and fiscal pressure, however indirectly, created the modern state. There is, within the historiography of the early modern state in Western Europe, a tendency to take Brewer's analysis as normative, which Brewer never intended. His analysis, like the work of Ardant and Braun, is at its most useful when discussing state building in early modern Europe; however, the Eurocentricity of much of the Western scholarship has meant that this scholarship is taken as the starting place for much of the scholarship on the non-Western experience too.

Empirically speaking, the wartime experience of most states does not conform to Brewer's scenario; more often, wartime fiscal pressure has led to increased revenue extraction, as predicted, but thence to economic or political collapse, and sometimes both. Even where wartime fiscal pressure led to fiscal state building, the outcome was not necessarily a modern state on the British model. Olga Crisp's work on the premodern Russian state demonstrates that there is another scenario for fiscal state building, in which higher levels of tax extraction do not lead to strengthened institutions in the sense of rational, efficient, and honest administrative structures, but instead lead to the development of a "bureaucratic revenue state," as described by Hicks.[16] In such a state, revenue-gathering bureaucracies are optimized, but only

---

14. Ardant, "Financial Policy and Economic Infrastructure"; Braun, "Taxation, Sociopolitical Structure, and State-Building."

15. Brewer, *The Sinews of Power*.

16. Crisp, *Studies in the Russian Economy*, pp. 10–11.

to maximize the self-interest of the members of that bureaucracy. In Brewer's scenario, members of the revenue-gathering bureaucracy are kept honest by their self-interest (they risk losing the benefits associated with their position, which outweigh any short-term gain), their professional ethic, and the checks built into the system. But such checks do not apply in Crisp's scenario. There are three points to take away from this discussion. First, Brewer's scenario is always the exception rather than the rule. Second, it is Crisp's scenario that may, in fact, describe the typical case much more accurately. And third, it may be useful to ask whether different parts of the same state may have belonged to either of these two very different scenarios at the same time.

An important recent work that takes the analysis beyond Europe is Wenkai He's *Paths toward the Modern Fiscal State*, which considers two East Asian cases of fiscal state building in relation to the English experience. By contrasting England's and Japan's successful paths toward a modern fiscal state with China's unsuccessful experience, He takes the debate beyond its Eurocentric limitations, arguing that the late-imperial Chinese state failed to turn itself into a tax state once more in the late nineteenth century (following the eighteenth-century example of the Qing state at the height of its power), owing to the unfavorable conjunction of a credit crisis and the lack of what He terms "proper socioeconomic circumstances."[17] In contrast, England (from 1642 to 1752) and Japan (from 1880 to 1895) benefited from favorable conjunctions: for example, their states ran out of funds at times that allowed them to experiment productively with new centralized ways to raise indirect taxes in order to meet new fiscal demands. The Chinese state, on the other hand, faced its credit crisis just as the mid-century rebellions of the nineteenth century began. In the ensuing unstable political climate, the imperial state lacked the political environment in which to launch either a new paper currency or the credit instruments to support new government tasks. For all the late Qing state's success at developing new taxes, as described in Halsey's more positive reading of late Qing finance, these two factors inhibited its

17. He, *Paths toward the Modern Fiscal State*, p. 186.

ability to stabilize China's fiscal system.[18] Wenkai He deals with the period from 1851 to 1911, when the imperial state came under attack in a series of rebellions, some along millenarian lines, others among ethnic and religious groups. His point about an unfavorable conjunction of credit crisis and socioeconomic environment also holds for the Nationalist period, though. Indeed, by then there was an added dimension of complexity: as Julia Strauss argues, although the administrative institutions of the Nationalist state relied on "raw materials . . . essentially unchanged from late imperial times," the political sentiments of nationalism and anti-imperialism demanded ever greater performance from the Nationalist state.[19]

In writing about the Nationalist government's political and economic mobilization strategies, Hans van de Ven offered another way of understanding the relationship between state building and fiscal expansion by proposing the model of the fiscal-military cycle: fiscal pressure necessitated military campaigns to widen the revenue base, and increased revenue was used to strengthen the military.[20] It is worth pointing out that there are both positive and negative versions of this scenario, depending on whether it is read as existential fiscal pressure stimulating rapacious military campaigns to prolong the Nationalist government's political survival, or as a rational strategy of maximizing revenue. The Maritime Customs came under the control of the Nationalists at the conclusion of the first phase of the Northern Expedition—the military campaign led by Chiang Kai-shek from 1926 to 1928 to unify China under Nationalist rule—and delivered an extra-cyclical lift to the finances of the Nationalist state.

Brewer and Crisp describe two scenarios to depict opposite experiences in the relationship between increasing taxation and state building, but there is also an older tradition of conceptualizing debt discussed in the literature that we need to take into account. In many ways, negative views of Guomindang governance on the part of Western observers had to do with negative perceptions of government debt

18. Halsey, "Money, Power, and the State."
19. Strauss, *Strong Institutions in Weak Polities*, p. 181.
20. Van de Ven, *War and Nationalism*, p. 93.

more generally. The view that the Nationalist government managed its government debt irresponsibly and failed to break the bad habits established by its Republican predecessors is a view that was held even at the time by contemporary observers. It was later adopted by Douglas Paauw, and later still by Lloyd Eastman.[21] In talking about the Nationalist government's debt management, we need to distinguish between payment habits in redeeming debt and paying interest, on the one hand, and incurring new debt and the total level of government debt, on the other. The view that government debt might be a bad way to finance government expenditures is associated in the Western tradition of economics with the classics of political economy, such as Adam Smith's *Wealth of Nations* (1776) and David Ricardo's *Principles of Political Economy and Taxation* (1817). In earlier writings on states and finance, government debt did not have the same negative connotation.[22] We need to remember, when discussing negative views of Guomindang governance based on the Nationalist government's increasing of the national debt, that since Adam Smith, economists trained in the Western tradition have been predisposed against government debt, although that view has not always held sway.

The question of government debt also needs to be seen within the context of our own time. Whether debt is a sound instrument for government financing, and whether there is a critical ratio of debt to gross domestic product that governments cannot surpass without damaging their fiscal and political integrity, are questions that continue to be debated today. The lack of consensus on this matter is illustrated by the attention devoted to Kenneth Rogoff and Carmen Reinhart's recent study of government debt across history, *This Time It's Different*, and also by the vehemence with which a subsequently discovered, comparatively minor methodological flaw was used by critics to discount Rogoff and Reinhart's entire argument.[23] Reinhart and Rogoff argue that, historically speaking, few governments have long survived a debt-

21. Paauw, "The Kuomintang and Economic Stagnation," pp. 213–20; Eastman, *The Abortive Revolution*.

22. Holtfrerich, "Government Debt," p. 3.

23. Reinhart and Rogoff, *This Time It's Different*; see also Reinhart and Rogoff, "Growth in a Time of Debt," pp. 573–78.

to-GDP ratio of 90 percent or more. They demonstrate this claim empirically, employing historical simplifications and stylized facts where necessary, in order to fit their cross-country study, covering eight centuries, between the covers of a book. The Nationalist government of China, in fact, is on Reinhart and Rogoff's list of governments that failed to survive beyond that fiscal frontier for a sustained period of time. When recalculating the figures in Reinhart and Rogoff's original work, however, Thomas Herndon, Michael Ash, and Robert Pollin noticed an error, and as a result they proposed that the entire argument was invalid.[24]

One reason for the vehemence of Herndon, Ash, and Pollin's criticism surely has to do with the use to which Reinhart and Rogoff's claim has been put: their work was the only piece of academic writing quoted by US congressman Paul Ryan in his 2013 budget resolution, in which he proposed to restore the United States to fiscal health by reducing taxes and spending in order to lower the United States' debt-to-GDP ratio.[25] The 90 percent threshold posited by Reinhart and Rogoff was also cited by Olli Rehn, the European Union's commissioner for financial affairs, in explaining the European Commission's pro-austerity stance in 2013.[26] Current debates about austerity point to the importance of government debt in the public eye, and the ongoing debate between Rogoff and Reinhart and their critics illustrates the lack of a consensus regarding the proper role of debt in government finance. Despite the methodological critique of that work, Reinhart and Rogoff's principal point stands—historically speaking, few governments have survived a debt-to-GDP ratio of more than 90 percent. So are they right, or is theirs an ahistorical approach, driven by present concerns? Scholarly writings on the extent of the Chinese Nationalist government's debt—as opposed to the quality of its debt service—have to be understood within the context of the ongoing debate about public debt and austerity, since it is impossible for historians to write about the role of government debt without reflecting the mood of their own times.

24. Herndon, Ash, and Pollin, "Does High Public Debt Consistently Stifle Economic Growth?"
25. US House Budget Committee, "The Path to Prosperity," p. 80.
26. Rehn, "Letter from Vice President Olli Rehn to ECOFIN Ministers."

The Nationalist Party-State

Since *The Abortive Revolution* (1974), Lloyd Eastman's seminal work on Nationalist China during the Nanjing decade, an important theme in English-language studies of the Chinese Nationalist Party has been the party's fiscal and budgetary incompetence as well as the ultimate failure of its military efforts against the Chinese Communist Party. This perception of the Nationalist Party is heavily influenced by what Hans van de Ven termed the Stilwell-White paradigm, which posits that the Nationalist regime failed because it was corrupt, authoritarian, and militarily incompetent.[27] General Joseph W. Stilwell, the chief US military adviser to the Nationalist government during the Second World War, wrote in an undated note found among his papers that the Chinese people could expect only "greed, corruption, favoritism, more taxes, a ruined currency, [and] terrible waste" from the Nationalists under Chiang Kai-shek.[28] Theodore H. White, drawing on six years of experience as *Time* magazine's correspondent in the Nationalist wartime capital, Chongqing, wrote in 1946 of both the "extravagance and debauchery of the Kuomintang's machine" and its "brutality and extortion."[29] The Stilwell-White paradigm found its most lucid expression in Barbara Tuchman's 1970 book *Stilwell and the American Experience in China*, which, to demonstrate that "China was a problem for which there was no American solution," went to great lengths to show that the Nationalist movement had been "overtaken by the compromises and corruption of climbing to power."[30] If, unlike Tuchman, we are trying to understand the Nationalist party-state on its own terms, there are three questions we need to consider. First, what were the aims of the Nationalist party-state, and how were they to be achieved? Second, were the Nationalists successful or did they fail to achieve those aims, and what does their success or failure mean for our understanding of the Nationalist period? And third, how was power disposed of in the Nationalist state, or, put more succinctly, who made Nationalist policy?

27. Van de Ven, *War and Nationalism*, p. 8.
28. Stilwell, *The Stilwell Papers*, p. 317.
29. White and Jacoby, *Thunder out of China*, p. 312.
30. Tuchman, *Stilwell and the American Experience in China*, pp. 115, 531.

What were the aims of the Nationalist party-state? Specifically, what kind of state did it want to be? For Chiang Kai-shek, the answer to that question was very clear: the aim was to be modern. As he said in a speech to military officers in 1934, a modern state was a civilized state. To be backward was uncivilized, and would lead China on a path to extinction. In the same speech, Chiang pointed out that China was still very far from that ideal, and that only a wholesale transformation of China under the leadership of the Guomindang could ever make it modern.[31] In 1934, when Chiang gave this speech, the Republic of China was a state that, in European terms, belonged much more to the nineteenth century than to the twentieth.

In his 1998 Reith Lectures, John Keegan argue that twentieth-century states were fundamentally different from their precursors: "Until very recent times the state gave little more than quite sketchy services of domestic law and order while, at times, taking very much indeed."[32] Keegan's contention was that a citizen's expectation that the state will be a "benevolent, not belligerent institution" was an innovation of the twentieth century, and applied most closely to nations in Western Europe and North America.[33] In contrast to the ideal of a democratic Western European or North American state based on a social contract, the political vision of the Nationalist party-state was formulated by the Guomindang. The aim of the Nationalist party-state was to make China a powerful country again and to end foreign-imposed constraints on her sovereignty by turning China into a modern state. Permitting a substantial foreign presence to continue to exist within the Maritime Customs was a clear contradiction, but we can resolve this by distinguishing between short-term and long-term goals. For China to become strong enough to withstand foreign interference, it had to modernize; and in that modernization process, foreign models, and foreign expertise, were important.

---

31. Chiang Kai-shek, "Xin shenghuo yundong zhi yaoyi," in Zhongguo Guomindang zhongyang weiyuanhui, *Xian zongtong Jiang gong sixiang yanlun zongji*, vol. 12, pp. 73–75.

32. Keegan, *War and Our World*, p. 33.

33. Keegan, *War and Our World*, p. 31.

If we want to understand how the Nationalists transformed, or attempted to transform, the Chinese state and the Chinese polity in the interwar period, we have to look at the models they used. Chiang Kai-shek looked to German and Italian fascism as a political model, at least until summer 1938, almost a year after the outbreak of the Second Sino-Japanese War.[34] Fascism not only provided a political model for Nationalist China, but it also served as a particular form of high modernity to which the Nationalist state aspired. That modernity was not fascist by default, but it was articulated with particular clarity in fascist ideology, although similar aspirations can be found in contemporary Soviet ideology. Its key elements included a respect, bordering on veneration, for scientific method and scientific truth for their purported ability to transcend political strife. The presumed intellectual superiority of apolitical science manifested itself in practical ways through the continuous optimization of technology and the promotion of its use in everyday life. A primary application for technology was public administration. There, too, the promise of the high-modernist vision was to lift the inherently political matter of public administration into the sphere of the apolitical through the use of modern scientific methods. Again, we may be struck by the seeming incongruity of a regime devoted to political mobilization promoting the apolitical nature of science and technology. But the incongruity becomes less acute when we consider that visions of science-based modernity existed in nontotalitarian societies too, as in, for example, the rise of Frederick Taylor's theory of scientific management in the United States, or Frank B. Gilbreth's movement analysis.

In Chiang Kai-shek's 1934 speech in which he explicitly linked modernity with civilization, he committed China to both as a matter of national survival. The modernity toward which the Nationalist state aimed was thus explicitly scientific and technological. While two different modernities developed in China, as posited by William Kirby—a metropolitan modernity in Shanghai, and a technocratic modernity in Nanjing—they were connected by the efforts of the Nationalist government to use modern technology and practices to gain control over

34. Chiang Kai-shek, "Yanbie Deji guwen zhici," in Zhongguo Guomindang zhongyang weiyuanhui, *Xian zongtong Jiang gong sixiang yanlun zongji*, vol. 15, p. 328.

people's material, everyday lives.[35] The latter forms of modernity were at least as important as the former. As Frank Dikötter points out, "Common sense dictates that the acquisition of a kerosene lamp to fight the dark and a cheap mirror to repel malign spirits was a far more widespread 'experience of modernity' for hundreds of millions of ordinary farmers in China who might only rarely travel beyond their village than the musings about the nature of time and space among a few self-absorbed writers."[36]

How successful was the Nationalist party-state in its modernization project and its attempt to restore the Chinese nation? The two constraints on sovereignty that most angered nationalists in China were China's lack of tariff autonomy and the practice of extraterritoriality. By 1929 the Nationalist Party government had negotiated the resumption of tariff autonomy with all treaty powers (a three-year exemption, until 1933, was applied to Japan). By 1943 the wartime Nationalist government had convinced the United States and Britain that extraterritoriality ill suited a relationship between allies (though at the price of a statute-of-forces agreement relating to allied troops based in China). Looking at the Nationalists' economic record, using Maddison's database, an average annual GDP growth rate of 1.5 percent for the period from 1929 to 1936 for China compares to -1.3 percent for France, 1.9 percent for Germany, 1 percent for Italy, 2.9 percent for Japan, 1.7 percent for the United Kingdom, and -0.8 percent for the United States for the same period.[37] Central government receipts increased more than threefold during the Nanjing decade, and in July 1937 the Nationalist government controlled 24.5 percent of China's territory, home to 66 percent of its population, compared with 7.6 percent of its territory and 20 percent of its population in March 1929.[38] Some authors, like William Kirby and Morris Bian, see the roots of postwar economic modernization on both sides of the Taiwan Strait in the policies of economic mobilization formulated by the Nationalists' wartime Chongqing state (1937–45).[39]

35. Kirby, "Engineering China," p. 137.
36. Dikötter, *Things Modern*, p. 12.
37. Maddison, "Statistics on World Population, GDP, and Per Capita GDP."
38. Strauss, *Strong Institutions in Weak Polities*, p. 120; Domes, *Vertagte Revolution*, pp. 680–81.
39. Kirby, "Continuity and Change in Modern China"; Bian, "How Crisis Shapes Change."

On the other hand, the Nationalist government did not achieve unified political and military control of all of China at any point during this period. The Guomindang remained a fragmented polity, and China a fragmented country. Living standards outside the cities, and for the urban nonelites, remained low in absolute terms, and the societal utility of wartime economic mobilization is debatable. My research on tariffs confirms the conclusion of others, that the Nationalists' increase in tax revenue came at a high social cost. The Nationalist regime's bloody beginnings, suppressing organized labor and Communists in Guangzhou and Shanghai, also made clear the cost of political dissent. For these reasons, and in spite of the recent revisionist scholarship, negative evaluations of the Nationalist state are predominant in the literature. Thus, it is worth pointing out that this book is not an apology for the Nationalist state but an attempt to understand more closely, on the basis of previously inaccessible archival records, its nature and the causes of its eventual demise.

Lastly, turning to the question of how political power was exercised and how political decisions were made in the Nationalist state: the ultimate source of political power for the Nationalists was their control of the military. Thus the most important decision-making body was the Military Affairs Commission of the Guomindang.[40] The most important individual in Nationalist politics was Chiang Kai-shek, who combined the role of senior military leader of the forces aligned with the Guomindang with a succession of senior political roles in the hierarchy of the party and state. Beyond Chiang, decisive political power was wielded by a small number of individuals, primarily as a function of their own power bases and their connections to Chiang, rather than because of the political offices they held. For all that we think of the Nationalist period as being dominated by a Guomindang party-state, it is worth noting the opinion of the Nationalists' longtime financial adviser, Arthur N. Young, who concluded that politics at the national level were dominated by the national government rather than the Guomindang, even if many members of the national government were also party members.[41] In the realm of fiscal policy,

40. Myers, "The Chinese State," p. 55.
41. Young, *China's Nation-Building Effort*, p. 424.

the most visible politician was Song Ziwen. Coble has argued that this owes more to Song's self-promotion than to political facts, and that Song lost political ground the moment he chose to disagree with Chiang on substantial issues.[42] With regard to policy making in the Nationalist state, it is important to remember the following: at the central level, political power was exercised by a small number of individuals; the political and military reach of the Nationalist state extended only over parts of the Chinese mainland, even before 1937; and the label "Nationalist" was ascriptive, especially the greater one's distance from Nanjing. The Nationalist polity, for all of Chiang's invocations of political unity, remained fragmented.[43]

There are two ways of challenging the traditional depiction of Nationalist governance as incompetent, corrupt, and disinterested. One is to point to the achievements of the Nationalist state at a time of ever-decreasing odds for its political survival, as Kirby, Strauss, van de Ven, and Bian, among others, have done. The other is to ask on what model the Nationalist state is best understood. We need not abandon political science models centered on Europe; all we need to do is use as the basis of our understanding the kind of European state for which the Nationalists professed so much admiration: the militarist, authoritarian, fascist state.[44] In writing about the politics of administration, especially that of the statistical profession during the Third Reich, Adam Tooze refers to Franz Neumann's memorable depiction of the Third Reich as a nonstate in which political power depended on access to the Führer, control of one of the means of violence, and command of the means of production.[45] Neumann proposed two ways of understanding the state, through the rule of law and as a rationally operating machine disposing of the monopoly of coercive power, and he took fascist Italy as the origin of that model.[46] This comes remarkably close

42. Coble, *The Shanghai Capitalists*, p. 266.

43. Zanasi, *Saving the Nation*, p. 82.

44. Chiang Kai-shek, "Xin shenghuo yundong zhi zhongxin zhunze," in Zhongguo Guomindang zhongyang weiyuanhui, *Xian zongtong Jiang gong sixiang yanlun zongji*, vol. 12, p. 89.

45. Tooze, *Statistics and the German State*, p. 246.

46. Neumann, *Behemoth*, p. 382.

to the totalitarian state to which Chiang aspired.[47] But, Neumann also argued, a state is ideologically characterized by the unity of the political power it wields. On that count, at least, the Chinese Nationalist state failed, much more conspicuously than the Nazi state about which Neumann wrote and which the Nationalists had so admired until the early months of the Second Sino-Japanese War.[48] Chiang's persistent stressing of the importance of ideological mobilization underscores this point.

Nationalist-controlled China never became that kind of state, a unified polity dominated and administered by a rationally operating machine, disposing of the monopoly of coercive power, but this remained the ambition of technocrats on the left and on the right of the Guomindang.[49] For all that its leaders wanted it to be a modern state, the Republic of China belonged to the earlier form of state described by Keegan rather than the later. Nationalist China failed to become modern in the way its leaders hoped it would.

The Maritime Customs Service in Chinese History

Within the Nationalist state, the Maritime Customs Service, as an institution, sat awkwardly. By the late 1920s the customs service was no longer the *imperium in imperio* that it had been in the late nineteenth century or during the Warlord period. Although still led by a foreigner, and with its senior ranks still dominated by other foreign appointments, the Maritime Customs was becoming less foreign and more Chinese every year. Indeed, at the beginning of the period, the head of the Maritime Customs Service, Inspector General Sir Frederick Maze, was criticized by members of the foreign community in China for being too accommodating toward the new Chinese Nationalist state. And yet that accommodation belied a structural and politi-

47. Chiang Kai-shek, "Xiandai junren xuzhi," in Zhongguo Guomindang zhong-yang weiyuanhui, *Xian zongtong Jiang gong sixiang yanlun zongji*, vol. 11, pp. 321–22.

48. Chiang Kai-shek, "Yanbie Deji guwen zhici," in Zhongguo Guomindang zhong-yang weiyuanhui, *Xian zongtong Jiang gong sixiang yanlun zongji*, vol. 15, p. 328.

49. Zanasi, *Saving the Nation*, p. 81.

cal problem for the Nationalists, in the matter of which they made a major, early policy choice: to tolerate an institution within the orbit of informal empire, inside the Nationalist state.

During the Nationalist era, the Maritime Customs served as a revenue-collection agency for international and some domestic trade, published trade statistics, and projected the image of the Nationalist government across China. Previously the Imperial Maritime Customs Service, the Maritime Customs originated as a tariff collectorate under foreign direction, set up by the local governor-general in a bid to use foreign know-how and protection to organize tariff collection in Shanghai during the Xiaodaohui Rebellion in 1853.[50] Although it was later used as an instrument of informal empire, the Maritime Customs was not a tool for imperialist domination in the beginning, even though it was paternalist in the sense that foreigners serving in the Maritime Customs in most cases thought they knew better what was good for China than did successive Chinese governments. Until the Chinese Revolution of 1911, foreigners did not dictate the course of events in Chinese fiscal affairs, and the Maritime Customs was therefore hardly an imperialist institution. Much has been written about the changing relationship between the Maritime Customs as a foreign-managed institution and the Ministry of Finance in the years between 1911 and 1929.[51] In contrast, this book focuses on the Maritime Customs as a revenue-collecting institution of the Nationalist government. It analyzes the relationship between the Maritime Customs and the Guomindang only to the extent that it is relevant to a revisionist argument about the success of Nationalist tariff policy in terms of revenue extraction and midterm sustainability.

The interpretation of the Chinese Maritime Customs Service in terms of the imperialist domination of China goes back to the writings of late-imperial commentators like Chen Chi, who argued in 1890 that Sir Robert Hart, the inspector general of the Imperial Maritime Customs, had "gradually gained control over court opinion, and had a

---

50. Bickers, "Revisiting the Chinese Maritime Customs Service," p. 222.
51. Chen Shiqi, *Zhongguo jindai haiguanshi*, pp. 589–616; Atkins, *Informal Empire in Crisis*; Aitchison, "The Chinese Maritime Customs Service"; Byrne, "The Dismissal of Sir Francis Aglen"; Brunero, *Britain's Imperial Cornerstone*.

tight grasp of the conduct of [China's] foreign relations." Also, according to Chen, Hart was "working for the good of his own country."[52] From 1858 until 1929, China's import tariffs were capped at a rate of 5 percent ad valorem under the terms of the Treaty of Tianjin, which ended the Second Opium War. Nationalist politicians, like Sun Yat-sen (1866–1925), and economists, such as Ma Yinchu (1882–1982), were critical of the effect of this tariff cap on China's economic development and blamed it, rather than the Maritime Customs as an institution, for what they saw as China's economic malaise.[53]

After the establishment of the People's Republic of China (PRC) in 1949, long-standing suspicions of the Maritime Customs as a foreign-administered institution were reinforced by the influence of the Leninist theory of imperialism as the highest stage of capitalism. Given the importance of debates on imperialism within China's political culture to this very day, PRC scholarship on the Maritime Customs Service is worth exploring a little further. It was dominated for a long time by explorations of the hierarchical relationship between foreigners and Chinese nationals within the Maritime Customs, and the origin of the Maritime Customs in the context of foreign aggression against China in the nineteenth century. Between 1957 and 1962, the Commission for the Compilation of Materials on Modern Chinese Economic History published a series consisting of materials translated from the archives of the Inspectorate General of Maritime Customs; this series was republished in 1983. In the preface to the second edition, Chen Hansheng and Qian Jiaju, two of the editors of the original series, wrote:

> We all know that in old China, control of Maritime Customs was in the hands of the imperialists, and that they used their control over Maritime Customs tariffs to manipulate China's fiscal policy, finance sector, foreign trade, and even the internal politics and foreign affairs of our country. Formerly, in China, our country's tariff revenue stood at 30 to 40 percent of budget revenue, and because tariffs were used as security for our country's foreign loans and indemnities, the imperialists used this as an excuse to demand and to grasp administrative control over the Maritime Customs. . . . Therefore, the Maritime Customs archives are

---

52. Chen Chi, *Yong shu*, pp. 293–94, corresponding to wai bian, shang juan, 35a–35b.
53. Sun Zhongshan, *Sanmin zhuyi*, p. 31; Ma Yinchu, *Woguo guanshui wenti*, p. 5.

not only records of China's Maritime Customs revenue and tax administrations but, importantly, also are irrefutable evidence of how the imperialists schemed, conspired, and implemented the colonialist policies of imperialism, and how they made our country lapse into becoming a colony or semicolony.[54]

These archival materials, they further stated, were not just valuable sources for modern history; they could also "make us understand the strategy and objectives of imperialism even more clearly, and are therefore valuable to us in carrying out patriotic education."[55]

Hu Sheng, one of the PRC's most prominent historians of the Republican era, argued in 1981 that the Maritime Customs was designed, from the very beginning, as a tool of Western imperialism. He claimed that "the significance of the control of the Chinese Maritime Customs by the imperialists lay in the fact that they used part of the spoils from the exploitation of the Chinese people to support the Qing regime, which they hoped would serve as an instrument to keep the people down."[56] Hu—incorrectly—claimed that "Hart . . . had devised and put into effect the whole system of foreign imperialist control over the Maritime Customs administration of China."[57] He also argued that, since the inspector general "was actually in a position to control the economic life-lines of the Qing government" through controlling the Maritime Customs, "the imperialists were able to step up their domination over Chinese politics."[58] As the title of a recent monograph attests, this understanding of the Maritime Customs is still influential, even beyond China.[59]

In 1990 the Second Historical Archives of China and the Institute of Modern History of the Chinese Academy of Social Sciences jointly published Chinese and English editions of the letters and telegrams between Sir Robert Hart and James Duncan Campbell, the Maritime

54. Zhongguo jindai jingjishi ziliao congkan bianji weiyuanhui, *Zhongguo haiguan yu ZhongFa zhanzheng*, p. 2.

55. Zhongguo jindai jingjishi ziliao congkan bianji weiyuanhui, *Zhongguo haiguan yu ZhongFa zhanzheng*, p. 2.

56. Hu Sheng, *Imperialism and Chinese Politics*, p. 65.

57. Hu Sheng, *Imperialism and Chinese Politics*, p. 64.

58. Hu Sheng, *Imperialism and Chinese Politics*, p. 65.

59. Brunero, *Britain's Imperial Cornerstone*.

Customs representative in London.[60] As Chen Xiafei, chief editor of the published correspondence, indicated, these editions were heavily indebted to John K. Fairbank's earlier edition of Hart's letters to Campbell.[61] However, Chen and Han's edition also contained Campbell's letters to Hart, as well as their telegraphic exchanges. In the series introduction to both editions, the Chinese Maritime Customs Study Association asserted that: "Maritime Customs is an important administrative organ for the supervision and control of border entry and exit. After the Opium War, when China was forcibly opened and entered by the Treaty Powers, our country's Maritime Customs for the first time lost control over the Maritime Customs duties, so that the Maritime Customs lost its role protecting our country's economy."[62] The series introduction further stated that "the Commissioner system, whereby the Chinese Maritime Customs was controlled by foreigners, and a whole range of systems of semicolonial Maritime Customs undertakings advantageous for the sale of the goods of the Western aggressors in China and the extraction of capital were designed by Hart and for a long time implemented by him in the Maritime Customs throughout China." Under the control of Hart and his successors, the Maritime Customs, "while nominally a Chinese administrative organ, was in reality the stronghold of the concerted aggression of other countries in China."[63] Importantly, for the purpose of this argument, the preface further stated:

> At the same time, it must be pointed out that although the modern Chinese Maritime Customs, while being controlled by foreigners, introduced a few rather scientific management techniques of the maritime customs services of Western capitalist countries; under the conditions of Chinese history at that point, these were just management techniques, and they were primarily for the benefit of Western aggression in China

60. Chen Xiafei, *Zhongguo haiguan midang*; Chen Xiafei and Han Rongfang, *Archives of China's Imperial Maritime Customs*.

61. Chen Xiafei, "Yuyan," in Chen Xiafei, *Zhongguo haiguan midang*, p. 14; Chen Xiafei, untitled contribution, in Cohen and Goldman, *Fairbank Remembered*, pp. 217–18; Fairbank, Bruner, and Matheson, *The I.G. in Peking*.

62. Chen Xiafei, *Zhongguo haiguan midang*, p. 1.

63. Chen Xiafei, *Zhongguo haiguan midang*, p. 1.

and for striking a semicolonial, semifeudal brand. For, just as Comrade Mao Zedong pointed out as early as forty years ago: the objective of the foreign capitalists in attacking China is not to make a feudal China into a capitalist China; it is to make China into their colony or semicolony.[64]

In other words, the Chinese Maritime Customs Study Association, while acknowledging the Maritime Customs' contribution to Chinese modernity, disqualified the contribution by pointing out that it served the wrong purpose. The thinking informing the authors' viewpoint may be inferred from their concluding assessment:

> The Chinese people conducted a long struggle to recover control over the Maritime Customs, but it was only under the leadership of the Chinese Communist Party, and through an arduous and lofty armed struggle, that they managed to bring about this aspiration truly to recover control over the Maritime Customs. At the same time that the People's Republic of China was established, a sovereign, unified, and socialist People's Maritime Customs Service and leadership were established throughout the entire country.[65]

In the PRC, academic monographs are subject to fewer structural constraints than collections of edited documents as regards the expression of scholarly opinions at variance with established narratives. In recent years there has been a trend toward a more balanced assessment of the Maritime Customs. The most important articulation of this approach is Chen Shiqi's *Zhongguo jindai haiguanshi* (History of the modern Chinese Maritime Customs), which is the standard monograph on the Maritime Customs Service available in China today. In the introduction to the 2002 edition of this work, Chen argues that scholarly approaches to the Maritime Customs Service should be defined by faithfulness to historical sources, historical context, and a comprehensive examination of each historical problem, in that order of importance.[66] Notably, Chen does not mention the importance of

---

64. Chen Xiafei, *Zhongguo haiguan midang*, p. 1.
65. Chen Xiafei, *Zhongguo haiguan midang*, p. 1.
66. Chen Shiqi, *Zhongguo jindai haiguanshi*, p. 3.

Marxist-Leninist theory in interpreting the history of the service, a departure from the previous historiography of the Maritime Customs in the PRC. Chen's overall assessment of the Maritime Customs' role in the development of modern China is that, on the one hand, it was one of the factors that brought about the emergence of capitalism in China, which he, in another departure from previous historiography, holds to be a positive development. On the other hand, as a tool for protecting the economic interests of the treaty powers—a term Chen uses in preference to "imperialists"—the Maritime Customs served to impede the development of Chinese society.[67]

In an assessment of the foreign-led Chinese Maritime Customs Service in terms of a revisionist interpretation of foreign influence in late nineteenth- and early twentieth-century China, Dai Yifeng writes that "while the illegality and the pillaging actions of the aggressors are apparent and easy to see, the subjective motives and objective effects of the reformers are confusing and can lead people rather astray [in their opinions]."[68] In a similar vein, Lian Xinhao states that "the role of the modern Chinese Maritime Customs . . . was very important and, in a wide-ranging fashion, touched on politics, economy, foreign relations, military affairs, thought, culture, education, and every other field of modern Chinese society, and it occupies an extremely important place in modern Chinese society."[69] But, Lian continues:

> Because the modern Chinese Maritime Customs was under the control of foreign commissioners of Maritime Customs, the files, archives, and materials, as well as the internal workings of the Maritime Customs, exercised a strict system of secrecy toward the outside. Therefore, those outside the Maritime Customs, and even Chinese Maritime Customs employees, had no means to carry out investigations and research. During the upsurge of Chinese national consciousness, and the Chinese democratic revolution after the bourgeois revolution of 1911, a few nationalists, based on the patriotic sentiment of winning back tariff autonomy, began to carry out research about the modern Chinese Maritime Customs under the control of foreign commissioners of Maritime Customs.[70]

67. Chen Shiqi, *Zhongguo jindai haiguanshi*, p. 2.
68. Dai Yifeng, *Jindai Zhongguo haiguan yu Zhongguo caizheng*, p. 299.
69. Lian Xinhao, *Zhongguo haiguan yu duiwai maoyi*, p. 1.
70. Lian Xinhao, *Zhongguo haiguan yu duiwai maoyi*, pp. 1–2.

In contrast to the Marxist-Leninist perspective, which saw the Maritime Customs as a tool of imperialist domination, John K. Fairbank claimed that it was an example of Sino-foreign cooperation. In discussing the phenomenon of non-Han Chinese participation in the administration of China throughout Chinese history, Fairbank posited the concept of synarchy—that is, "*joint administration* by a mixed Chinese and non-Chinese bureaucracy," with "foreign participation in [China's] government."[71] Using this concept, he claimed that the Maritime Customs, prior to the 1911 Revolution, functioned as a "partnership" in which the foreign commissioners of Maritime Customs maintained a "careful parallel relationship [with] the Chinese Superintendents of Maritime Customs." While foreign Maritime Customs officials exercised administrative supervision over the assessment and collection of Maritime Customs revenue, they did not handle Maritime Customs revenue until 1911, since Chinese local officials handled the financial side of tariff collection.[72] This partnership was brought down by the "cognate developments of nationalism and industrialism" introduced into China through contact with the West, Fairbank argued. Nationalism and industrialism "remade... Western and modern Chinese evaluations of China's political institutions, including synarchy."[73] In doing so, they destroyed a delicately balanced system based on Sino-foreign partnership rather than foreign domination of China.

Both the classic Marxist-Leninist view of the Maritime Customs, predominant in the PRC until the early 1990s, and Fairbank's idealistic synarchic perspective are economical with the truth. The idealistic synarchic perspective belittles, to the point of deliberately ignoring, the role of Chinese revenue-collecting agencies before the Taiping Wars, when control of the Maritime Customs' tariff collection was handed to the foreign consuls, a change that preceded the establishment of the foreign-run Inspectorate General of Maritime Customs. The classic Marxist-Leninist view avoids the fact that the Maritime Customs Service, which politicians and scholars sought to reclaim from foreign control during the Republican period, and which Chinese

71. Fairbank, "Synarchy under the Treaties," p. 205, emphasis in the original.
72. Fairbank, "Synarchy under the Treaties," pp. 222–23.
73. Fairbank, "Synarchy under the Treaties," p. 225.

historians have since described as under foreign control, was inextricably linked to the outside expertise brought into China during the period of the foreign-run inspectorate. Furthermore, neither view makes sufficient allowance for the development of the Maritime Customs' structure and role over time.

In the PRC, the works of Chen Shiqi, Dai Yifeng, Lian Xinhao, and others, published in recent years, adopt what one might call a realistic synarchic view. This view acknowledges the contribution that the Maritime Customs made to Chinese modernity as well as the elements of joint control over China's Maritime Customs, while still emphasizing its existence "as an agency in the British orbit."[74] A new perspective in the English-language historiography of the Maritime Customs Service is that of Hans van de Ven, discussed above, who argues that Maritime Customs was an institution that "facilitated China's globalization . . . by drawing up rules applicable to goods which were to be obeyed by all regardless of status and connections and which were enforced through an efficient and centralized bureaucracy differentiated from local society."[75] This perspective is shared by James Hevia, who claims that, through the publication of its trade statistics, Maritime Customs "helped to integrate China into the global capitalist economy of the late nineteenth century by generating returns on trade between China and the West."[76]

The Chinese Economy

A brief description of the state of the Chinese economy in the interwar period will illustrate both the size of the Nationalists' modernization task and the tax base that the regime had to work with. China's economy in the interwar period is best understood in terms of regional economies. That was how the economy had been traditionally structured, owing to its climatic and geographical variations, natural barriers, great distances, and transport technology. Changes in trans-

74. Bickers, "The Chinese Maritime Customs at War," p. 301.
75. Van de Ven, "The Onrush of Modern Globalization in China," p. 177.
76. Hevia, *English Lessons*, p. 143.

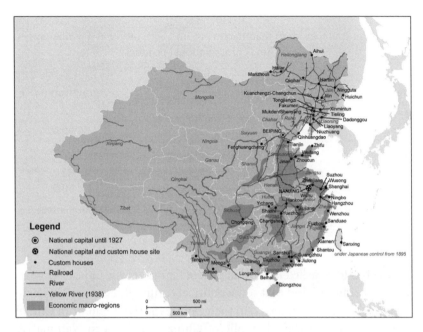

Map 0.1. Custom houses, economic regions, and major transport routes.

portation and increasing interregional trade led to increasing integration of the regional economies during the nineteenth and early twentieth centuries, but in the prewar period, the Republic of China did not yet possess an integrated national economy like those in Western Europe. This is worth noting because so many political models for the emergence of a modern state assume the economic basis of a national economy.

China's economic macro-regions sometimes, but not always, overlapped with its political macro-regions—that is, those regions controlled by a particular regime or power holder. This is useful to remember, since Nationalist policies reached only to the parts of China over which the Nationalists had political and military control. As map 0.1 shows, the Maritime Customs was an important exception to this rule; despite operating under the Nationalist government in Nanjing, it maintained custom houses in areas beyond the Nationalists' control. This creates challenges in interpreting even the limited number of quantitative indicators that are available for this period. The question that

Table 0.1.
Foreign trade, modern manufacturing, and agriculture as a percentage
of China's gross national product

Year	Foreign trade/GNP	Modern manufacturing/GNP	Agriculture/GNP
1931	7.9	4.7	69.3
1932	7.3	5.4	66.6
1933	8.1	6.5	63.5
1934	7.3	7.1	61.3
1935	6.3	7.3	62.2
1936	3.6	8.1	60.5

Source: Data from Liu, China's National Income, pp. 10, 69. The figures exclude the three northeastern provinces.

always has to be asked is, to what part of China are the indicators referring, bearing in mind that some political competitors of the Nationalist government also referred to their polities as the Republic of China? Do indicators for the "Republic of China" refer just to Nationalist-controlled areas, to all the areas labeled "Republic of China," or to all of China? Again, the custom houses are an important exception, since they recorded statistics from beyond the boundaries of particular economic or political macro-regions.

Under the Nationalists, central government revenue was particularly dependent on two parts of the Chinese economy, the modern manufacturing sector and foreign trade, both of which were concentrated on the eastern seaboard. Table 0.1 illustrates the low level of industrialization in China at this point, and also the relatively low importance of foreign trade in terms of gross national product. And yet, the taxation of foreign trade and the modern manufacturing sector provided the bulk of central government revenue.[77] Hence, China's small modern manufacturing sector and its foreign trade largely had to support an entire modernizing government. The size of the manufacturing sector and the structure of the Nationalist government's tax base give us a more precise idea of the size of the modernization task facing the Nationalist government.

77. Strauss, Strong Institutions in Weak Polities, p. 124.

Outline of the Book

This study is divided into six chapters. In chapter 1, I discuss how Chinese Nationalists, beginning with Sun Yat-sen, conceptualized China's foreign trade and the role of the Chinese Maritime Customs Service in administering it. As economic nationalists, Guomindang thinkers believed in protectionism; as political nationalists, they believed that allowing foreigners to have a substantial role in the performance of one of China's sovereign rights, the policing of trade, diminished China's sovereignty. As the Guomindang emerged as a leading contender for political dominance in China in the mid-1920s, it had to consider the benefits of uninterrupted revenue flows from a customs service that continued to operate as a semiforeign hybrid against the political satisfaction to be gained from ending foreign influence in the Maritime Customs. The Guomindang's rise to national political preeminence took place against a changed foreign-policy environment in the 1920s, which brought a retrenched Western presence in China and a new Japanese presence that, while not yet as aggressive as it would become in the 1930s, was strongly assertive about its rights and privileges in China.

Chapter 2 describes the process by which the Nationalist administration of Chiang Kai-shek took over the Chinese Maritime Customs Service, and the uses to which the customs service was put in Chinese Nationalist fiscal policy. The takeover necessitated twin accommodations. On the one hand, the Nationalists decided to accommodate a remaining foreign presence within the Maritime Customs in the interest of stable revenue collection, meanwhile continuing the process of gradually diminishing the foreign presence within the Maritime Customs that had begun under the previous Beiyang government rather than risking foreign noncompliance with Chinese tariff laws by making a unilateral change to the status quo. The Maritime Customs Service, on the other hand, had to accommodate a new political master, one that was more assertive about China's sovereign rights than the immediate predecessor, and an increased Chinese presence within the senior ranks of the service. Even as that accommodation was negotiated over the course of the Nanjing decade, tariff revenue became the most important source of revenue for the Guomindang, consistently accounting for more than a third of central government revenue during the decade and thus underwriting a large part of Nationalist Party governance in the prewar period.

Delivering that very significant share of government revenue was the most important contribution the Maritime Customs made to Nationalist governance. But it also produced valuable statistics, which served as both a tool of Nationalist governance and evidence of the Nationalists' modern, scientific administration. Chapter 3 discusses the Maritime Customs' use of modern technology to appraise trade goods, the process by which statistics were collected, and the methodological assumptions that underlie most Maritime Customs statistics. These assumptions, in particular, are notable, given the important role customs statistics played in the economic history of late imperial and republican China.

Having discussed the intellectual antecedents of Nationalist tariff policy, its role in Nationalist fiscal policy, and the process by which customs statistics were collected, I turn to the tariff policy's effect on trade in chapter 4. Throughout the Nanjing decade, Nationalist leaders stressed that their tariff policy had two aims of equal importance: protecting infant industries and assuring a stable flow of revenue. Four case studies of individual imported commodities lead me to conclude that, for the Nationalist government, revenue considerations consistently outweighed protectionist ambitions.

Chapter 5 looks at how the Nationalist government and the Maritime Customs dealt with the most important challenge to their fiscal sovereignty, smuggling. I begin by examining the way in which the notion of smuggling is tied to concepts of territorial sovereignty, and I propose that, for the fragmented Chinese polity of the Nanjing period, the concepts of legitimate and illegitimate trade are more helpful. What the Nationalists, and the Maritime Customs, defined as smuggling could often also be read as a challenge to the Nationalists' political authority. During the Nanjing period, the customs service managed to contain smuggling at a level which did not call into question the continued stability of revenue collection, and thus the Nationalist regime's ability to finance itself.

Chapter 6 deals with the impact of the Second Sino-Japanese War (1937–45) on Nationalist tariff policy, Nationalist fiscal policy, and the

Maritime Customs Service. In the opening stages of the war, the Nationalists lost control of China's most productive economic regions, which had delivered the bulk of its tax revenue, including that from tariffs, precisely as wartime fiscal pressure mounted. Not even older, previously discredited forms of taxation could deliver enough revenue to make up for the lost tariffs, and so the Nationalists resorted to deficit financing and extortion. As a result, they emerged from the war a politically discredited party, with their project of administrative modernization but a memory. The Maritime Customs, which had been such an important part of that modernization project, lost both its power and it relative independence within the Nationalist polity as trade and tariff revenue declined during the war.

ONE

Nationalism, Nationalists, and Informal Empire

Foreign Control of the Customs—The establishment of the Customs is not only responsible for the collection of the revenue for immediate needs of the country and the examination of the goods coming and going through it but also the protection of home commodities. The English persuaded the Manchus to let them have the control of the Customs as a means for paying off external debts, but really had in view using it as the basis of operations for their intrusion into China. The administrative power has been vested in the hands of the foreigners. A Chinese dared not hope for ever so small a post as an appraiser of goods. From an organisation of self-defence, as is the Customs in other countries, it has become in this country an instrument for the protection of foreign international capitalism. Chinese Customs tariff rates are perhaps the lowest in the world; a levy of five percent *ad valorem* is by no means an effective one as the prices of goods, being appraised only once every ten years, have soared so high that the amount charged now is no more than an effective one percent. Even in the revision of the tariff rates the foreigners took care that any increase in the Customs revenue should just suffice for the payment of the foreign debts. They do not care the slightest whether China gets anything or not.[1]

Few things mattered more. Tariffs—taxes on imports and exports—were the main source of revenue for the Chinese Nationalist government between 1927 and 1937. Chiang Kai-shek's Guomindang government

---

1. Hu, "Foreign Economic Domination in China," p. 710.

relied on tariff revenue to finance its rule over those parts of the Republic of China that it controlled politically and militarily. It also sought to control tariff revenue in order to weaken its political and military competitors for control of China. Yet until 1929 this important source of government revenue was outside China's control in many ways. The text quoted above was originally published in *Dongfang zazhi* (Eastern miscellany), one of China's leading intellectual magazines in 1929. Written by Hu Huaishen, a Chinese economist, it contains many elements of contemporary Chinese opinion on the Chinese tariff system. The main charge was that the Maritime Customs Service, because it was under foreign administration, could not be used to enforce protective import tariffs in order to encourage the growth of domestic industries. Nationalist fiscal policy during the Nanjing decade relied on tariff receipts as one of its main sources of central government revenue, but to make full use of tariffs for revenue purposes the Nationalists first had to regain tariff autonomy.

Regaining tariff autonomy was one of the key aims of Chinese Nationalist foreign policy. Sun Yat-sen, the dominant figure in early Chinese political nationalism, wrote as early as 1919 that China could not "find a solution for the livelihood problem in the economic field alone; we must first take hold on the political side, abolish all unequal treaties and take back the Maritime Customs from foreign control."[2] At the time, Sun Yat-sen was proposing to abolish the 5 percent maximum ad valorem import tariff imposed by the Treaty of Tianjin concluded between Britain and China in 1858. In 1911, Prime Minister Yuan Shikai of the imperial government had arranged, with the assistance of the British minister to China, Sir John Jordan, and the inspector general of Maritime Customs, Sir Francis Aglen, to have Maritime Customs revenue placed with the Hong Kong and Shanghai Bank rather than with local government banks, thus stopping "a main source of funds to both the Qing and the revolutionary provinces."[3] Thereafter, regaining control over the disposal of revenue became part of the Nationalists' ambitions for regaining tariff autonomy. China attempted in vain to recover

2. Sun Zhongshan, *Sanmin zhuyi*, p. 396.

3. Van de Ven, "Military and Financial Reform," pp. 35–36; Wright, *Collection and Disposal*, p. 4.

tariff autonomy at the Paris Peace Conference in 1919.[4] The restoration of tariff autonomy was promised in principle by the treaty powers at the Washington Conference of 1921–22, but no specific action to grant it was taken, not least because of the unstable political situation in China at the time. The Beijing Tariff Conference, convened in 1925 following a recommendation of the Washington Conference, proposed that full tariff autonomy be restored to China, on the condition that it would abolish all internal taxes on imported goods, particularly the transit tax, or *lijin* (釐金). However, because of the continued unstable political situation in China, no specific measures toward restoring tariff autonomy to China were taken at the time.[5]

After moving the seat of government to Nanjing in 1927, the Nationalists unilaterally reclaimed tariff autonomy, promulgated a new tariff law, and announced that tariffs at the rates agreed on at the Beijing Tariff Conference in 1925 would be implemented as of the first of January 1929.[6] This announcement met with strong opposition from the treaty powers and the foreign community in China. It also attracted criticism from senior Maritime Customs officials, who complained of insufficient notice to implement the new tariffs and a problematic legal situation for collecting them, the tariffs being in violation of bilateral treaties between China and other countries.[7] The eventual resumption of tariff autonomy in 1929 was as much a result of foreign-policy shifts on the part of the treaty powers as it was of a new, successful Chinese negotiating strategy.

The first part of this chapter discusses how Chinese intellectuals and politicians conceptualized China's foreign trade and the position

4. Xu, *China and the Great War*, pp. 258–70.

5. Young, *China's Nation-Building Effort*, p. 18; Sun Ruoyi, "'Guanshui tebie huiyi,'" p. 241.

6. Foreign Office Memorandum of 8 January 1930, on British Policy in China [F 6720/3/10], in Rohan Butler and J. P. T. Bury, *Documents on British Foreign Policy* [hereafter cited as *DBFP*], 2nd ser., vol. 8, p. 7.

7. Second Historical Archives of China, Inspectorate General of Maritime Customs Records [hereafter cited as SHAC]; see SHAC 679/17973, A. H. F. Edwardes, Officiating Inspector-General, to R. F. C. Hedgeland, Commissioner, Canton, 13 October 1927.

of Maritime Customs in administering it. The second part offers an analysis of the foreign policy of Great Britain, the United States, and Japan toward China, and the Chinese negotiating strategy that led to the granting of tariff autonomy to China by the treaty powers in 1929. By the late 1920s Great Britain, still preeminent among the treaty powers, was committed to accommodating Chinese nationalism. The US government, then led by President Calvin Coolidge and still under the influence of the horrors of the First World War, was committed to an isolationist foreign policy that entailed a retreat from international involvement. France was beset by domestic struggles, Japan on its own was not strong enough to maintain the status quo, and Germany and the Soviet Union had renounced their treaty rights early on.

Conceptualizing Trade

In the century between the signing of the Nanjing Treaty in 1842 and the beginning of the Second Sino-Japanese War, Chinese opinion on the role of external trade changed fundamentally. In the early nineteenth century, the dominant opinion in statecraft circles was that external trade was, at best, superfluous, and more often than not harmful to the Chinese empire. Some scholars advocated a limited opening of China to external trade; however, imperial policy sided with the negative view of external trade. That view changed, however, with the advent of legally imported foreign commodities, increased government revenue from tariffs, and the exposure of Chinese intellectuals to the concepts of Western political economy. External trade was now viewed as an integral part of the Chinese economy, although it required the close supervision and regulation of the state; it was certainly legitimate, and could be beneficial if advantageously regulated by the state. This paradigm shift was not a Nationalist project, but because the Nationalist state relied on tariffs as its single greatest source of government revenue, it also relied on the changed view of external trade to justify this economic activity as legitimate.

Consumer taste and state policy were at variance with each other during the Qing dynasty, as is evidenced by the Qianlong emperor's closure of all seaports other than Guangzhou to foreign trade, on the one hand, and the continued existence of illicit trade, or smuggling, to meet consumer demand for foreign goods, on the other. In his analysis of the "everyday changes in the material landscape of China" from the mid-nineteenth to the mid-twentieth century, Frank Dikötter shows that foreign commodities were widespread in China as early as the early nineteenth century: "What was considered a luxury in the past is now viewed as perfectly ordinary, and only things foreign are considered to be superior."[8] This perception was not a matter of social rank: "As Chen Zhongshu noted with alarm, the entire population, from servants and footmen down to prostitutes and slaves, admired the ingenious and exquisite goods imported from abroad."[9] According to Dikötter, "While some of these observations gleaned from literary notes (筆記; biji) deplored foreign influence on material culture, a more widespread discourse portrayed 'ocean goods' (洋貨; yanghuo) as intricate and exotic"; this taste for the exotic extended to the emperor himself, as reflected in the imperial collections.[10] After the opening of the first five treaty ports and imposition of the 5 percent ad valorem limit on import tariffs, foreign goods spread throughout China; Duan Guangqing noted in 1857 that "everything produced by Westerners is used all over the empire."[11]

If these widespread consumer preferences existed, one wonders why the Qing state did not tap into them for revenue. The idea of legitimizing trade on a wider scale than previously allowed was repeatedly mooted by Chinese scholar-officials during the nineteenth century, both before and after the opening of the first five treaty ports under the Treaty of Nanjing in 1842.[12] And yet, this was not the dominant paradigm in understanding external trade in nineteenth-century China. Huangchao jingshi wenbian 皇朝經世文編 (Collected writings on

8. Liang Zhangju, Tui'an suibi, vol. 7, pp. 7–8a, in Biji xiaoshuo daguan, vol. 1, p. 172, quoted in Dikötter, Things Modern, p. 26.

9. Chen Zhongshu, quoted in Dikötter, Things Modern, p. 26.

10. Dikötter, Things Modern, p. 27.

11. Duan Guangqing, Jinghu zixuan nianpu, quoted in Dikötter, Things Modern, p. 27.

12. Dikötter, Things Modern, p. 39; Levenson, Confucian China and Its Modern Fate, p. 62.

the statecraft of the reigning dynasty), the great statecraft compilation of the nineteenth century, contains an essay from 1827 by a scholar identified only by his surname or pen name, Guan, entitled "Jinyong yanghuo yi" (Suggestion to prohibit the use of foreign goods), in which the author argues that "all foreign goods that come to China are ingenious, but they are also useless."[13] Guan goes on to say that "abroad, they have wool, but China has never lacked the means to clothe itself; abroad, they have knives and mirrors, but China has never lacked the means to make tools."[14] Goods from abroad were unnecessary and caused an outflow of money, he concluded. Therefore, China should not allow foreign trade, and if it did not, China's fiscal strength would stabilize within a few years. As Jerome Ch'en writes, the problem with China's "mercantilist policies [was that they] were adopted when the sovereignty of the sovereign was crippled; therefore they, too, were crippled in the sense that the mercantilists could not protect fully their home economy against foreign competition."[15]

Beginning in the late nineteenth century, Chinese economists broke with their indigenous intellectual legacy, under the influence of Western economic theory; however, early translations into Chinese of Western works on economics are still framed in terms of statecraft philosophy. One of the first works of political economy to be translated into Chinese was an abbreviated version of Henry Fawcett's *Manual of Political Economy*, translated into Chinese by W. A. P. Martin and Wang Fengzao as *Fuguo ce* (Strategy for enriching the country); it was followed by others in the same vein—such as *Fuguo yangmin ce* (Strategy to enrich the country and nourish the people), Joseph Edkins's translation of William Stanley Jevons's *Political Economy*.[16]

In their assessment of the government's success in protecting domestic industries, Chinese economists were leaving the intellectual terrain of statecraft and entering the world of civil society. Many commentators in late Qing and Republican China associated China's

13. Guan, "Jinyong yanghuo yi," in He Changling, *Huangchao jingshi wenbian*, p. 42.

14. Guan, "Jinyong yanghuo yi," in He Changling, *Huangchao jingshi wenbian*, pp. 42–43.

15. Ch'en, *State Economic Policies of the Ch'ing Government*, p. 137.

16. Casalin, *L'introduzione del pensiero economico occidentale*, p. 60.

political and economic decline in the late nineteenth century with Manchu rule, arguing that the Qing dynasty concluded humiliating bilateral treaties that limited China's sovereign rights with respect to the imperialist powers because, being ethnically foreign, the Manchus were uninterested in China's fate. Chinese Han nationalists used what they regarded as the Qing's neglect of China's national interests to justify their call for an end to Qing rule. This interpretation was artic-ulated most prominently by Sun Yat-sen, who traced China's con-temporary predicament back to the nineteenth century: "After the Manchu government had carried on wars with foreign nations and had been defeated, China was forced to sign many unequal treaties. . . . Foreign nations are still using these treaties to bind China, and as a result China fails at whatever she attempts."[17]

Even after Sun Yat-sen's death in 1925, political discourse within the Guomindang was dominated by his theoretical legacy. Sun's writ-ings provided a theoretical reference point for Chinese nationalism and he achieved, posthumously, the paramount status in Chinese political discourse that had eluded him throughout his life. The rev-erence with which Sun's writings were regarded after his death was part of a Guomindang strategy to unify the Nationalist Party under Chiang Kai-shek's leadership through continuous references to the legacy of the *guofu* (國父; father of the nation), as Sun became known in Guomindang rhetoric.[18] Both Chiang Kai-shek and Wang Jingwei, for a time Chiang's chief rival for Guomindang leadership, claimed Sun's intellectual legacy—Chiang, in justifying "a vigorous military reunification followed by the establishment of a military regime rely-ing on a strong, military-oriented heavy industry," and Wang, in ex-pounding the merits of national unity brought about by economic reconstruction.[19]

Sun was a physician by training, not an economist; his visions for the development of China, as set forth in *Shiye jihua* (Industrializa-tion plan) and *Sanmin zhuyi* (Three principles of the people), both

17. Sun, *San min chu i*, p. 104.
18. Spence, *The Search for Modern China*, p. 347.
19. Zanasi, *Saving the Nation*, p. 30.

published in 1919, are impressive for their ambition and scope rather than for their attention to detail or practicality.[20] Nevertheless, while Sun's plans lack a grasp of infrastructure and technical problems, his pronouncements on the importance of tariffs show an understanding of the basic issue of free trade versus protectionism. Sun Yat-sen's economic thinking, which shaped economic debates in the 1920s and 1930s, was based on his understanding of the concept of infant-industry protection developed by Western economists in the nineteenth century.

Sun believed that "since China opened to foreign trade, the unfavorable balance of trade . . . had steadily [become] rampant."[21] In his view, regaining tariff autonomy was only one element in a necessary comprehensive strategy to limit foreign economic influence in China. Protectionist tariffs were to be accompanied by a wide range of boycott activities: "The common people . . . can do things such as these— refuse to work for foreigners, refuse to be foreign slaves or to use foreign goods manufactured abroad, push the use of native goods, decline to use foreign bank notes, use only Chinese government money, and sever economic relationships with foreigners."[22] Sun also refers to the example of economic protest set by Mahatma Gandhi's noncooperation movement: "What does noncooperation mean? What the British needed, like labor, the Indians did not provide them with; and what the British offered, like foreign goods, the Indians did not need, since they consumed indigenous goods only."[23] In his study of the relationship between consumerism and nationalism in China, Karl Gerth points out the parallels between Gandhi's *swadeshi* ("of our own country") and the noncooperation movement (1904–8 and 1920–22) and the protectionist National Products Movement promoted by the Nationalist government during the Nanjing decade that was to a large extent based on Sun's ideas.[24] However, Chinese economic

20. Sun's *Shiye jihua* is more commonly known by the title of the English ed., *The International Development of China*.
21. Sun Zhongshan, *Sanmin zhuyi*, p. 33.
22. Sun Zhongshan, *Sanmin zhuyi*, p. 94.
23. Sun Zhongshan, *Sanmin zhuyi*, p. 94.
24. Gerth, *China Made*, p. 33.

nationalism never attained the importance of the *swadeshi* movement, not least because Chinese consumers were keen to consume modern, imported commodities.

At the same time, tariff reform was only one part of Sun Yat-sen's vision for a reformed Chinese taxation system. This vision was very much shaped by Sun's perception of economic modernity in the West and Japan, as becomes apparent from his plans to introduce direct taxation. A graduated income tax, which Sun advocated, is a form of taxation that, because of the degree of its intrusiveness into citizens' lives, had become common in Western countries only during the First World War in order to fund military expenditures (with the exception of Britain, where it had been adopted during the Napoleonic Wars for the same purpose).[25]

> The third feature of modern economic reform, direct taxation, is also a very recent development in the socioeconomic method. It is applied by means of a graduated tax scale, which levies a heavy income tax and inheritance tax on capitalists and secures financial resources for the state directly from the capitalists. Because of the large income of capitalists, direct taxation by the state brings in much revenue without being oppressive.[26]

Sun Yat-sen asserted that fairness should be the basis of taxation. One may suspect that in denouncing the supposedly privileged position of capitalists under the traditional Chinese system of taxation, Sun was influenced by his Soviet advisers, just as they had influenced his critique of imperialist domination in China. However, Sun's proposals for national taxation were still based on a capitalist economy.

> The old system of taxation depended entirely on the tax on money and grain and on the Maritime Customs tariff. These methods laid the burden of national income entirely on the poor people and let the capitalists enjoy all the privileges of the state without shouldering any financial re-

25. Nehring and Schui, "Introduction"; Nehring, "The Paradoxes of State-Building."
26. Sun Zhongshan, *Sanmin zhuyi*, p. 302.

sponsibility, which was exceedingly unjust. Germany and Great Britain long ago became aware of this injustice and put into effect a plan of direct taxation.[27]

Sun Yat-sen's thinking was heavily influenced by Leninism, both politically and economically. In his economic thought, Sun was influenced by the New Economic Policy, which had succeeded War Communism as the official economic reconstruction policy of the Soviet Union in 1921.[28] The New Economic Policy was characterized by the role it allocated to privately run small-scale enterprises and the limited economic role assigned to the market. Also, it reintroduced taxation in place of forced grain requisitions, and allowed peasants to retain their surplus produce and sell it for a profit. Large industries remained under state control and operated on the open market, but the state controlled the fixing of prices and the appointment of boards of directors. Private trade and wages were restored, and compulsory labor abolished.[29] The influence of this policy is demonstrated in Sun Yat-sen's conclusion to *The International Development of China*, in which he outlines plans for state-led industrialization in China and concludes by stating that China, in its quest for development, must adopt the best of both capitalism and socialism.[30]

Sun Yat-sen's thinking shaped the debate about political and economic issues in Republican China; his intellectual support for protectionism provided the basis for Nationalist government tariff policies during the Nanjing decade. Philip Richardson even argues that "the dominant ideology behind the pursuit of economic modernization [in China] in the twentieth century was provided by Sun Zhongshan (Sun Yat-sen)."[31] However, debates about economic issues were also influenced decisively by the advice of academically qualified economists. Chinese students had begun to study economics at China's recently established Western-style universities during the last years of the

27. Sun Zhongshan, *Sanmin zhuyi*, p. 302.
28. Bergère, *Sun Yat-sen*, p. 308.
29. Davies, *Soviet Economic Development*, pp. 23–37.
30. Sun, *The International Development of China*, p. 161.
31. Richardson, *Economic Change in China*, p. 92.

Qing dynasty. The subject was subsequently introduced throughout Chinese universities, where it was taught with an emphasis on applied economics, the primary purpose of its study being the training of future administrators. The most renowned institution for the study of economics in China was the Institute of Economics at Tianjin's Nankai University. The Nankai Institute of Economics stood out both in terms of the volume and quality of its empirical research on the Chinese economy and because it was led by Chinese economists from its inception. Chinese economists trained at Nankai and elsewhere would become influential in later economic debates during the Nanjing decade.

In the late 1920s and early 1930s, the Institute of Economics was headed by Franklin Ho (He Lian) and his deputy, H. D. Fong (Fang Xianting). Both had received part of their training in the United States at Yale University, and thus they belonged to the ranks of the Chinese academic elite trained at leading Western universities. Like many other Chinese academics and intellectuals, Franklin Ho joined the nationalist government in the late 1930s during a climate of national emergency. Ho served as director of the Department of Political Affairs of the Executive Yuan, the executive branch of the Nationalist government, in 1936 and became vice minister of economic affairs in 1938.[32] Because he joined the government at a time of national crisis, Ho's government service cannot necessarily be interpreted as the action of a Guomindang loyalist. Ho reflected critically on the regime's developmental agenda and added to the economic expertise among Guomindang policy makers.

Both Ho and Fong had advocated protective tariffs for "infant industries" since the 1920s and provided theoretical support for the Guomindang national government when it increased tariffs after achieving tariff autonomy in 1929.[33] Based on his reading of their work, Paul B. Trescott argues that "protectionism was never a big element in the Ho-Fong policy outlook."[34] However, he further states that both

---

32. Shih, *The Strenuous Decade*, pp. 332–33.

33. Franklin Ho and H. D. Fong, "Extent and Effects of Industrialization in China" (1929), quoted in Trescott, "Economics at China's Nankai University," p. 56.

34. Trescott, "Economics at China's Nankai University," p. 58.

economists persistently stressed the damage being done to Chinese industries by competition from foreign imports. Looking back on the interwar period, Fong wrote in 1942:

> The failure of the Government to adopt a persistent policy for the encouragement and protection of industry has considerably impeded the course of China's industrialization. . . . As a colony in fact if not in name, China was bound to leave her industries unprotected. She had thus in the early forties of the last century given away her tariff autonomy, a very important instrument of tariff protection, until its recovery in 1929. . . . Nay, she had to stand a further loss of industrial protection under the 1895 Treaty of Shimonoseki, according to which foreigners were allowed to erect factories on Chinese soil, thus evading the payment of a stipulated tariff of five per cent *ad valorem* altogether. . . . Not "protection to infant industries," but "protection to foreign industries" carried the day.[35]

In this statement, Fong echoes Sun Yat-sen's statement about the 5 percent ad valorem tariff cap having worked in favor of foreign imports; he also addresses the issue of foreign-owned enterprises based in the foreign concessions that were not subject to any import tariffs. Reflecting the nationalist trend in economics following the works of Friedrich List and John Stuart Mill, Fong did not commend foreign-owned enterprises in China as foreign direct investment but saw their role in strictly nationalistic terms.

The economist Zheng Youkui, who was based at the Academia Sinica, observed in 1939 that "taking a comprehensive view of our country's tariff policy, it is clear that it is concerned first of all with increasing revenue, and only secondarily with protecting the industry."[36] Zheng derived this conclusion from observing the correlations between the development in tariff rates on competitive and noncompetitive imports and the relative shares of competitive and noncompetitive imports. He defined a competitive import as the import of a commodity that was also produced domestically. Correspondingly, a

35. Fong, "The Prospect for China's Industrialization," pp. 56–57.
36. Zheng Youkui, *Woguo guanshui zizhu hou jinkou shuilü bianqian*, p. 23.

noncompetitive import is the import of a commodity that faces no domestic competition. His conclusion was that since the average tariff rate on noncompetitive imports was higher than that on competitive imports, the government was changing the tariff schedule in such a way as to maximize its tariff revenue rather than to protect domestic industries.[37] Zheng claimed that in its quest for increased tariff revenue, the government significantly increased the tariff rate on imported necessities.

Critical analysis of Guomindang tariff policy was accompanied in many cases by an awareness of the changing nature of the Chinese taxation system. Yau-Pik Chau, who was awarded a PhD in economics from the University of Chicago in 1942 for his comprehensive examination of the Nationalist government's tax reforms during the Nanjing decade, addressed the rationale underlying taxation. He argued that "the notion of taxes as contributions by free citizens for the rendering of public services by a popularly elected government did not arise until the necessary political arrangements were developed."[38] One may question Chau's implication that the political system of the Nanjing decade was that of a popularly elected government. Nevertheless, this passage reflects one Chinese economist's awareness of the changed social contract behind taxation under a republican constitution, however nominal some aspects of popular representation in this republican system remained. Besides this more systemic appreciation, Chau also had a number of suggestions to make about the reform of the Chinese tariff schedule. He observed that, in many cases, tariffs and taxes disadvantageous to industrial development were retained for fiscal reasons. Examples included both the interport tax and the import taxes levied on industrial raw materials: "In most industrialized countries, industrial raw materials are exempt from import duties, whereas in China a non-protective fiscal policy has been adopted."[39]

37. Zheng Youkui, *Woguo guanshui zizhu hou jinkou shuilü bianqian*, pp. 23–28; Cheng, *Foreign Trade and Industrial Development of China*, p. 61.

38. Chau, "Taxation Reforms of the Chinese National Government," p. 319.

39. Chau, "Taxation Reforms of the Chinese National Government," p. 344.

By Republican times, Chinese economists accepted China's foreign trade as legitimate, if rarely beneficial for China's economic development. They objected to the 5 percent ad valorem limit on import taxes imposed by the Treaty of Tianjin, and demanded tariff protection for China's indigenous industries. The Maritime Customs Service, and the trade statistics it published, were essential in establishing the notion of China as an international economic player. Fong pointed out the potential benefits of foreign trade for China's economic development and the prosperity of some of China's industries during the First World War, when China's economic rivals had to concentrate their economic resources on their respective war economies: "Except for the temporary relief afforded to Chinese manufacturers, especially cotton mill owners, during the World War of 1914–1918, Chinese industries could not have prospered the way they did in those years."[40] Compared with the Qianlong emperor's attitude—foreign trade was essentially unnecessary for China and was permitted only to allow foreigners to purchase Chinese goods—this was a significant change. Chinese economists repeatedly referred to the insufficiency of the Nationalist government's tariffs for keeping out foreign goods with which Chinese goods could not compete, but there were no more demands to close China completely to foreign trade. Indeed, even Sun Yat-sen, for all his rhetoric about tariffs acting like fortresses guarding China against the outside world, suggested a scheme of large-scale international investment in China, including the creation of planned port cities.[41]

A Changed Foreign-Policy Environment: British Policy on China

Britain's policy toward China underwent a major change in the 1920s. The change has been interpreted variously as a strategic retreat based on the preservation of Britain's economic interests in China and as a reaction to political and economic events in East Asia on the part of

40. Fong, "The Prospect for China's Industrialization," p. 56.
41. Sun Zhongshan, *Sanmin zhuyi*, p. 31; *The International Development of China*, pp. 160, 178.

British politicians and diplomats.[42] Britain's economic interests in China in the 1920s and 1930s notably included loans financed by British banks and stockholders' interests in British companies operating in China, such as Imperial Chemical Industries (ICI) and the Hong Kong and Shanghai Bank (HSBC).[43] In the most important recent work on this topic, Robert Bickers argues that British diplomats and politicians reacted to political and economic pressures brought to bear on the British presence in China in the 1920s by reconfiguring that presence.[44]

The interplay between strategic retrenchment and reaction to political and economic pressure becomes apparent from the official British reactions to Chinese protests and boycotts. The May Thirtieth Incident (30 May 1925), in which Chinese demonstrators were killed by members of the Shanghai Municipal Police, led to strikes and boycotts in Shanghai and other urban centers. During a demonstration of solidarity in Guangzhou on 23 June 1925, Chinese demonstrators and bystanders were killed by British and French troops as the demonstration marched past the foreign concession on Shamian Island. This violent response led to a boycott of British shipping that lasted for almost a year and greatly affected the British colony of Hong Kong.

Given the deleterious economic effect on British interests of this boycott and other similar boycotts elsewhere in China, and Britain's inability and unwillingness to protect its interests through the use of force, the British legation in Beijing acknowledged in its annual report to the Foreign Office that Britain's policy on China might have to change to guard British economic interests.

It is, however, doubtful whether the use of armed force by His Majesty's Government to bring the Cantonese [i.e., the Guomindang] to reason and to exact compensation for the outrages committed by them against the British communities in Shameen [Shamian] and Swatow [Shantou]

---

42. Fung, *The Diplomacy of Imperial Retreat,* pp. 3–6; Louis, *British Strategy in the Far East,* pp. 1–4.
43. Cain and Hopkins, *British Imperialism,* p. 607.
44. Bickers, *Britain in China,* p. 115.

and the colony of Hong Kong would result in the establishment of improved relations between Canton and the Government of the colony, and
whether the remedy might not prove worse than the disease by permanently diverting from Hong Kong and Canton a large volume of trade
which has already been forced to take other channels by continuance of
the strike and the boycott.[45]

Summarizing the official British negotiating position with regard
to the Guangzhou boycott, John Pratt, a long-time member of the British consular service in China then seconded to the Foreign Office as
an adviser on Chinese affairs, stated that "His Majesty's Government
have decided to acquiesce in these new taxes and to favour assistance
being rendered by the customs solely because that seems to be the only
means of terminating the boycott and because the price we are being
called upon to pay is not too heavy." In fact, however, Pratt noted that
the decision was also made for less immediately practical reasons: "If
the question be examined from the point of view of high policy, it is
probable that, on the ground, this decision will be found to be both
wise and far-sighted." In Pratt's view, "China must some day acquire
tariff autonomy and resume control over her customs revenues—a control which she only lost in 1911—and this seems as smooth and easy a
way of achieving that end as any."[46]

  While Pratt represented the position within the Foreign Office
most sympathetic to Chinese nationalism, that institution was on the
whole more committed to what Edmund Fung refers to as the policy
of "imperial retreat," a policy that aimed to preserve British economic
interests in China, if necessary at the expense of political interests.[47]
The British minister in Beijing from 1923 until 1926, Sir Ronald Macleay, was noticeably less sympathetic toward Chinese nationalism

  45. "China, Annual Report, 1925" [F 3028/3028/10], in Trotter, *British Documents
on Foreign Affairs*, Part 2, Series E, Asia [hereafter cited as *BDFA*], vol. 19: *China,
1919–1926*, p. 332.

  46. J. T. Pratt, "The Customs Administration and the New Taxation Proposals at
Canton," 29 September 1926, *BDFA*, vol. 31: *China, July 1926–December 1926*, p. 132.

  47. Atkins, *Informal Empire in Crisis*, pp. 15–16; Fung, *The Diplomacy of Imperial
Retreat*, p. 8.

than Pratt or Pratt's superior, Sir Victor Wellesley, head of the Foreign Office's Far Eastern Department. In November 1926, Macleay wrote that he did not believe that the Guomindang was "either able or anxious to throw off the Soviet yoke." Still mindful of the demonstrations and boycotts in Guangzhou and elsewhere, Macleay said he also believed that the "policy of a Kuo-min-tang Government, if ever one is to be in control of the country, [would] under Soviet instigation be aggressively Nationalist and primarily and intensely anti-British." Macleay wrote this dispatch shortly before the end of his tenure as British minister in Beijing to correct what he regarded as the "unfounded" assumptions of the Foreign Office about "moderate and reasonable elements" within the Guomindang.[48] Macleay's successor as British minister in Beijing, Miles Lampson, while stopping in Hong Kong en route to his new post, telegraphed to the foreign secretary that in Hong Kong and Guangzhou there was the "strongest possible opinion in all British circles, shared by the Governor [of Hong Kong] and Mr Brenan [acting consul general in Guangzhou] that [sic] time has come when the South should be recognized." Lampson himself expressed his reserve on the issue of recognition but stated that he was convinced that he should make contact with the Guomindang-led southern government as soon as possible.[49] In the British legation's annual report for 1927, Lampson wrote that "the term 'Nationalist Government' of China [was] again a mere name, around which the Southern politicians wrangle and dispute in interminable controversies which lead to no result."[50] In early 1929, although Lampson wrote that China was "more than nominally united," he also stated that "progress has been slower than even the less optimistic anticipated, and in many directions is hardly discernible."[51] Thereafter, the British legation and the British consular service remained more reserved in their attitudes

48. Sir R. Macleay to Sir Austen Chamberlain, 24 November 1926 [F 5016/1/10], BDFA, vol. 31, p. 276.

49. Mr. Lampson to Sir Austen Chamberlain, 27 November 1926 [F 5058/933/10], BDFA, vol. 31, p. 283.

50. "China, Annual Report, 1927," 30 January 1928 [F 1807/1807/10], BDFA, vol. 20, p. 4.

51. Sir M. Lampson to Sir Austen Chamberlain, 4 January 1929 [F 1054/3/10], BDFA, vol. 36, p. 146.

toward Chinese nationalism and the Guomindang than the British government and the Foreign Office.

The change of opinion in the Foreign Office was encapsulated in what is known as the December Memorandum of 1926, which signaled a shift in British policy on China. Having at first acknowledged the Nationalists only as a threat to British economic interests and then as a probable contender for rule over China, the Foreign Office eventually began to see the rhetoric of Chinese nationalism in a more favorable light. In the memorandum, the British government called on the other treaty powers to "make it clear that in their constructive policy they desire to go as far as possible in meeting the legitimate aspirations of the Chinese nation." The treaty powers should "abandon the idea that the political and economic development of China can only be secured under foreign tutelage" and "declare their readiness to recognize her right to the enjoyment of tariff autonomy, as soon as she herself has settled and promulgated a new national tariff law." The reason for this conciliatory attitude, according to the December Memorandum, was the fact that "there will continue to be in the future as there have been in the past breaches of treaties as a result either of lawlessness or of deliberate intent, but it will be equally difficult to secure the enforcement of treaty stipulations or to effect their much needed revision."[52] The difficulty of revising the duties lay in the fact that "in any attempt to secure revision the Chinese are faced on the one hand with the internal difficulty of their own disunion and on the other with the external difficulty of obtaining the unanimous consent of the Powers."[53] In conclusion, the memorandum stated that the treaty powers should declare "their readiness to negotiate on treaty revision and all other outstanding questions as soon as the Chinese themselves have constituted a Government with authority to negotiate." That the Foreign Office considered the Guomindang to be the most likely party to establish such a government is apparent in the preceding passage: "The political disintegration of China has,

52. "Statement of British Policy in China, Approved by the Cabinet on 1st December, 1926" [F 5298/10/10], *BDFA*, vol. 31, p. 298.
53. "Statement of British Policy in China, Approved by the Cabinet on 1st December, 1926" [F 5298/10/10], *BDFA*, vol. 31, p. 300.

however, been accompanied by the growth of a powerful Nationalist movement, which aimed at gaining for China an equal place among the nations."[54] Besides this declaration of intent, the British government "strongly urged that the [Treaty] Powers should now authorize the immediate levy of the Washington surtaxes unconditionally throughout China" and hoped that this step would "provide a basis for regularizing the position at Canton."[55]

Once the British government had officially changed its policy on China, it remained committed to the policy of recognizing Chinese Nationalist claims as legitimate, despite antiforeign incidents that were at least sponsored, if not actively organized, by left-wing elements within the Guomindang. One such occurrence was the Nanjing Incident in March 1927, when Nationalist troops that had conquered Nanjing during the Northern Expedition looted foreign-owned property in the city and engaged in antiforeign violence. In a dispatch summarizing the events leading up to the negotiation of the Anglo-Chinese Commerce Treaty, Lampson stated that "the continuance of civil war between North and South throughout . . . 1927, and in particular the Nanking outrage of March 1927 made it difficult, if not impossible for us to take any further steps in the direction of the recognizing [of] China's right to tariff autonomy, and we were obliged to adopt a waiting attitude, which lasted well into the spring of 1927."[56] The successful completion of the second phase of the Northern Expedition, which ended with the occupation of Beijing by Nationalist troops in June 1928, and the signing of the Sino-US tariff treaty on 25 July 1928, also known as the Soong-MacMurray Agreement, stimulated the British government to take further action with regard to negotiating both a settlement of the Nanjing Incident and a bilateral tariff treaty. In the settlement of the Nanjing Incident, the Chinese Nationalist government accepted full responsibility for damages to British lives and property

54. "Statement of British Policy in China, Approved by the Cabinet on 1st December, 1926" [F 5298/10/10], *BDFA*, vol. 31, p. 298.

55. "Statement of British Policy in China, Approved by the Cabinet on 1st December, 1926" [F 5298/10/10], *BDFA*, vol. 31, p. 300.

56. Sir M. Lampson to Sir Austen Chamberlain, 4 January 1929 [F 1056/11/10], *BDFA*, vol. 36, p. 153.

and undertook to pay compensation.[57] In exchange, the British consul general in Shanghai, acting for the British minister in Beijing, expressed the willingness of the British government to enter into negotiations regarding tariff revision "in due course."[58] This deal represented a departure from the earlier British negotiating position, since in April the British foreign secretary, Sir Austen Chamberlain, had stated that he was "strongly averse to the inclusion of so extraneous a matter as treaty revision in any documentary settlement of the Nanking incident, because [he could not] admit that, in what should constitute a unilateral act of reparation for a gross outrage, the Nanking Government should be able to claim that as the price of making such reparation they have been able to secure the introduction of other matters into the actual terms of settlement."[59] However, the publication of the Sino-US tariff treaty on 26 July 1928, providing for US recognition of Chinese tariff autonomy pending the consent of the other treaty powers, caused Sir Austen Chamberlain to announce in a speech in the House of Commons on 30 July that "as soon as the Nanking incident was settled, [the British government would be] prepared to negotiate a commercial treaty with China to take the place of the existing system of restriction of China's tariff freedom."[60] Once that obstacle was overcome, a bilateral commercial treaty that provided, among other things, for mutual most-favored-nation treatment was negotiated and ratified on 14 March 1929.[61] By 1930, the Foreign Office stated that British policy on China was determined by the following principles:

> As regards the principles of British policy in China, these can be stated in a very few words. We have no territorial or imperialistic aims. Our first concern is to maintain our position in the trade of China, which is

57. Dr. C. T. Wang to Sir M. Lampson, 9 August 1928 [F 4378/156/10], *BDFA*, vol. 34, p. 166.

58. Sir M. Lampson to Dr. C. T. Wang, 9 August 1928 [F 4378/156/10], *BDFA*, vol. 34, p. 168.

59. Sir Austen Chamberlain to Sir M. Lampson, 28 March 1928 [F 1423/156/10], *BDFA*, vol. 34, p. 282.

60. Sir M. Lampson to Sir A. Chamberlain, 4 January 1929 [F 1056/11/10], *BDFA*, vol. 36, p. 151.

61. Sir Austen Chamberlain to Sir M. Lampson, 14 March 1929 [F 1093/11/10], *BDFA*, vol. 36, p. 177.

largely bound up with the prosperity of Hong Kong and the fortunes of the Maritime Customs Administration, and to secure adequate protection for British lives, property and business enterprises. Our second concern is to maintain the principle of the "open door" and opportunity for all, and to see that China does not fall under the tutelage of any single Power. For these reasons we desire to see a united, well-ordered, prosperous and peaceful China, and it is our policy to endeavour to co-operate to that end with the other Great Powers concerned. These are the root principles underlying all our efforts in China.[62]

While British policy on China was also influenced by other factors, such as the British view of China as the "front line in the struggle of the empire against the USSR and its support for anti-colonial movements and Asian communism," its trajectory, after late 1926, was one of reforming and decolonizing the British presence in China.[63] The commitment of the British political and diplomatic establishment to this policy of retrenchment was an outcome of the successful Nationalist boycott strategy that threatened British economic interests in China.

United States Policy on China

While the United States shared Britain's economic and financial interests in China, it did not have leased territories or a colony in China. Therefore the US government was less vulnerable to the pressures of domestic foreign-policy lobbies and stood to lose less from the demands of Chinese nationalism. At the same time, the United States was committed, at least rhetorically, to a new diplomatic approach in dealing with China, based on President Woodrow Wilson's condemnation of the practices and concepts of "old diplomacy." This new approach opposed establishing new "particularistic policies and power rivalries in the Far East at the expense of China."[64] At a time when the

---

62. Foreign Office Memorandum of 8 January 1930 on British Policy in China [F 6720/3/10], *DBFP*, 2nd ser., vol. 8, p. 4.

63. Bickers, *Britain in China*, pp. 17, 117; quotation on p. 117.

64. Iriye, *After Imperialism*, pp. 10–11.

United States was still reeling from the impact of the First World War, a negotiated solution to conflict among the treaty powers in China also offered the chance to avoid further overseas conflicts.

In 1922 the US government convened the Washington Conference on the Limitation of Armament in order to negotiate a framework of treaties aimed at containing Japanese expansion in the Pacific. At the conference, all those powers that still maintained bilateral treaties with China that were concluded under conditions of inequality committed themselves, in principle, to restoring tariff autonomy to China; details of the process would be settled at a conference to be convened in Beijing especially for that purpose. The Beijing Conference was delayed until 1925, both because of the unstable political situation in China and because of the French government's refusal to negotiate with the Chinese until China had committed to paying France's portion of the Boxer Protocol indemnity at the rate of exchange demanded by the French government.

The US attitude toward China in the 1920s can be summarized as an attempt to protect American economic and financial interests as well as extraterritoriality in China by granting concessions to the Chinese government. This attitude was illustrated in an exchange of notes between the United States and France in 1924. In November 1924, the French government wanted to use a change in government in Beijing as an opportunity to extract an agreement to France's demands in exchange for diplomatic recognition of the new government. In its response to the French proposal, the US Department of State declared that "while recognizing the fact that the Chinese Government has of late manifested an increasing tendency to ignore the rights of the foreign Powers, this Government cannot blind itself to the fact that this tendency has found an excuse and an encouragement in the minds of the Chinese by reason of the fact that they conceive the foreign Powers to have abandoned the policy of cooperation and mutual accommodation embodied in the decisions with respect to Chinese affairs adopted by the Washington Conference on the Limitation of Armament." The State Department further noted that "the Powers are ... prejudiced and weakened in their insistence that China should observe their treaty rights in full, unless and until these treaty rights may be modified by mutual consent; and in the opinion of the American Government there is grave danger of the inculcation of a spirit of distrust which might even more seriously attenuate the sense of responsibility of the Chinese with respect to their obligations."[65] Couched in the evasive language of international diplomacy, the US Department of State advocated the gradual diminution of some American privileges in China. When the Beijing Tariff Conference was eventually convened in 1925, Secretary of State Frank Kellogg wrote in his instructions to the American delegation that he was "sympathetic to the aims of the Chinese, and [desired] to bring about such modifications in the [US] treaties with China as may be just and practicable."[66]

A comparison with the British position is illuminating. The economic effect of the boycotts occasioned by the Shanghai and Shamian incidents in 1925 was one of the main factors that changed British policy with relation to Chinese nationalism. Those protests were directed chiefly against British and Japanese goods; the economic interests of the United States were much less affected by the strikes and boycotts. However, the Guangzhou boycott did make an impression on the resident American consul general, Douglas Jenkins, who reported to the American minister in Beijing as follows:

> The Canton government is using the strike to further its aims. There could be no valid objection, of course, to the strike as such were it not encouraged and directed by the authorities, but there is, it seems to me, a very serious cause for complaint in the fact that the local government has permitted the strikers to uniform and arm themselves and to arrest foreigners alleged to have broken the strike regulations as well as [to] seize foodstuff and other merchandise in the possession of foreigners. . . . The local authorities say that they are not responsible for the strike and yet they not only fail to prevent outrages of this sort but have actually promulgated laws conferring extensive police and other powers on the strikers.
>
> The ultimate aim of the Kuomintang, or the Canton branch of it at least, is clearly to force the United States and the other Powers to sur-

65. Memorandum, Department of State to the French Embassy, 25 November 1924 [893.01/134], in US Department of State, *Foreign Relations of the United States* [hereafter cited as *FRUS*], 1924, vol. 1, pp. 427–28.

66. Secretary of State to American Delegation, 9 September 1925 [500.A 4e/352b], *FRUS*, 1925, vol. 1, p. 843.

render extraterritorial rights and it seems to me quite clear that as long as the Powers submit to the present methods of attack the campaign will gradually become more and more reckless of treaty rights to the very grave discomfort of Americans and other foreigners residing here.[67]

In other words, the Nationalists had found an efficient strategy to use against the treaty powers and it was anticipated that this strategy could also be used specifically against the United States at some point in the future.

Its growing awareness of American vulnerability in China, earlier commitments to the peaceful resolution of conflicts of interest in China in the 1922 Washington Treaty—intended as a restraint against the Japanese use of force in China—and the need to respond to Britain's 1926 December Memorandum led the US government to seek negotiations with China on the subject of tariff autonomy in early 1927. In January, Kellogg publicly stated that "the United States is now, and always has been, ever since the negotiation of the Washington Treaty, prepared to enter into negotiations with any Government of China or delegates who can represent or speak for China not only for the putting into force of the surtaxes of the Washington Treaty but [also for] entirely releasing tariff control and restoring complete tariff autonomy to China."[68]

The negotiations were delayed both because, as MacMurray complained to Kellogg, the Nationalist government was reluctant to begin actual negotiations owing to continuing power struggles within the Guomindang and because the American government insisted on settling the Nanjing Incident before beginning negotiations with the Nationalist government.[69] The Nanjing Incident was settled with an exchange of notes on 30 March 1928, several months before Great Britain reached a similar settlement with the Nationalist government. In both settlements, the Nationalist government accepted responsibility for the

67. Consul General, Canton (Jenkins), to Minister in China (MacMurray), 6 February 1926 [893.00/7190], *FRUS*, 1926, vol. 1, p. 691.

68. Secretary of State to Chargé in China (Mayers), 25 January 1927 [711.93/116a: Telegram], *FRUS*, 1927, vol. 2, p. 350.

69. Memorandum by the Assistant Secretary of State (Johnson), 5 January 1928 [711.93/164], *FRUS*, 1928, vol. 2, p. 401.

loss of foreign lives and promised to pay compensation, while also resolutely maintaining that the incident had been the fault of leftist elements within the Guomindang.[70] In exchange, in settling the Nanjing Incident the US minister stated that the bombardment of Nanjing by US Navy vessels had been necessary to defend American lives and declined to apologize for the consequent loss of Chinese lives. However, he consented to begin negotiating a treaty revision, despite stating that there was no connection between the settlement of the Nanjing Incident and the beginning of bilateral negotiations. As a Nationalist victory over northern troops became increasingly likely in the early summer of 1927, Kellogg articulated the State Department's position on negotiations with the Nationalist government in a telegram to the American minister in Beijing, writing that "although it may be that the time has not arrived for the taking of definite action toward recognition of the existing Nationalist Government as the Government of China, it is felt that if the internal warfare should appear to be actually at an end it will be necessary soon for us to deal with that Government, as the de facto Government of China at least, and that we be prepared to fulfil the promises set forth in my statement of January 27, 1927."[71]

Just one day later, the Nationalist government publicly stated its intention to begin renegotiating China's bilateral treaties so as to "realize its hope of a new state." Claiming that the provisions in the unequal treaties were "a contravention of the principle in international law, of mutual respect and sovereignty and are not allowed by any sovereign state," the Nationalist government stated that it wished to "begin at once to negotiate—in accordance with diplomatic procedure—new treaties on a basis of complete equality and mutual respect for each other's sovereignty." In the same declaration, the Nationalist government went some way toward allaying concerns on the part of the treaty powers by asserting that it would "not disregard, nor has it disregarded, any international responsibility in consequence of agree-

70. Minister in China (MacMurray) to Secretary of State, 30 March 1928, *FRUS*, 1928, vol. 2, pp. 331–32.
71. Secretary of State to Minister in China (MacMurray), 15 June 1928 [893.01/284a: Telegram], *FRUS*, 1928, vol. 2, p. 181.

ments and understandings properly and legally concluded on a basis of equality."[72] In response, Kellogg authorized MacMurray to "commence at an appropriate time (and an early date is suggested) conversations with the Nationalist authorities with a view to the revision of tariff provisions of our treaties."[73]

Wu Chaogui, present in the United States as a special representative of the Nationalist government, as the Nationalist government had not yet been recognized by the US government, informed the secretary of state on 11 July that "in view of the traditional friendship between the United States and China, and your statement of January [27,] 1927, it [was] the hope and expectation of the Nationalist Government of China that the Government of the United States of America [would] be prepared at once to enter into negotiations with it for a new treaty between the two countries on a footing of equality and reciprocity."[74] The State Department was keen to complete negotiations quickly, the secretary of state having told the minister in Beijing in his earlier authorization that the January 1927 statement, "fairly interpreted, places us under an obligation to proceed, either with the other powers or alone, to negotiate on tariff matters."[75] In seeking President Coolidge's authorization to begin negotiations, Secretary of State Kellogg also stated that the United States stood "pledged to the release of tariff control and if China guarantees us equal treatment under a treaty I do not think we can suffer." In his letter to the president, Kellogg's main argument for negotiating a new tariff treaty was that "tariff control of China is doomed." Happily, the impending loss of this American prerogative also had a beneficial aspect, Kellogg noted, since "any encouragement which can be given [to the Nationalist

72. Nationalist Gvt. Declaration, Reuters, Shanghai, 16th June, in Minister in China (MacMurray) to Secretary of State, 17 June 1928 [793.00/202], *FRUS*, 1928, vol. 2, pp. 413–14.

73. Secretary of State to Minister in China (MacMurray), 23 June 1928 [893.01/289], *FRUS*, 1928, vol. 2, p. 449.

74. Special Representative of the Chinese Nationalist Government (C. C. Wu) to the Secretary of State, 11 July 1928 [711.93/184], *FRUS*, 1928, vol. 2, p. 415.

75. Secretary of State to Minister in China (MacMurray), 15 June 1928 [893.01/284a: Telegram], *FRUS*, 1928, vol. 2, p. 181.

government] by the world powers [would] strengthen their hands in dealing with the enormously difficult domestic situation."[76] The president's authority to negotiate was duly granted, and MacMurray negotiated a new tariff treaty with Song Ziwen that was signed on 25 July 1928. This treaty provided for mutual recognition of national tariff autonomy and nondiscriminatory tariff treatment. In submitting the treaty to President Coolidge for ratification by Congress, Kellogg commented that the "underlying principles of national autonomy and equality of treatment are those that apply generally among independent nations."[77] As Akira Iriye notes, in the Wilsonian worldview, of which Kellogg's China policy was an example, the concepts of national sovereignty and self-determination of peoples "applied primarily to Europe."[78]

Japan's China Policy

The 1920s saw a reconfiguring of international relations in East Asia, as the Western imperial powers scaled down their presence and Japan emerged as the preeminent foreign power with strategic interests in China. Still, when analyzing Japan's China policy between the two world wars one needs to be bear in mind that, from the late 1920s onward, the imperial government in Tokyo did not have full control of the Japanese armed forces, particularly those stationed in Korea, and that consequently, prior to the attempted military coup of 26 February 1936, Japan had several different policies on matters of foreign relations.[79] At the time of the bilateral tariff-autonomy negotiations with China in 1928, the Japanese embassy in the United States, representing the imperial government in Tokyo, wrote to the US State Department as follows:

76. Secretary of State to President Coolidge, 11 July 1928 [711.93/184a], *FRUS*, 1928, vol. 2, p. 455.

77. Secretary of State to President Coolidge, 1 December 1928 [611.9331/122a], *FRUS*, 1928, vol. 2, p. 490.

78. Iriye, *After Imperialism*, pp. 10–11.

79. Iriye, *After Imperialism*, p. 222.

The Japanese Government have watched with deep and sympathetic interest the progress of the Nationalist movement in China and, together with the other Governments concerned, have always shown their willingness to make their best possible efforts to facilitate the realization by China of her legitimate national aspirations. At the same time, they are convinced that if this movement were to be crowned with success and if international complications were to be avoided, it is imperative that counsel of reason and moderation should prevail.[80]

The moderate Japanese policy toward China of the cabinets of Baron Tanaka Giichi (1927–29), Hamaguchi Osachi (1929–31), and Baron Shidehara Kijūrō (1931) was nevertheless based on the assumption that Japanese economic interests, especially trade with China and investment in Manchuria, were safeguarded as constituted at the time.[81] China's desire to terminate the Sino-Japanese Treaty of Commerce of 1896, concluded after China's defeat in the Sino-Japanese War of 1895, was anathema to Japan's imperial government.

The Treaty of Commerce [of 21 July 1896] constitutes the backbone of mutual friendship between Japan and China. Its revision is a matter of the greatest importance. In fact the Japanese Government have made a most careful study of the whole subject by taking into consideration both the national aims of China and the economic position of Japan in that country and have agreed most willingly to the demand of China for the revision of the Treaty. Many difficulties arose in the course of the negotiations[,] due principally to the unsettled political condition of China, but Japan has consistently done her utmost to expedite the negotiations with a view to reaching a satisfactory settlement. In entire disregard, however, of these circumstances, and in explicit defiance of the provision of the Treaty, the Nationalist Government sent to Japan some time ago the abrupt notice that the Commercial Treaty between China and Japan would be abrogated and that, pending conclusion of a new treaty, the

---

80. Japanese Embassy to Department of State, 9 September 1928 [793.94/1694], *FRUS*, 1928, vol. 2, p. 425.
81. Iriye, *After Imperialism*, p. 222; Drea, *Japan's Imperial Army*, pp. 163–64.

Japanese nationals and commerce would be governed by provisional regulations unilaterally adopted by China.[82]

According to this statement, in acknowledgment of the importance that the United States attached to the declaration of intent of the Washington Conference with regard to restoring tariff autonomy to China, the Japanese imperial government was willing to proceed with bilateral negotiations, provided that Japanese interests in China were guaranteed by a separate bilateral agreement.

Independent of the question of the sanctity of treaties, Japan is deeply concerned that if this kind of procedure is once concurred in, it may lead to the subversion of all the rights and interests legitimately secured by Japan under treaties or agreements. Nevertheless, the Japanese Government have been and are ready to enter upon negotiations for treaty revision [as] soon as the policy of the Nationalist Government makes it possible for them to do so. It is sincerely hoped that ways and means may be found by which the treaty question may be settled to the mutual satisfaction of both countries. Further, the Japanese Government are willing to cooperate with the other Governments concerned in the completion of tasks started at the time of the Tariff Conference at Peking and by the Commission of Extraterritoriality if only the demands of China are fair and reasonable.[83]

Japan's insistence on a bilateral agreement granting preferential tariffs on Japanese goods, at least for a transitory period, meant that it was the last of the nine treaty powers to sign a bilateral treaty restoring tariff autonomy to China; as late as December 1928, the Japanese position was still that the Chinese government had broken its obligations to Japan under international law:

82. Japanese Embassy to Department of State, 9 September 1928 [793.94/1694], *FRUS*, 1928, vol. 2, p. 425.

83. Japanese Embassy to Department of State, 9 September 1928 [793.94/1694], *FRUS*, 1928, vol. 2, p. 425.

The difference between the Japanese and Chinese Governments arising from the repudiation by the latter of the Sino-Japanese Commercial Treaty not being settled, the Japanese Government find themselves for the moment in a position somewhat different from that of either the United States or the British Empire [which have] no such questions pending with China.[84]

The Japanese imperial government also insisted, like its British and US counterparts, on extracting apologies for the loss of its citizens' lives and damage to their property during the Nanjing and Hankou incidents, and for a clash between Chinese Nationalists and Japanese troops in the Ji'nan area in Shandong Province during the second phase of the Northern Expedition in May 1928. Those apologies were made in March and May 1929, respectively, after which bilateral tariff treaty negotiations began. The Sino-Japanese Treaty of Commerce and Friendship was signed on 6 May 1930; in an exchange of notes appended to the treaty, China guaranteed Japan that it would maintain 1929 duty levels (that is, the first duties fixed under tariff autonomy) for a period of three years from the date of the signing of the treaty.[85]

This arrangement, by which the Chinese Nationalist government granted to Japanese economic interests a degree of consideration that it did not grant to British or US interests, was negotiated between representatives of the Chinese Nationalist government and the Japanese imperial government. As in other areas of Sino-Japanese relations at this time, Japanese military interests, acting independently from the Japanese imperial government, derailed an accommodation reached between political actors on both sides. When, in 1931, Zhang Fuyun, the director general of the Office of Customs Affairs in the Nationalist Ministry of Finance, asked the Japanese minister to China, Shigemitsu Mamoru, to intercede with the imperial government to put a stop to smuggling from occupied Manchuria into the North China Plain,

---

84. Aide-Mémoire, Japanese Embassy to Department of State, 29 December 1928 [793.003/92], *FRUS*, 1928, vol. 2, p. 455.

85. SHAC 679/1/26909 IG Circular No. 4089, 2nd ser.; Wright, *China's Struggle for Tariff Autonomy*, p. 639.

Shigemitsu replied that he was unable to stop it because the imperial government did not know what the Japanese military did in occupied Manchuria.[86]

Conclusion

Chinese writers throughout this period referred to what they regarded as the illegality of having foreigners in control of the administration of China's Maritime Customs; this is hardly surprising given the upsurge of nationalist sentiment. What is notable is that they did not describe the existence of the Maritime Customs itself as illegal, for two reasons: first, because they placed the Maritime Customs in the tradition of China's indigenous, domestic customs service, and second, because foreign trade itself was no longer deemed illegal or immoral—only China's inability to direct the inflow of foreign commodities through tariffs was. For these same reasons, the fact that the statistics essential for protectionist arguments were provided by the Maritime Customs Service itself—a foreign-administered Chinese government agency—was not seen as problematic because it was not the existence of the Maritime Customs but rather its mode of administration and governance that was the object of criticism.

The treaties regarding the restoration of tariff autonomy that the Nationalist government signed with the United States, Britain, and Japan in 1928, 1929, and 1930, respectively, constituted the Nationalists' first major foreign-policy achievement. In securing, through bilateral diplomacy, one of Sun Yat-sen's constant demands of the treaty powers, the Guomindang acquired political legitimacy with its domestic constituency of Chinese nationalists, beyond the core supporters of the Nationalist government. Abroad, the Guomindang came to be seen as a reliable state-level actor, especially when measured against the standards of many competing power holders in China. The Guomindang's ascendancy in Chinese national politics was paralleled by a foreign-policy paradigm shift on the part of one of the main treaty powers, Britain. Following the Guangzhou boycott, the British Foreign Office

86. Zhang, "Chang Fu-yun: Reformer," p. 166.

advised the British government that Britain could preserve its political position in China only by military force, and Britain was not willing to commit that force to foreign military campaigns in the aftermath of the First World War. The United States had been willing for some time to relinquish its political influence in China, under the twin influences of a Wilsonian commitment to the right of national self-determination and the isolationism that resulted from the human and financial costs of the First World War. Faced with a Chinese government on the rise, and now lacking the support of the other two major treaty powers, Japan, too, agreed to restore tariff autonomy to China, albeit with a delay of three years. The Guomindang had finally achieved the necessary conditions for making Nationalist tariff policy.

TWO

Making Nationalist
Tariff Policy

U nderstanding tariff policy is crucial to understanding the nature of Nationalist governance on the Chinese mainland. Import tariffs were an important instrument of Chinese economic nationalism, and tariffs made up the single greatest share of central government revenue between 1927 and 1937, accounting for a far greater percentage of central government revenue in China than in the public finances of any other major country during this period, as table 2.1 demonstrates. Nationalist tariff policy was designed to promote fiscal stability and ensure the government's ability to meet foreign and domestic financial obligations. But to implement this policy, the Nationalist government first had to gain control over Maritime Customs. This chapter describes that takeover process and then analyzes the role of tariff policy within Nationalist fiscal policy.

The Nationalists' public debt management was successful until the Second Sino-Japanese War. Increasing tariff revenue and designing sustainable import tariffs were integral parts of Guomindang fiscal management. Therefore, I make the revisionist argument that Nationalist fiscal policy was in fact successful in many areas. In Cicero's phrase, echoed in the title of John Brewer's monograph on the emergence of the British military-fiscal state in the seventeenth century, money is equivalent to the "sinews of power."[1] By arguing for the soundness of

1. Brewer, *The Sinews of Power.*

Table 2.1.

Customs revenue and income tax as a percentage of central government revenue, selected countries, 1928–37

Year	China		Japan		United Kingdom		United States	
	Customs	Income tax	Customs and excise	Income tax	Customs and excise	Income tax	Customs and excise	Income tax
1929	72.8	—	12.0	10.9	30.4	36.0	10.6	11.5
1930	61.2	—	11.5	12.6	28.6	37.8	9.3	10.2
1931	59.0	—	12.5	9.4	30.1	42.8	9.5	6.3
1932	60.1	—	8.7	6.7	34.2	37.8	9.0	4.5
1933	56.0	—	8.0	6.8	35.4	34.9	16.0	5.3
1934	53.3	—	9.8	8.7	36.0	34.8	20.0	4.8
1935	54.4	—	10.5	10.1	36.0	34.2	18.4	6.1
1936	43.7	—	11.7	11.7	35.8	34.7	16.2	6.9
1937	49.3	0.9	10.1	16.4	35.4	37.4	15.0	9.7

Year	Italy		France	
	Customs	Income tax	Customs and excise	Income tax
1928	7.3	19.3	23.7	6.5
1929	10.4	18.7	24.8	5.5
1930	9.3	19.2	25.9	6.7
1931	8.2	17.8	29.9	7.1
1932	10.0	18.1	27.8	8.3
1933	10.3	18.2	29.2	6.2
1934	10.2	17.8	28.0	6.6
1935	9.2	16.9	28.9	4.8
1936	6.9	15.5	30.2	5.4
1937	5.3	13.7	28.7	6.6

Sources: Data from Strauss, *Strong Institutions in Weak Polities*, p. 124; Liesner, *One Hundred Years of Economic Statistics*, pp. 58, 112, 194, 244, 268.
— = not available.

the sinews, I also argue for a more positive appraisal of Nationalist state building.

Chinese Nationalism
and the Maritime Customs

Bringing the Maritime Customs Service back under the control of the Chinese government and implementing a protective tariff schedule were two of the central demands of Chinese nationalism, both for fiscal reasons and for reasons of national prestige. In his *The Three Principles of the People*, which the Nationalists regarded as a formative text, Sun Yat-sen compares import tariffs with coastal defenses in their role of protecting the Chinese economy from foreign aggression: "Just as forts are built at the entrances of harbors for protection against foreign military invasion, so a tariff against foreign goods protects a nation's revenue and gives native industries a chance to develop."[2] In the context of developmental strategies, Sun goes on to say that China's economic development depends on political development: "We cannot find a solution for the livelihood problem in the economic field alone; we must first take hold on the political side, abolish all unequal treaties, and take back Maritime Customs from foreign control. Then we can freely increase the tariff and put into effect a protective policy. Such a policy will prevent foreign goods from pouring into China, and our home industries will naturally be able to develop."[3]

Like contemporary statesmen in other countries, Sun subscribed to the prevailing economic doctrine of the interwar years; that is to say, protectionism. The concept of infant-industry protection is based on the work of the German economist Friedrich List (1789–1846), who advocated protective national import tariffs as a means of defending nascent domestic industries against the competition of more economically advanced countries.[4] This conception of tariffs is reflected by Sun Yat-sen: "The idea of a protective tariff is to put a heavy duty on imports.

2. Sun Zhongshan, *Sanmin zhuyi*, p. 31.
3. Sun Zhongshan, *Sanmin zhuyi*, p. 396.
4. Irwin, *Against the Tide*, pp. 124–28.

The high duty makes foreign goods expensive so that they cannot circulate, while [domestic] goods free from duty are reasonably priced and widely distributed."[5] W. O. Henderson, one of List's biographers, points out the influence of List's thinking on China, one of many predominantly agrarian countries endeavoring in the twentieth century to increase their national wealth and living standards by stimulating industrial growth.[6]

Frank Dikötter observes that in China "the notion of a commercial war with the foreign powers grew in the early years of the twentieth century, as increasingly nationalist voices pointed at an onslaught of foreign goods."[7] In the course of this analysis, it will become apparent that infant-industry protection through tariffs became a dominant paradigm of Chinese economic policy in the 1930s, enjoying the support of both politicians and academic economists. Sun's writings show that the attraction of infant-industry protection was that it was accepted internationally and was being pursued by fully sovereign countries: "Now how do other countries meet foreign economic pressure and check the invasion of economic forces from abroad?—Usually by means of a tariff, which protects economic development within these countries."[8]

Sun used the Chinese native cotton industry as an example of the effects of the absence of tariff protection on China's domestic industries. The example also shows the connection between economic and nationalist considerations that existed in the minds of Chinese intellectuals at the time. "Because of the low tariff, foreign cloth is cheaper than native cloth. Since, moreover, certain classes of the people prefer the foreign to the native cloth, native industry has been ruined. With the destruction of this native handicraft industry, many people have been thrown out of work and have become idlers. This is a result of foreign economic oppression."[9]

Sun did not understand foreign trade under the theory of comparative advantage: "Although China produces a great deal of cotton of good

5. Sun Zhongshan, *Sanmin zhuyi*, p. 32.
6. Henderson, *Friedrich List*, p. 217.
7. Dikötter, *Things Modern*, p. 39.
8. Sun Zhongshan, *Sanmin zhuyi*, p. 31.
9. Sun Zhongshan, *Sanmin zhuyi*, p. 32.

natural quality, because her industries are undeveloped, she cannot herself use the raw cotton in the manufacture of good fabrics and yarn; she can only ship it for sale abroad. The clothes we wear every day are made of imported material for which we have to pay a high price. The high price we pay is the sending of our valuable money and food abroad in settlement."[10] Sun's analysis of the harmful effects of unregulated international trade on underdeveloped countries is based on his understanding of the writings of John Stuart Mill and those of his own contemporary, the scholar and reformer Liang Qichao (1873–1929).[11]

Sun Yat-sen's understanding of international trade and the international economic system was also heavily influenced by Leninist economic theory, which regards imperialism as the highest form of capitalism, thus linking the political and economic motives behind the exertion of foreign influence in China.[12] Sun suggested that there was comprehensive coordination between political interests at the state level and economic interests at the enterprise level on the part of the foreign powers: "When foreign nations at times find their economic strength weak and cannot attain their objectives in other ways, they add political force."[13] Having externalized the reason for China's economic predicaments in this way, Sun Yat-sen goes on to point out the necessity of improving China's political standing in order to improve her economic condition:

If we want to solve our livelihood problem and protect our native industries so that they cannot be attacked by foreign industries, we must first have the political power to protect them. But China today, in the grip of the treaties, not only has lost her sovereign rights and the power to protect her own industries, but also is actually giving protection to foreign industries. This comes of the capitalistic expansion, mechanical progress, and economic superiority of foreign countries; besides, foreign economic power is backed up by political power.[14]

10. Sun Zhongshan, *Sanmin zhuyi*, p. 388.
11. Wilbur, *Sun Yat-Sen*, p. 17.
12. Bergère, *Sun Yat-sen*, p. 364.
13. Sun Zhongshan, *Sanmin zhuyi*, p. 392.
14. Sun Zhongshan, *Sanmin zhuyi*, pp. 294–95.

In this statement, protectionism was linked to treaty revision and thus became part of the central foreign-policy aim of the Guomindang. Sun's assertion that China provided tariff protection to foreign industries was based on the 5 percent ad valorem cap on import tariffs imposed in the Treaty of Tianjin. Since tariff readjustments had to be sanctioned by the treaty powers and because commodity prices continually rose, the actual amount of duty revenue quickly fell below the supposed percentage after each readjustment. In an article for the *Far Eastern Survey* in 1936, Frank Kai-Ming Su and Alvin Barber estimated an effective average import tariff rate of about 3.4 percent for 1927.[15] At a time when other countries were resorting to protectionist measures to encourage the growth of indigenous industries, an effective import tariff rate below 5 percent made China an export market of continued attractiveness. In the same year, the average import tariff rates for Germany, France, and Italy were 20.4 percent, 23 percent, and 27.8 percent, respectively.[16] It was precisely those protectionist policies that Sun Yat-sen aimed to imitate: "In order to compete with other countries, we must imitate the tariff policy of the Western nations. . . . It is clear from this that if we want Chinese industries to flourish, we must follow the protective policy of the United States and of Germany, resist the invasion of foreign goods, and protect our native industries."[17]

Sun Yat-sen's demands for the renationalization of the Maritime Customs became part of the Nationalist Party's policy agenda. The first Guomindang national congress in January 1924 called for the elimination of all powers exercised by foreigners in China as a result of the unequal treaties: "foreigners' leased territories, consular jurisdiction, foreigners' management of customs duties, [and] all political power exercised by foreigners in China at the cost of Chinese sovereignty."[18] This remained the Guomindang's policy after Sun Yat-sen's death. In the same way, protectionism was introduced into Chinese political debate as part of Sun's theoretical legacy. Song Ziwen, then the Nationalist minister of finance, stated in his opening address to the First

15. Su and Barber, "China's Tariff Autonomy," p. 119.
16. Liepman, *Tariff Levels*, p. 415.
17. Sun Zhongshan, *Sanmin zhuyi*, p. 396.
18. Iriye, *After Imperialism*, p. 41.

National Economic Conference in 1928 that "the completion of the war sees a chance for shifting expenditure in great measure from wasteful to productive enterprises, and it is our duty to seize this opportunity to carry out the rehabilitation plans of our revered late Leader, Dr. Sun."[19]

Nationalist views on the effect of foreign imports and the connection between tariff autonomy and sovereignty were shared by economists. Jia Shiyi (1887–1965), a prominent Chinese economist at the time, was able to draw on his experiences as a superintendent of customs for his book *Guanshui yu guoquan* (Tariffs and national sovereignty). After graduating from Meiji University in Tokyo in 1913, Jia served in the Beiyang Ministry of Finance before being appointed superintendent of customs and commissioner of foreign affairs at Zhenjiang in 1920. In 1927 he became a member of the Jiangsu provincial government; in 1928 he was appointed director of the taxation department of the Nationalist government's Ministry of Finance.[20] In *Guanshui yu guoquan*, Jia argued that tariff autonomy was explicitly linked to national sovereignty, that enjoyment of tariff autonomy was crucial to the self-definition of a modern state, and that China was being denied what was rightfully hers by the treaty powers: "A country's tariff sovereignty is part of that country's national sovereignty. Sovereign countries set their own tariff schedules, without being limited by others. This is the same in countries East and West, but our country is different. . . . If we want to restore our sovereignty, we must restore our tariff sovereignty."[21] Discussing the international impact of the Beijing Tariff Conference, he argued that "if [the Chinese government does] not set national tariff rates and regulations . . . , we will be the laughingstock of the foreigners," thus introducing matters of national prestige into the debate in addition to the revenue and protectionist considerations that formed the bulk of his argument.[22]

Another economist inside the Nanjing political establishment who demanded a protectionist tariff policy was Ma Yinchu (1882–1982). Ma

---

19. Soong, "Opening Address to the National Economic Conference," p. 628.
20. Woodhead, *The China Year Book: 1929–30*, p. 932.
21. Jia Shiyi, *Guanshui yu guoquan*, preface, p. 1.
22. Jia Shiyi, *Guanshui yu guoquan*, part 4, p. 164.

had been trained as an economist at Beiyang University (later Tianjin University) and at Yale University and Columbia University in the United States. After the Guomindang national government moved to Nanjing in 1927, he served as a member of the Zhejiang Provincial Government Committee, the National Legislative Yuan Legislative Committee, and the National Legislative Yuan Economics Committee, in addition to teaching at National Central University. In his monograph *Woguo guanshui wenti* (Our country's tariff problem), published in 1927, Ma analyzed the historical background of China's lack of tariff sovereignty, ascribing it to the unequal treaties. He then described the deleterious effects of low import tariffs on the Chinese textile industry: "Take the Jiangxi cotton industry in our country as an example. . . . Japanese cottons compete with it. If we used a protective tariff, we could contain [Japanese cottons]. Since we are limited to 5 percent, there is nothing we can do."[23]

The Nationalist state-building endeavor required significant financial resources. Realizing they were unable to implement their desired tariff policy in the face of treaty obligations and opposition from within the Maritime Customs, the Nationalists were even more set on regaining tariff autonomy and gaining control of the customs service. In 1933, Song Ziwen summed up Nationalist sentiment about the Maritime Customs before the regaining of tariff autonomy in 1929:

At the time that the National Government was [moved] to Nanking, many grievances were harboured against the Customs Service by the Government and the people. It was said that the Customs had become an *imperium in imperio*; that it was an adjunct of Legation Street; that the word of the Inspector-General had become law in national finances; that the Inspector-General had played the role of king-maker to every Finance Minister at Peking; that the Customs funds were deposited almost *in toto* with foreign banking institutions, and had served merely to build up their credit to the neglect of Chinese banks; and that the higher ranks of the service were exclusively occupied by foreigners and were not open to the Chinese.[24]

23. Ma Yinchu, *Woguo guanshui wenti*, p. 5.
24. Song Ziwen, *North China Daily News*, 9 November 1933, quoted in Young, *China's Nation-Building Effort*, p. 40.

Renewed efforts by the Nationalists to gain control of the Maritime Customs took the form of changes in personnel policy and the extension of their political control throughout the rest of China. In terms of personnel, the most important change was the appointment of the pro-Nationalist Frederick Maze as inspector general of customs.[25] Maze, partly out of a genuine commitment to the Chinese Nationalist cause and partly because he realized early on the career advantages of allying himself with the Nationalists, substantially helped the Nationalists increase their control over the Maritime Customs. In 1927, Sir Francis Aglen, then inspector general, was dismissed by the Beiyang government and the Guomindang Nationalist government, both of which cited his lack of support for their interests. The Beiyang government appointed Aglen's deputy, A. H. F. Edwardes, as Aglen's successor. The Nationalists, meanwhile, cultivated good relations with Maze, then the commissioner of customs in Shanghai. When Beijing fell to Nationalist forces in the summer of 1928, ending the second stage of the Northern Expedition, Edwardes's position soon became precarious owing to his previous association with the Beiyang government and Aglen.[26] Popular Chinese attitudes toward the Maritime Customs were summed up by Arthur Lyall, a commissioner of customs who retired from the Maritime Customs in 1927.

> The present anti-foreign feeling running through China is perhaps more widely spread than such exhibitions were in the past, but it is not different from those that have gone before. The attitude adopted by the local authorities towards the Customs seems, on the other hand, to be quite different from what it was in the past. In the past local authorities always did their best to protect the Customs. They now seem generally to display ill-will towards the Service. The reason is evident. In the past a great part of the revenue that passed through the hands of the local officials was collected by the Customs. It was therefore in their interest to protect us. To-day they have nothing to gain by protecting the Customs, and the Service having become hateful to them, owing to the support it has given to their enemies the Northern militarists, they naturally take a pleasure [sic] in seeing it humiliated. It is possible that the assistance we are now giving the

25. Wu Jingping, *Song Ziwen pingzhuan*, pp. 108–9.
26. Brunero, *Britain's Imperial Cornerstone*, pp. 72–85.

local authorities in the collection of the Surtax may improve this state of affairs. But as the revenue collected at most ports in the interior, where the danger to the Service is greatest, is almost entirely export and coast trade duties, it is not to be expected that any great improvement will result.[27]

Edwardes finally resigned in August 1928, leaving the way open for the Nationalists to appoint their chosen candidate, Frederick Maze, as inspector general, although they faced strong initial opposition from the foreign community in China, the foreign legations, and foreign governments.[28] The official British position on Maze at the time was summed up in a 1928 dispatch from Miles Lampson, the British minister in China, to Foreign Secretary Sir Austen Chamberlain, in which he wrote that "Maze's substitution for Edwardes would be regarded by the extremists of all parties as a victory against foreign influence in the Customs and would thus militate against the future foreign interest in the Service."[29] Lampson also told Zhang Fuyun, the director general of the Office of Customs Affairs in the Ministry of Finance, that the British government "had confidence in Edwardes but none in the other competitor [i.e., Maze]."[30]

The manner in which Maze achieved his appointment as inspector general was viewed with criticism within the Maritime Customs as well. B. E. F. Hall, then a senior assistant in what was called the Indoor Staff, recorded in his diary in January 1929 that "Maze [was] appointed IG in place of Edwardes after much unpleasant intrigue."[31] In autumn 1928, Maze described his close acquaintance with and support for the Nationalist movement:

I have had, perhaps, closer relations with the Kuo-min-tang than most foreigners: I was Commissioner in Canton in 1911 when the first Republican

27. SHAC 679/17980, Arthur Lyall to IG of Customs, 28 May 1927.
28. Lester Knox Little Diaries, 82M-103, 2 January 1946, Houghton Library, Harvard University.
29. FO 228/3740/5A/48 1928, Lampson (Hong Kong) dispatch to Chamberlain, 22 February 1928, quoted in Atkins, *Informal Empire in Crisis*, p. 73n1.
30. Zhang, "Chang Fu-yun: Reformer," p. 126.
31. B. E. F. Hall diary, 10 January 1929. Quoted by kind permission of Mrs. Patricia Hayward.

Government was established there and for some years following I had relations with that Government; and on many occasions met the founder of the Republic, Dr. Sun Yat-sen. And later on, from 1927 onward I have, as you know, been in close touch with the Nanking Government. I have always been one of those who held the view that the Nationalist movement in China would prevail, and although the party may have more obstacles to overcome, and further difficult problems to solve, I feel confident that in the end it will successfully attain the goal—peace and prosperity throughout China.[32]

The impression that Maze owed his appointment to political intrigue persisted for some time after he was named to the position. A number of years later Maze discussed the circumstances of his appointment with a retired Chinese Maritime Customs official in England, W. F. Tyler, who had recently published a memoir of his time in the Maritime Customs, titled *Pulling Strings in China*. Tyler praised Maze for his initiative in preserving the Maritime Customs as an institution, but suggested that "as the Hunghutzu [*hong huzi* 紅鬍子, red beard, a traditional Chinese term for bandits] who becomes a tuchun [*dujun* 督軍, provincial governor] sheds the cruder characteristics that raised him to his place, so you should drop those of yours."[33] Maze crisply replied to Tyler that "your analysis of our respective characters is not too good" and noted on Tyler's letter that "it should not be overlooked that men who have to make their own positions sometimes write and do things or say things which are not necessary for those for whom those *positions are provided*."[34] More telling still is a statement Maze made in another letter to Tyler: "Mere rectitude of character and honesty of intention—good in themselves—are not sufficient:

32. Sir Frederick Maze Papers, School of Oriental and African Studies, London [hereafter cited as Maze Papers, SOAS], vol. 2, Confidential Letters etc. of Sir Frederick Maze, 1926–29, F. W. Maze, "Speech Delivered at Informal Chinese Official Gathering," n.d. (most likely autumn 1928).

33. Maze Papers, SOAS, vol. 5, Confidential Letters etc., 1930–31, W. F. Tyler to F. W. Maze, 19 December 1930.

34. Maze Papers, SOAS, vol. 5, Confidential Letters etc., 1930–31, F. W. Maze to W. F. Tyler, 4 February 1931; emphasis in the original.

the *statesman* must have more than that!"[35] In commenting on the retirement of Father Louis Froc S.J., a Jesuit priest who had been in charge of the Xujiahui Observatory in Shanghai, Maze summed up his principles of leadership:

> Your unimaginative Administrator specializes in stability only—prophets, on the other hand, specialize in change and progress. Father Froc—and I, in my modest Irish way!—belong to the latter category. Perhaps we even have, or try to have, the Administrator's appreciation of stability combined with the prophet's appreciation of change: if this is really so, then it can be truly said that our leadership is uplifted! To have real progress you must mix routine and revolution! It has been aptly said, and most truly so, that "in the absence of statesmanship, routine and revolution alternate—in its presence they amalgamate!"[36]

The opinion that Maze was too accommodating to Chinese nationalism was widely shared in the foreign community in China throughout the late 1920s. The *Peking and Tientsin Times*, one of the main English-language treaty-port newspapers, opined in 1929 that "[the appointment of Mr. Maze] would be unacceptable both to the Service and to the British and other Foreign Governments... [and] the conditions which have been allowed to grow up in Shanghai during the past year have resulted in a form of dual control of the Service which is destroying the fine traditions of efficiency and discipline which have characterized the Customs Service during the past 70 years."[37]

Maze further antagonized the foreign community through the manner of his induction into the position of inspector general of Maritime Customs, swearing "to obey the will of the President and to accept the principles of the Kuomintang." In the event that he broke his oath of office, Maze swore to "submit myself to punishment of the severest

---

35. Maze Papers, SOAS, vol. 6, Confidential Letters etc., 1931–1932, F. W. Maze to W. F. Tyler, 30 September 1931; emphasis in the original.

36. Maze Papers, SOAS, vol. 6, Confidential Letters etc., 1931–1932, F. W. Maze to W. F. Tyler, 30 September 1931.

37. *Peking and Tientsin Times*, 5 January 1929, in Wright Collection (Official Correspondence), Queens University Library Special Collections, MS 16, hand list, n.d.

kind which may be imposed by the Kuomintang."[38] The *North China Daily News* commented on this swearing in as follows:

> Throughout the long list of China's foreign servants no parallel can be recalled for the humiliating oath which Mr Maze demeaned himself to take. Had he sworn to be true and faithful to the service of China it might . . . have been understandable, although any oath of this nature appears incompatible with his duty as a British subject. . . . The pointed dragging in of the Kuomintang as the special object of allegiance and arbiter of punishment, which is but one party in the state, and . . . may have blown to pieces a year hence . . . [intensifies] the fear that the Customs service has become a mere political plaything.[39]

Maze defended his actions by referring to the example of Sir Robert Hart and his relationship with China and the imperial government. Earlier, both Aglen and Maze had claimed to be acting in Hart's spirit. Aglen claimed that Hart had kept the Maritime Customs out of domestic Chinese politics but for that reason had served China well. Therefore, Aglen claimed that he was acting in the sense that Hart had when he undertook such projects as the Custodian Bank Agreement and the Consolidated Loan Fund, which diminished the authority of the Chinese government of the day.[40] Maze, on the other hand, claimed that since Hart had been the servant of the imperial government, it

38. *Peking and Tientsin Times*, 18 January 1929, in Wright Collection, Queens University Library Special Collections.

39. "The Customs," *North-China Herald and Supreme Court & Consular Gazette*, 12 January 1929. The *North-China Herald* was the weekly edition of the *North China Daily News*.

40. The Custodian Bank Agreement was concluded between the Chinese government and the diplomatic body resident in Beijing in early 1912. It made the inspector general of customs accountable to the foreign banks involved in handling China's foreign loans and indemnities until "such time as the Chinese Government are in a position to resume payments of loans and indemnity." See Wright, *Collection and Disposal*, pp. 5–6. The Consolidated Loan Office was established in 1921 by Minister of Finance Zhou Ziqi and Inspector General Sir Francis Aglen to reassure holders of domestic Chinese government debt that sufficient funds were available from Maritime Customs revenue to service their loans. Crucially, control of this office lay with the inspector general of Maritime Customs. See Wright, *Collection and Disposal*, pp. 169–70.

was in a similar sense that Maze acknowledged the Guomindang as the national government of China and acceded to its requests whenever they were compatible with the treaty framework. In a letter to Tyler, Maze wrote that "as you remark, my career savours of a Fairy-story—except that I was my own Fairy-godmother:... unlike Bredon, Aglen, Bowra and Edwardes ... I did not inherit the throne from the King my father; was not made Inspector General through Legation or any other influence: I was selected by the Chinese Government independently!"[41] Maze's claim to have been appointed entirely on his own merits is somewhat disingenuous, given his frequent rhetorical use of Hart's image to defend his vision of serving China, and the fact that he was Hart's nephew. Robert Hart had been criticized for nepotism concerning the appointment of recruits to the Indoor Staff, which comprised the administrative staff of the Maritime Customs, during his time in office.[42] L. K. Little, the last foreign inspector general of Maritime Customs, sought to lessen the force of these charges by pointing out the high standards to which Hart held all his employees, even when they were members of his own family.[43] Nevertheless, a family connection to Hart was in most cases a career asset, and this certainly applied to Maze's appointment as inspector general in 1929.

Maze's appointment in January of 1929 was greeted with dismay by the English-language treaty-port press. The *North-China Herald* wrote that "it would be idle to pretend that Mr Maze's appointment [would be] pleasing either to foreigners or the most responsible Chinese."[44] Maze countered their criticism by circulating to the newspaper editors a document containing his own version of events and his vision for serving China. In it, he used a quotation by Sir Robert Hart to justify his own position toward the Guomindang:

41. Maze Papers, SOAS, vol. 4, Confidential Letters etc., 1930, F. W. Maze to W. F. Tyler, 19 March 1930.

42. See, e.g., King, *In the Chinese Customs Service*, pp. 20–21.

43. Little, "Introduction," in Fairbank, Bruner, and Smith, *The IG in Peking*, vol. 1, p. 24.

44. "The Customs," *North-China Herald and Supreme Court & Consular Gazette*, 12 January 1929.

Although the growth of the Customs establishment has been encouraged, yet it has, with foreign intercourse, been to some extent forced
upon China; and moreover, its existence implies that Chinese officials
cannot do their own work! It should not be forgotten, therefore, that a
foreign-controlled Inspectorate may come to an end: it may flourish, do
good work, and be appreciated for a time; but the day must come when
natural and national forces, silently but constantly in operation, will eject
us from so anomalous a position. Meanwhile we are here to act with and
assist, and not to ignore or displace Native authority.[45]

When Hart wrote these lines in 1873, Chinese nationalism was still
in its infancy. The strikes, boycotts, and violence of nationalist protest
in the 1920s had damaged any notion foreigners working in China
might still have entertained about the silent nature of Chinese nationalism. Being ejected from China, on the other hand, was becoming an
increasingly likely option. Hart's conception of Chinese nationalism
as a natural force owes much to the intellectual climate of the late nineteenth century. What is also apparent, though, is Hart's notion of the
foreign-managed Maritime Customs as a temporary expedient. While
the transitory nature of the Maritime Customs was a cause of regret for
Aglen, Hart accepted it as part of the Maritime Customs establishment
he had created. During Hart's time in office, no Chinese member of the
Indoor Staff, the senior branch of the service, was promoted to the rank
of commissioner of customs or to the position of inspectorate secretary.
Hart, therefore, may well have granted the eventual return of the Maritime Customs to Chinese control in the knowledge, or with the intention, that the transfer would not occur during his time in office.

After Maze's appointment as inspector general, his victory in the
succession struggle found visible representation in his remodeling of
the memorial to Sir Robert Hart that overlooked the Bund, the river-
front thoroughfare in Shanghai. When the Shanghai Municipal
Council undertook to widen the Bund, Hart's statue had to be moved
from its original position. Maze had it moved to a position outside the
Custom House on the Bund, facing toward the Custom House and

45. Maze Press Release, 10 January 1929, quoted in Atkins, *Informal Empire in
Crisis*, p. 47.

away from the waterfront. He also commissioned a much higher plinth, to which were added tablets describing Hart's career. After these alterations had been completed, Maze commissioned a brochure showing the new design and circulated it among current and former members of the Indoor Staff.[46] In this way he used his new position to impose his own representation on the public memorial for Hart in Shanghai. Throughout the 1930s, Maze quoted Hart's example as a precedent and as the intellectual authority for many of his policies, confirming the ongoing importance of Hart's image for Chinese tariff policy.

Maze strengthened his relationship with the Nationalist government by arguing early on for the promotion of Chinese members of the Indoor Staff to the rank of commissioner. Making use of the appointment structure of the Maritime Customs, he also promoted his own allies and followers in preference to those of his predecessors, Sir Francis Aglen and A. H. F. Edwardes. In the Maritime Customs appointments process, patronage had played an important role since the days of Sir Robert Hart.[47] As a result of this system of patronage, within a few years the majority of higher officials within the Maritime Customs at the very least professed loyalty to the Nationalist government. In addition, appointments of Chinese nationals to the rank of commissioner and to the position of port commissioner insured greater loyalty toward the Chinese government among the ranks of the Maritime Customs. The effect of the new hiring policies on the composition of the service's staff is demonstrated in table 2.2.

The Maritime Customs staff, which numbered a few thousand by the late 1920s, was divided into two main groups, the Indoor Staff, as mentioned, and the Outdoor Staff. The Outdoor Staff dealt with manual and menial jobs in the customs service, and the Indoor Staff handled administrative tasks.[48] At the head of the Maritime Customs stood the inspector general, responsible initially to the Zongli Yamen,

---

46. IG Circular No. 3901, 2nd ser., 26 April 1929, in Inspectorate General of Customs, *Documents Illustrative*, vol. 4, p. 203.

47. King, *In the Chinese Customs Service*, pp. 20–21.

48. Ladds, *Empire Careers*, p. 87.

Table 2.2.
Chinese and foreign Maritime Customs staff, 1926–48

Year	Total number of staff	Foreign staff		Chinese staff	
		Number	Percent of total	Number	Percent of total
1926	8,684	1,231	14.0	7,453	86.0
1927	8,724	1,184	14.0	7,540	86.0
1928	8,568	1,101	13.0	7,467	87.0
1929	8,623	1,059	12.0	7,564	88.0
1930	8,671	994	11.0	7,677	89.0
1932	8,832	924	9.0	7,908	91.0
1933	8,294	815	10.0	7,479	90.0
1934	9,351	821	9.0	8,530	91.0
1935	9,182	774	8.0	8,408	92.0
1936	9,371	751	8.0	8,620	92.0
1937	9,614	720	7.5	8,894	92.5
1948	11,705	234	2.0	11,471	98.0

Source: Data from Cheng Linsun, "Zhang Fuyun yu jindai Zhongguo haiguan xingzheng guanli gaige," p. 34.

which dealt with the foreign relations of the late Qing state, then to the Shuiwu chu, a board of taxation jointly responsible to the Ministry of Finance and the Ministry of Foreign Affairs and ultimately to the Guanwu shu, the Office of Customs Affairs in the Ministry of Finance. Until the mid-1920s, the higher ranks of the Indoor Staff, leading up to the position of port commissioner, the Maritime Customs official in charge of a port, were closed to Chinese nationals. By then, the majority of entrants recruited into the Indoor Staff hailed from Britain, the United States, and Japan. The first Chinese commissioner was appointed in 1925. Recruitment of foreigners into the Indoor Staff of the Maritime Customs was suspended in 1927 and finally discontinued in 1929.[49] The end of foreign recruitment was intended to be permanent, the recruitment of foreigners into the Outdoor Staff having been discontinued as

49. IG Semi-Official Circular No. 54, 24 February 1927, and Enclosure No. 2, IG Circular No. 3873, 2nd ser., 14 March 1929, in Inspectorate General of Customs, *Documents Illustrative*, vol. 4, pp. 126, 187.

early as 1925.[50] After the outbreak of the Second Sino-Japanese War in 1937, the Japanese authorities in Shanghai pressured the inspector general of Maritime Customs into accepting new Japanese recruits, but with that exception, recruitment of foreigners into the customs service had ceased.

Huang Qingxun joined the Maritime Customs in the spring of 1944 because, as he wrote in his memoirs, his family was neither rich nor influential enough for him to join the diplomatic service and his mother wanted him to have a career in a stable environment.[51] While his mother's wish for a stable environment was undoubtedly disappointed by the Nationalists' retreat to Taiwan, Huang enjoyed the successful career she may have intended for him, finally attaining the post of inspector general of the Republic of China's Maritime Customs Service, which he held from 1977 until his retirement in 1980. To be sure, Huang achieved the post of inspector general at a time when foreigners had long since ceased to serve in the Maritime Customs. However, when he entered the service it was already possible for Chinese nationals to rise to the leading ranks. This was due in large measure to the changes implemented under Frederick Maze. In 1929, Maze wrote that "natural and national development must necessarily result in the Chinese members of the Service becoming eligible in the future for positions of greater responsibility."[52] One may question whether, as one former Chinese Maritime Customs official recalls it, Maze "was the first to advocate the equal treatment of Chinese nationals and foreign employees [in the Maritime Customs], assign people work according to their capabilities, and throw out the discrimination and prejudice of the past," or indeed whether Maze implemented those changes out of a genuine commitment to Chinese nationalism or to advance his own career.[53] However, before Maze no Chinese national had been promoted above the rank of assistant commissioner. When Maze resigned in 1943, a Chinese national, Ding Guitang, was serving as deputy inspector general. The advancement of

50. IG Circular No. 3661, 2nd ser., 1 December 1925, in Inspectorate General of Customs, *Documents Illustrative*, vol. 4, p. 89.

51. Huang Qingxun, *Haiguan suiyue*, p. i.

52. IG Circular No. 3846, 2nd ser., 21 January 1929, in Inspectorate General of Customs, *Documents Illustrative*, vol. 4, p. 149.

53. Wang Wenju, *Lanyu haiguan sishi nian*, p. 1.

Chinese officials to the highest ranks in the customs service was crucial to the Nationalist takeover of the Maritime Customs as well as to the Maritime Customs' continued existence as an institution.

By preserving the Maritime Customs as an institution, Maze also managed to reestablish relations with the treaty-port community. His appointment as inspector general had been met with open hostility by English-language treaty-port newspapers, such as the *North China Daily News* and the *Peking and Tientsin Times*, as quoted above. The same papers expressed quite a different attitude when Maze departed on home leave in 1937. Most of the English-language treaty-port newspapers marked the occasion with a tribute to his work as inspector general; the following is one example:

> Sir Frederick's countrymen and fellow-subjects of His Majesty have every reason to be proud of the manner in which the Inspector-General of Maritime Customs has upheld the traditions of public service in conditions of extreme difficulty. His unswerving fidelity to the interests of China and to the policies of the Government under which he holds his many-sided office has been marked by courage and tact of a high order. It has fortunately found response in the trust and confidence imposed in him by successive Finance Ministers who will certainly be gratified to note that the British Government's official representative here, on the eve of transfer to the inner counsels of Whitehall, has so cordially drawn attention to Sir Frederick Maze's achievements.[54]

Maze made similar progress in his relations with the Chinese government, although in this case the mistrust he had to overcome was not as strong. As the revenue-producing capacity of the Maritime Customs increased as a consequence of tariff autonomy and subsequent tariff revisions, both Minister of Finance Song Ziwen and his eventual successor, Kong Xiangxi, came to rely heavily on the tariffs for revenue, and they developed a good working relationship with Maze until the outbreak of the Second Sino-Japanese War.[55] Until the late 1940s,

---

54. SHAC 679/11614, "Irish Services," *North China Daily News*, 12 March 1937.
55. Wu Jingping, *Song Ziwen pingzhuan*, pp. 106–7; Li Maosheng, *Kong Xiangxi zhuan*, pp. 60–62.

the Nationalist government did not have full control over the Maritime Customs, since it remained under the direction of a foreign inspector general and retained a certain amount of administrative independence from the Nationalist state. However, successive Beijing governments and the Nationalist government in Guangzhou had attempted several times to gain more influence, or any influence at all, over the Maritime Customs. The Nationalists' domestic and foreign-policy successes in 1929—in securing the appointment of an inspector general sympathetic to Chinese nationalism, achieving tariff autonomy, and revising tariff rates—need to be seen in this context.

The Nationalists succeeded largely because of the changed foreign-policy environment—a paradigm shift in their own foreign policy making from revolutionary diplomacy to a more consensual, negotiated approach, as demonstrated in the bilateral negotiations leading to the restoration of tariff autonomy following their unsuccessful unilateral declaration of autonomy—and because of the cooperation of some elements within the Maritime Customs, chiefly the new inspector general, Frederick Maze.[56] The success of the Nationalist government's takeover of the Maritime Customs can be seen in the following passage from a British Foreign Office memorandum on British policy in China, written in 1930:

> But already it is clear that it will become increasingly a Chinese Service, and that the days of a Chinese Inspector-General are not far distant. So far as the personnel are concerned, the Customs Service is therefore much less important a British interest than it was even as late as 1925; but as regards its function as a mediator between the Chinese Government and the foreign merchant, its importance is as great as ever, and every effort should be made to see that, however much the Chinese share in it may be increased, the old spirit of Sir Robert Hart's creation should be, so far as possible, maintained.[57]

56. Shan Guanchu, *Zhongguo shoufu guanshui zizhuquan de licheng*, pp. 68–69.
57. Foreign Office Memorandum of 8 January 1930 on British Policy in China [F 6720/3/10], *DBFP*, 2nd ser., vol. 8, p. 24.

Nationalist Tariff Policy as Fiscal Policy

At the heart of the argument for the soundness of Nationalist fiscal policy is Guomindang public debt management. The large percentage of its expenditures that the Nationalist government had to devote to debt service, especially when compared with other governments, as demonstrated in table 2.3, makes this clear. When the Nationalist government moved to Nanjing in 1927, borrowing abroad was not a feasible option, owing to earlier defaults by successive Republican governments in Beijing. Tariff revenue increased significantly after the Nationalists regained tariff autonomy in 1929. The increased tariff revenue was used as a source of funds for the repayment of principal and payment of interest on foreign and domestic loans, and also as security for new domestic loans. There is an issue of perception here, since using revenue to finance borrowing can be interpreted in different ways: as a fiscally responsible way of maximizing government expenditures while also providing a low-risk, low-interest investment, or as a means of addressing short-term financial obligations at the cost of using future government revenue to pay bondholders, thus redistributing government revenue in favor of bondholders.[58] Using revenue to secure borrowing was a common tool of fiscal policy in states with supposedly sounder fiscal policies than those of the Republic of China. Overall, Nationalist debt management until 1937 was successful. Two-thirds of the government deficit represented payments to retire earlier debt; by 1937, 10 percent of China's national debt was in arrears, compared with 50 percent in 1928.[59] As figures 2.1 and 2.2 show, after tariff autonomy, up until 1937 tariff revenue consistently exceeded the extent of China's fiscal obligations. The Nationalists used increased tariff revenue as a way of inspiring bondholders' confidence, both domestically and abroad.

One way to measure the confidence that the Nationalist government's fiscal policy inspired abroad is to examine the fluctuations in bond prices of Chinese government bonds traded abroad. Douglas Paauw notes in his highly pessimistic assessment of Nationalist fiscal

58. Vries and van der Woude, *The First Modern Economy*, p. 115.
59. Young, *China's Nation-Building Effort*, pp. 149, 141.

Table 2.3.
Foreign and domestic debt interest paid, as a percentage of central
government expenditures, selected countries, 1928–37

Fiscal year	China	Year	Japan	Italy	UK	US
1928–29	38.3	1928	15.7	15.8	27.9	—
1929–30	37.2	1929	16.1	21.5	27.5	6.8
1930–31	40.5	1930	17.5	22.1	25.4	6.3
1931–32	39.5	1931	14.5	17.9	24.7	7.3
1932–33	32.6	1932	12.4	19.1	24.7	10.6
1933–34	31.8	1933	14.8	22.7	21.4	—
1934–35	33.2	1934	16.7	28.4	19.6	11.5
1935–36	26.9	1935	16.9	20.5	18.5	—
1936–37	24.1	1936	15.9	7.7	17.3	8.7
		1937	14.7	11.8	16.1	—

Sources: Data from Liesner, *One Hundred Years of Economic Statistics*, pp. 58, 112, 268, 244, 194; Spence, *The Search for Modern China*, p. 394.

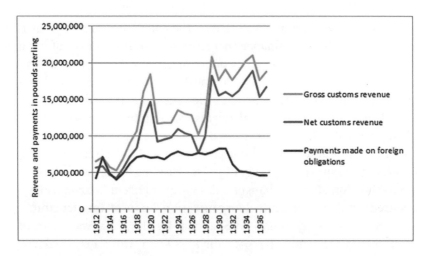

Figure 2.1. Relation of combined Maritime and Native Customs revenue to China's foreign loans and indemnities, 1912-37, in pounds sterling. *Source*: Data from Inspectorate General of Customs, *Trade of China: 1938*, p. 110.

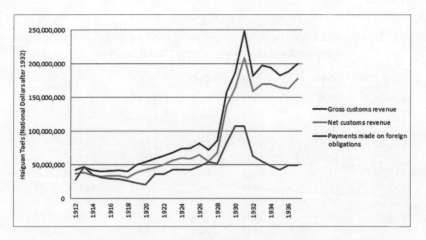

Figure 2.2. Relation of combined Maritime and Native Customs revenue to China's foreign loans and indemnities, 1912–37, in Haiguan taels and National Dollars from 1932. *Source*: Data from Inspectorate General of Customs, *Trade of China: 1938*, p. 110.

policy that it was "paradoxical that . . . the confidence of foreign governments in Nanking finance increased during this period of fiscal demoralization in China," since prices of Chinese bonds held abroad rose between 1933 and 1937.[60] The most common indicator of bond price fluctuations is their current yield. The current yield of bonds is calculated by dividing annual interest payable by the percentage of their nominal value at which the bonds are being traded. Thus, the lower the price at which the bonds are being sold, the higher the yield. In 1927, "The approximate range of yields of leading foreign loans [traded on the London Stock Exchange] was: 1898 4½ per cent Loan (customs-secured), 7 to 11 per cent; Reorganization Loan of 1913 (customs-secured), 9 to 12 per cent; and Shanghai-Nanking Railway Loan of 1903, 11 to 15 per cent."[61] By 1937, "the 1898 Loan with a 1943 final maturity sold in London on a 3¾ per cent basis; the 1913 Reorganization Loan with 1960 final maturity yielded 4.9 per cent; the Crisp Loan of 1912 with 1952 maturity yielded 5.5 per cent; and the Shanghai-Nanking

60. Paauw, "Chinese National Expenditures during the Nanking Period," p. 10.

61. Young, *China's Nation-Building Effort*, pp. 98–99; data based on *Central Bank of China Bulletin*, March 1938, pp. 81–82.

Railway Loan of 1903 with 1953 maturity yielded 6 per cent."[62] The increase in Chinese government bond prices (expressed by the drop in current yields) indicates that by 1937 investors on the London Stock Exchange had more confidence in the Nationalist government's fiscal policy than they had had in 1927. This increase in confidence can at least partly be explained by the increase in Maritime Customs revenue, which provided a greater margin of safety that the interest and principal payments would be met. The fact that the payment of interest and principal on foreign loans was not suspended until January 1939 (see chapter 6) indicates that the foreign bondholders' confidence was not misplaced.

The increase in Maritime Customs revenue also facilitated an increase in domestic borrowing. Under the Nationalist government, domestic bond issues increased significantly. Between 1927 and 1935, the government issued $1,636 million worth of domestic bonds, or $182 million each year on average. This is compared with a total domestic bond issue of $612 million, or an average of $38.3 million annually, issued by successive Republican governments between 1911 and 1927.[63] The increase in domestic borrowing was helped by the bank coup of 1935 in which the Nationalist government brought the Bank of China and the Bank of Communications, China's two largest banks, back under central government control by forcing them to purchase large amounts of government bonds; the Nationalists then used the receipts to purchase majority shares in the two banks.[64] Thereafter, the Nationalist government was in a much stronger position to place government bonds. But allowance must also be made for the organic growth of China's domestic bond market and for the Nationalist government's role in fostering this growth. Hans van de Ven has pointed out that the imperial Chinese state began to issue bonds at a late point compared with Western states.[65] Unlike Western European states, China possessed no tradition of government bonds as conservative, dependable investments for small

62. Young, *China's Nation-Building Effort*, pp. 99–102; data based on *Central Bank of China Bulletin*, March 1938, pp. 82–84.

63. Cheng, *Banking in Modern China*, p. 116.

64. Cheng, *Banking in Modern China*, p. 99.

65. Van de Ven, "Military and Financial Reform," p. 35. See also Halsey, "Money, Power, and the State," p. 427.

private investors. In the Republican era, the Chinese domestic bond market grew largely through speculation; government bonds were issued at significant discounts on their face values, making them attractive for speculators. Banks were frequently reluctant to take on bonds, fearing that they would not be able to sell them fast enough.

Linsun Cheng characterizes the bond market of the Nationalist prewar period as "highly sensitive and speculative." Bond prices were affected, at various times, by seasonal fluctuations in the Shanghai financial market, changes in the political situation, natural disasters, exchange rate fluctuations, and the actions of major speculators. To give but one example, the Japanese attack on Shanghai in late 1931 and early 1932 led to a 50 percent drop in the prices of major government bonds.[66] An awareness of this political instability was reflected in the attitude of private banks towards government transactions in general. The management of the Shanghai Commercial and Savings Bank (Shanghai Shangye Chuxu Yinhang), one of Shanghai's most important private banks, argued in 1934 that the bank "should not make a lot of government loans since [it was] a commercial bank." Such government loans as were to be made had to be based on "scrutiny of the government's financial situation... conducted in advance"; the feasibility of the loan had to be "based on the government's financial credit," and the "fluidity and ease of disposal [of the loans] had to be kept."[67]

That this concern was justified is demonstrated by the debt consolidations of the Nationalist government. Debt consolidation, in this case, is a euphemism for partial default, since the 1932 debt consolidation was based on cutting interest rates and extending the amortization period of existing loans. Again, in 1936, debt consolidation meant that the amortization period of existing loans was extended. In the 1932 debt consolidation, security for internal loans was transferred from revenue from China's salt monopoly and unspecified other internal revenue to tariff revenue.[68] Despite two partial defaults within the

66. Cheng, *Banking in Modern China*, p. 124.

67. Shanghai Shangye Chuxu Yinhang, "Benhang zhengfu jiekuan zhi yanjiu," December 1934, Shangye Chuxu Yinhang file, No. 1625, quoted in Cheng, *Banking in Modern China*, p. 134.

68. Young, *China's Nation-Building Effort*, pp. 104–8.

space of four years, domestic bond prices began to rise again in 1937, not least because the Nationalist government had issued no new domestic bonds since the 1936 debt consolidation. The average current yield of domestic bonds in June 1937 was 8.7 percent, compared with 11.6 percent in 1936, 24.4 percent in 1932, and 17.3 percent in 1928.[69] From the government's point of view, using the expanding domestic bond market was a way of legitimately financing its deficit without resorting to excessive indirect taxation or irregular levies. In increasing domestic bond issues, the Nationalists relied on their partial control over the banking sector to place bond issues (such as in the 1935 bank coup), but the subsequent development of bond prices demonstrates that, despite this measure of coercion, the government did not destroy public confidence in the bond market permanently. In both the 1932 and the 1936 internal debt consolidations, tariff revenue was used as security. Increased tariff revenue suggested a margin of safety for meeting the costs of China's domestic obligations.

The government's perceived competence in managing its fiscal affairs was also important in creating public trust in Guomindang monetary policy. Niv Horesh has argued for the "efficacy of the Kuomintang's monetary policy," based on the Nationalists' success in ending private banknote issues in 1935 and limiting the influence of foreign banks on the Chinese banking market.[70] Because money "issued by organizations such as banks and governments relies on impersonal trust in these organizations, as well as trust that society in general will accept the tokens produced by those organizations," the Nationalists had to demonstrate fiscal competence in order to create public confidence in their currency.[71] In analyzing relations between the state and the banking sector in Republican-era Tianjin, Brett Sheehan concludes that, in extending loans, "Tianjin's modern bankers sought stable government institutions with the legitimacy to commit verifiable sources of revenue to the banks in return for loans."[72] Taking the exchange rates of the new Chinese currency introduced in 1935 as an indication

---

69. Young, *China's Nation-Building Effort*, p. 99.
70. Horesh, "'Many a Long Day,'" p. 38.
71. Sheehan, *Trust in Troubled Times*, p. 5.
72. Sheehan, *Trust in Troubled Times*, p. 150.

of public confidence, those rates remained stable as long as the money supply remained constant and the government deficit was sustainable. Once the Nationalist government resorted to issuing insufficiently backed currency during the Second Sino-Japanese War, public confidence in the new currency, which had also been damaged by Japanese currency warfare, decreased and exchange rates declined.[73] As Horesh points out, "Statehood, nation building and monetary reform were inextricably interwoven in Republican China."[74] In 1935, the Nationalists' paying habits in retiring public debt, as well as the midterm increase in government revenue through the increase in tariff revenue, facilitated the beginnings of a territorial currency, and thus contributed to the Nationalist state-building project.

Conclusion

The evidence indicates that, up until 1937, the Nationalists successfully used increased government revenue to maintain bondholders' confidence both domestically and abroad. Through the appearance of fiscal competence, the Nationalists also created public acceptance of its national currency after 1935. All this was possible because the Guomindang made skillful use of those sympathetic to the Nationalist cause within the Indoor Staff of the Maritime Customs—in particular, Frederick Maze, the erstwhile commissioner of customs in Shanghai. Maze was as susceptible to the Nationalists' overtures of confidence in his abilities as he was determined to rise to the top of the Maritime Customs, to the position that his uncle, Sir Robert Hart, had occupied. It is impossible to determine at this point whether Maze was motivated by careerism, genuine sympathy for the Nationalist cause, or both. (The majority of those in the foreign treaty-port community in China, and many of his foreign colleagues, attributed his actions to professional self-interest.) Whatever Maze's motives, the Nationalists had found their necessary ally, and they continued to find Maze useful until the outbreak of the Second Sino-Japanese War. In the interim,

73. Lin Meili, *Kangzhan shiqi de huobi zhanzheng*, p. 28.
74. Horesh, "'Many a Long Day,'" p. 37.

foreign opinion of Maze also markedly improved. The cooperation between the Nationalists and Maze formed the basis for the midterm success of Guomindang fiscal policy during the prewar decade. Stabilizing China's desolate fiscal situation by increasing central government revenue took precedence over other policies, and the increased tariff revenue from international trade after the restoration of tariff autonomy was crucial to the continued existence of the Nationalist government after 1927. That revenue was used chiefly to pay off government debt and to promote fiscal stability by creating the impression of fiscal probity.

THREE

The Maritime Customs as
Economic Modernity

What did the Maritime Customs do? Its most important purpose was its primary one, to assess and collect tariffs, although it is worth noting that it also managed harbors and maintained navigational aids, among other things—activities that were important in themselves since they helped to produce tariff revenue. The Maritime Customs had a further dimension, though: assessing commodity values enabled the Maritime Customs to collect and publish trade statistics, one of the activities of a modern state. In assessing commodity values, the customs service made use of modern technologies and administrative practices, many adapted from abroad; thus the Maritime Customs also served as a conduit for the kind of bureaucratic and technocratic modernity that Guomindang leaders aspired to bring to China.[1] Hence, the Maritime Customs fulfilled a dual function for the Nationalist government. While the Guomindang regarded it as primarily a revenue-collecting agency, its subsidiary function in producing trade statistics was a source of authoritative Western modernity. A technocratic, modernist vision of governance was central to the Nationalists' claim to political legitimacy,[2] and the Maritime Customs was key to realizing that vision. This chapter looks at the

1. Song Ziwen, "Message to the Customs Staff," in Inspectorate General of Customs, *Documents Illustrative*, vol. 5, p. 332.
2. Chiang Kai-shek, "Geming dangyuan banshi de jingshen he fangfa," p. 174; "Kexue de daoli," pp. 29–30.

process by which the customs service contributed to modern techno-cratic governance by assessing the value of goods and producing vital trade statistics.

The Maritime Customs in the Nanjing Decade

To understand the importance of valuation and statistics to the customs service's work, it is useful to examine the process of assessing and collecting tariffs. This is not a history of the Maritime Customs but a description and explanation of the institution as it existed in 1927, when the Nationalists moved the seat of their government to Nanjing. With the appointment of Frederick Maze as inspector general of Maritime Customs, the Nationalist government believed that it had an administrator in place who was supportive of its vision and its aims for governance. Nationalist tariff policy was determined by a variety of actors. The most obvious were the ministers of finance: Song Ziwen (served 1925–31 and 1932–1933), Huang Hanliang (1931–32), and Kong Xiangxi (1933–44). The inspector general was charged with implementing tariff policy and was therefore also in a good position to help to shape it, especially given that the Maritime Customs continued to enjoy some measure of administrative independence under the Guomindang. The inspector general's direct superior, the director general of the Office of Customs Affairs, was also important, as were other senior Guomindang members, from Chiang Kai-shek downward. Between 1927 and 1945, the position of director general was held, successively, by Fu Bingchang (in 1927), Zhang Fuyun (1928–32), Shen Shuyu (1932–35), Zheng Lai (1935–43), Li Tang (1943–45), and Zhang Fuyun once more (1945). Like other government regulations, tariff schedules had to be approved by both the Executive and the Legislative Yuan.

By 1927, the Maritime Customs was split vertically into two departments: the Revenue Department, which contained the Indoor and Outdoor Staffs, and the Marine Department. Earlier functions, such as the postal service and the quarantine service, had already been spun off into separate agencies directly under the control of the Nationalist government. The Indoor Staff did the white-collar administrative

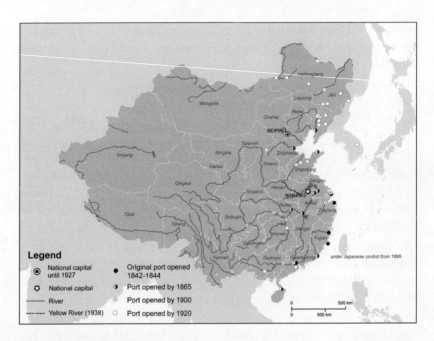

Map. 3.1. Distribution of custom houses.

work; the Outdoor Staff performed blue-collar tasks related to the collection of revenue. The Marine Department looked after the lighthouses and the vessels of the preventive fleet.[3] Horizontally, the important division was between the Inspectorate General, first in Beijing and then in Shanghai, and ultimately in Nanjing (but, much to the annoyance of successive ministers of finance and directors general of the Office of Customs Affairs, always with a substantial presence in Shanghai), and the custom houses, which were spread through China in every treaty port (see map 3.1).

After the Revolution of 1911, local custom houses were responsible for both assessing and collecting tariff revenue, at the request of Yuan Shikai; prior to the revolution, the custom houses had only assessed the value of tariffs to be collected; the revenue had been collected by the superintendent of customs, a Chinese official who was part of the

3. Ladds, *Empire Careers*, pp. 85–92.

local hierarchy.[4] In Yuan's reasoning, the customs service, being "in the orbit of empire," in Bickers's phrase, was less susceptible to interference from his political competitors. One can also read this move as an effort to buy political goodwill from the foreign diplomatic and consular presence in China. Whatever the reason behind the change, in 1911 the superintendents of customs lost the power to collect tariff revenue, and that power was transferred to the most senior customs employee in each custom house, the local commissioner of customs. By the late 1920s these officials performed a range of tasks beyond overseeing the assessment and collection of tariff revenue, as is apparent from the following portion of a speech by Inspector General Maze to the Royal Empire Society:

> I will outline, for the purpose of comparison, the work and responsibilities of the Collector of Customs in London and the Commissioner of Customs in Shanghai: the Collector of Revenue in [London] merely collected revenue, as indicated by his title, and has nothing to do with conservancy operations; nothing to do with general finance or National Debts; and nothing to do with the Thames River Police. His sphere of activity is limited in area to the actual port of London. On the other hand, the Commissioner of Customs in Shanghai is assigned a large District within which he has responsibilities over and above the mere collection of dues and duties. He is the Receiver of Wrecks; in the case of non-treaty-power ships—i.e., vessels belonging to nations having no Treaty relations in China—he sometimes acts as the Consul of the crew; he is empowered to function notarially; he controls the Shanghai River Police, a very useful and extensive organization; he is in charge of an elaborate Preventive service; he acts as the Port Authority and is thus in direct control of the Harbour—that is to say, there is [sic] vested in him responsibilities which may be compared with the Port of London Authority, and the extent of these responsibilities will be realized when it is remembered that the Port of Shanghai in point of tonnage is now the sixth or seventh in the world, while in terms of population it is now the fifth city in the world; he is also one of three directors of the local Conservancy Board, and as such is directly concerned with the important work of improving and conserving the sea-approaches to the Port, as well as the Shanghai

4. Van de Ven, *Breaking with the Past*, pp. 166–68.

river—the Whangpoo. He is thus a man of many parts, and is directly responsible to the Inspector General, who, in turn, is responsible to the Chinese Government.[5]

As map 3.1 illustrates, throughout the Nanjing decade custom houses existed in parts of China that the Nationalists did not control. The fact that tariffs were a national revenue source led to frequent disputes among local power holders, the Nationalist government in Nanjing, and the Maritime Customs, as occurred in Guangzhou, Tianjin, and Fuzhou.[6] The customs service had a separate agenda from the Nationalist government, at least at times, being interested in both institutional survival and the continued ability to operate within local circumstances.[7] This was apparent not least from the fact that, during all disputes, commissioners of customs negotiated directly with the insurgents regarding revenue-sharing arrangements. It was demonstrated even more clearly during the early years of the Second Sino-Japanese War, when the Maritime Customs continued to operate from Shanghai after the government had moved to Chongqing, and also when the Maritime Customs argued for remaining outside the scope of the National Treasury Law. Even after the ending of foreign hires for the Indoor Staff, the appointment of Frederick Maze as inspector general, and the express recognition on the part of the Maritime Customs that its role was subordinate to the Nationalist state, its relationship with the Nationalist state continued to illustrate the limited reach of the Nationalists' political control; its network of custom houses throughout China suggest an extent of control that the Nationalists did not in fact possess.

At the central government level, the Inspectorate General of Customs coordinated the assessment and collection of revenue, and reported to the Office of Customs Affairs in the Ministry of Finance, the

---

5. SHAC 679/11614, Sir F. W. Maze's Career, Sir Frederick Maze, speech to Royal Empire Society, 20 November 1934, reproduced in *North China Daily News*, 11 December 1934.

6. Van de Ven, *Breaking with the Past*, pp. 247–57; Chang, *Government, Imperialism and Nationalism*, pp. 95–104.

7. Van de Ven, *Breaking with the Past*, p. 233.

Maritime Customs' superior in the Nationalist hierarchy. Much to the frustration of successive directors general in that office, in practice the inspector general of customs often dealt directly with the minister of finance rather than going through the proper channels. The range of the Inspectorate General's tasks can be seen from the purviews of its department heads. In 1927, Maritime Customs had a chief secretary, who deputized for the inspector general; an audit secretary; a Chinese secretary, who dealt with government correspondence and language matters; and a staff secretary. When the Nationalist government took over the service of China's foreign financial obligations, a financial secretary, who dealt with matters relating to the revenue needed for the repayment of loans, was added in 1929.[8] Also in 1929, because of the Republic of China's recovery of tariff autonomy, a tariff secretary was appointed to advise on tariff rates.[9] When increased tariffs led to an upsurge in smuggling and the customs service expanded its trade-policing operations, a preventive secretary was appointed in 1931 to oversee those operations.[10] In theory, the Inspectorate General's role by 1927 was to implement policies designed by the Ministry of Finance and to advise on policy making, through the means, for instance, of the National Tariff Commission, which consisted of three representatives from the Ministry of Finance and two representatives from the Maritime Customs. In practice, the customs service also shaped Nationalist tariff policy by varying its implementation, arguing against Nationalist proposals that were impractical or unfeasible, and setting up or condoning revenue-sharing or parallel-taxation arrangements with local power holders.

The fact that these arrangements became possible or necessary stemmed from the way in which tariff revenue was assessed, collected, and remitted to the Inspectorate General, which in turn transmitted it to the Ministry of Finance after deducting the authorized cost of revenue collection. When ships docked in a treaty port, merchants,

8. IG Circular No. 3855, 2nd ser., in Inspectorate General of Customs, *Documents Illustrative*, vol. 4, p. 160.

9. IG Circular No. 3935, 2nd ser., in Inspectorate General of Customs, *Documents Illustrative*, vol. 4, p. 205.

10. IG Circular No. 4172, 2nd ser., in Inspectorate General of Customs, *Documents Illustrative*, vol. 4, p. 366.

shipping agents, or specialized customs brokers would submit a cargo manifest to the local custom house, which would assess the amount of tariff to be paid. Once the custom house received notice that the tariff had been paid at the local branch of the appropriate bank, it issued a customs clearance, which allowed the goods to be imported or moved onward. Inspections by employees of the Outdoor Staff established that goods declared matched goods carried aboard and goods landed.[11] To function effectively, customs officials thus needed to have access to the quayside, have access to the custom house, have the custom house accessible to the public, and have access to the local branch of the Central Bank of China, where such a branch existed, or the branch of whichever bank with which the Customs had its account. The fact that local power holders were able to prevent all of these things explains to an extent (and notwithstanding a fatal Customs habit of hedging its bets) how the Maritime Customs arrived at its revenue-sharing and parallel-taxation arrangements.

Modern Administration and Modern Technology

In the process of assessing tariff values, the Maritime Customs in effect disseminated modern, scientific expertise by using scientific equipment and defining "scientific" tariff schedules. An example of this is seen in the valuation of imported sugar. In 1931–32, the Maritime Customs switched from using the Dutch Sugar Standard, a visual classification tool, to using the polarimeter, a device for chemical analysis. Both the Dutch Sugar Standard and the polarimeter were foreign inventions. The Dutch Sugar Standard was abandoned after the Dutch government stopped regulating measurements and standard samples began to be offered by a commercial enterprise. The government had been regulating sugar valuation with the Dutch Sugar Standard since 1884 and did so until the late 1920s, when the valuation process was taken over by Nederlandsche Handels-Maatschappij (the Netherlands Trading Company).[12]

11. Inspectorate General of Customs, *Code of Customs Regulations and Procedure*, pp. 13–58.
12. SHAC 679/30511, Explanatory Notes regarding the Proposed New Tariff Rates on Sugar, 24 November 1931.

While Javanese sugar, originating from a Dutch colony, was valued by Javanese exporters according to the Dutch Sugar Standard, Cuban sugar was more commonly measured by its degree of polarization, using the polarimeter.

Replacing Dutch Sugar Standard sample sets cost 30 Shanghai taels every other year. Continued use of the Dutch Sugar Standard meant replacing the sample sets in use throughout China; in 1931, for example, "a minimum of 41 sets [would] be required at an approximate cost of $4,100."[13] Meanwhile the saccharimeter required a single outlay of 200 Haiguan taels.[14] As a cost-cutting and modernizing measure, Maritime Customs initially bought seventeen Winkel Half-Shadow polarimeters for use in ports, and a single more-complex "Bates"-type Polariscope-Saccharimeter for the Maritime Customs laboratory in Shanghai for use in appeal cases.[15] Later, the Maritime Customs added another nineteen polarimeters to ensure the use of chemical analysis for sugar valuation in ports throughout China.[16]

Chemical analysis allowed for more differentiated measurements, creating the potential for both increasing revenue and scientifically adapting tariffs to the developmental needs of China's economy. That this was a consideration is evidenced by the increase in the number of items on China's tariff schedule; the trend is apparent in the tariff classification of sugar as well as other items. The switch to chemical analysis necessitated the hiring of a foreign-trained chemist at the Inspectorate General, owing to the increased complexity of the procedures involved. However, as the customs service was assured, "it does not require any highly technical skill in handling the instrument, nor deep mathematical knowledge in determining its reading."[17] The Inspectorate General's chemist would then train customs examiners throughout China in the correct use of the equipment. In 1929, W. S. Myers, the commissioner of customs at Shanghai, wrote to the inspector general of Maritime Customs to recommend the appointment of a German-trained chemist to head the Maritime Customs laboratory at

13. SHAC 679/30511, IG of Customs Draft Despatch to Guanwu shu, 18 August 1931.
14. SHAC 679/30510, Memorandum, Joseph Y. S. Huang, 12 April 1930 (Yu Shi).
15. SHAC 679(8) 86, IG of Customs to Guanwu shu, D. 1595, 13 December 1930.
16. SHAC 679/30511, Tariff Secretary's Printed Memorandum, No. 7, 4 July 1931.
17. SHAC 679/30510, Memorandum, Joseph Y. S. Huang, 12 April 1930.

Shanghai.[18] Myers's candidate was Huang Guojie (Joseph K.C. Huang), who had obtained his doctorate in chemistry from the Institute of Chemistry of the Academy of Veterinary Medicine at the Friedrich-Wilhelms-Universität in Berlin.[19]

In response to a request from the inspector general to provide various items of information on the valuation of sugar, Tariff Secretary Carlo Bos stated that he had "always held [the] 'Dutch Standard' to be inaccurate and a source of interminable discussions between Customs and merchants." This was because, he wrote, "the classification of sugar by the colour must in the nature be unreliable, since the colours of the standard samples are liable to change in a comparatively short time, thereby rendering a precise grading impossible." Assessing the value of sugar with the aid of a polarimeter, by measuring the degree of refraction of single-plane light in a dissolved sugar solution, was both "more scientific and accurate," according to Bos.[20]

The most obvious question to ask in this context is how important technical innovations like the polarimeter were to Chinese fiscal policy and Chinese consumers. Revenue collected on imported sugar increased sharply after the introduction of the 1931 tariff requiring greater specificity in the classification of imported sugar. That increase in specificity was made possible by the new technology used to establish the classification of imported sugar, particularly when Maritime Customs disputed the importer's declared value. As to consumers, the increased tariff was passed on to them through the retail price of sugar. They were therefore also affected by the technological innovation.

The new measurement procedures were costly and delayed the clearing of goods through customs, even when goods were allowed to be removed "on deposit," meaning an additional duty as might be assessed

18. SHAC 679/8586, W.S. Myers to IG of Customs, No 23292, 3 March 1930.

19. Joseph K.C. Huang is also referred to as Joseph H.S. Huang. Joseph H.S. Huang, *Über Synthesen und Spaltungen in der Hydrophanten-Reihe* (Syntheses and cleavages in the hydrophanten-series), Chemisches Institut der Tierärztlichen Hochschule zu Berlin, Direktor G. Schroeter, genehmigt von der philosophischen Fakultät der Friedrich-Wilhelms-Universität zu Berlin, 24 July 1929, in SHAC 679/8586, Dr. Joseph H.S. Huang's Career.

20. SHAC 679/30510, C. Bos, Tariff Secretary, to F.W. Maze, S/O No. 8, 22 April 1930.

based on laboratory analysis to be settled later. For this reason, the polarimeter technique was used sparingly. Of Maritime Customs assessment procedures in general, Carl Neprud, the director of the Shanghai Appraising Department, wrote to Carlo Bos, the tariff secretary, in 1930: "It is recognized by the Appraising Department that examination, however carefully performed, is vexatious and unpopular, and it is therefore sparingly resorted to, and mainly in cases where the views regarding the valuation are hopelessly conflicting."[21]

Turning to the impact of the new assessment procedures on tariff revenue, the change in tariff rates and revenue brought about by the introduction of the polarization method of classification was minor initially. The Maritime Customs estimated that, had it charged duty on sugar imported into Shanghai between September and November 1931 at the new rates rather than the old tariff rates, tariff revenue in customs gold units (CGU) would have been CGU 1,730,523 rather than CGU 1,728,955.[22] However, the Maritime Customs' annual trade reports for 1933 state clearly that the effect of the increased tariff rates on imported sugar was to "[price] imported sugar out of the range of most consumers."[23]

The fate of the next technical innovation introduced by the Maritime Customs illuminates one of the reasons for the ultimate failure of the Nationalist modernization project. In April 1937 the Shanghai commissioner of customs asked the inspector general's permission to purchase a portable X-ray machine.[24] This machine was to be used to screen liquid and baled goods for concealed smuggled objects without having to open and unpack the goods to be examined. While by this time X-ray machines were small and light enough to be used quayside, they were still very expensive. The chief secretary, in reply to the Shanghai commissioner's letter, authorized the necessary expenditure; because of the high cost, the technology was to be tested at Shanghai,

21. SHAC 679/30590, Report on Shanghai Appraising Department, in Neprud to Bos, S/O, 2 May 1930.
22. SHAC 679/30511, Explanatory Notes regarding the Proposed New Tariff Rates on Sugar, 24 November 1931.
23. Inspectorate General of China, *Trade of China: 1933*, vol. 1, p. 46.
24. SHAC 679/20863, P. G. S. Barentzen, Commissioner, Shanghai, to IG of Customs, No. 28,648, 6 April 1937.

the busiest port, before the purchase of X-ray machines for other ports would be considered.[25] There is no further record in the file indicating whether the X-ray machine ever came into use. One conjecture, based on a delivery time of two to three months as stated in the manufacturer's prospectus, is that that X-ray machine would have arrived around the end of June 1937. Given that the Marco Polo Bridge Incident, which provided the Guandong Army with a pretext for invading the North China Plain, took place on 7 July 1937, the machine would have been received at a time when the Shanghai import trade was severely disrupted by the Japanese attack on Shanghai that paralleled the invasion of the North China Plain.[26] Thus the use of the X-ray machine to detect smuggled goods was most likely prevented by the onset of war, and gains in the modernization and effectiveness of revenue collection and trade policing did not materialize.

Even within the Maritime Customs, economic modernity was not uncontested. The tariff secretary, Carlo Bos, who had backed the new inspection technology, replied to comments on one of his working reports that, "having been asked to go," he was "able to take a much more detached view of these questions than before." No trail of Bos's having been reprimanded or prematurely removed from his position as tariff secretary remains in his career file. Following an average-length term as tariff secretary, Bos was granted the long leave to which he was entitled. However, his reforms must have caused friction, especially with the statistical secretary. In responding to his colleagues' comments on his final report, Bos refers to the statistical secretary's remarks in particular, declaring them to be "pure undiluted poison," and goes on to conclude:

> Among other wise sayings from hoary antiquity, I was told also, several
> times during the first two years of my career in the Inspectorate in con-

25. SHAC 679/29863, H. Kishimoto, Chief Secretary, to Commissioner, Shanghai, No. 165,719/28,143, 20 April 1937.

26. The Guandong Army was the Japanese army group based in the Japanese-leased territory on the Liaodong Peninsula and along the South Manchuria Railway Zone. The Marco Polo Bridge Incident marked the start of the Second Sino-Japanese War.

nection with quite reasonable suggestions, that *"natura non facit saltus"* [nature does not leap]. . . . The Customs is not a product of the laws of nature, but a man-made institution which must move with the times, unless we wish to be *told* to "leap" and in what direction—in other words—unless we wish our heads to be twisted perforce towards realities which we refuse to see, and unless we wish the initiative for timely progress to be taken from our hands.[27]

The Maritime Customs and the Rise of Statistics in China

In compiling and publishing trade statistics based on nationwide standards and introducing a national unit of account, the customs gold unit, the Maritime Customs made a significant contribution to the emergence of economic statistics in China. Record keeping for fiscal purposes had existed in China long before the Maritime Customs Service was established, but those records were limited in terms of their precision and reliability. In his critique of Ming governance, based on a study of the Grand Canal, Ray Huang claims that "the Ming emperor and ministers had never been methodical and cost-conscious in financial administration."[28] Huang goes on to point out, however, that "in their [defense], it may be said that the Ming officials administered what was then the largest empire in the world without the benefit of statistical techniques."[29] The statistics compiled by the Maritime Customs complemented and eventually replaced earlier types of economic statistics collected by the local Chinese bureaucracies, as described by Madeline Zelin.[30] According to Andrea Eberhard-Bréard, Qing statistics did not need to be very precise, since they served to determine local revenue quotas and were therefore "based on heterogeneous local

27. SHAC 679/1/17350, Tariff Secretary's Remarks on Various Secretary's [sic] Comments on Tariff Secretary's Confidential Memo to IG, 11 May 1932. Emphasis in the original.
28. Huang, "The Grand Canal," p. 251.
29. Huang, "The Grand Canal," p. 252.
30. Zelin, *The Magistrate's Tael*, pp. 18–21.

conditions, with substantial differences in measures of weight and value, and [had an] unstandardized nomenclature."[31] Because Maritime Customs trade statistics addressed these shortcomings, they were welcomed by some statecraft scholars, such as Xue Fucheng, who was close to the self-strengthening movement. Xue noted that the figures on duties levied "were a mirror reflecting the seclusion or accessibility of the land, poverty or wealth of the people, flourishing or declining of material well-being, and swelling or shrinking of revenues."[32]

Later, Western-trained economists, such as Yau-Pik Chau, Franklin Ho, and Zheng Youkui, described and analyzed China's national economy in the 1920s and 1930s in ways shaped by the concepts of Western economics, and their research heavily relied on Maritime Customs statistics. On the applied end of economic theory, Chinese students returning from abroad brought with them the latest business management theories, which also relied on statistics collected in certain ways. The methodology used by Chinese economists relied on empirical material provided by Maritime Customs publications. Works such as Zheng Youkui's 1939 *Woguo guanshui zizhu hou jinkou shuilü zhi bianqian* (Fluctuations of import tariff rates after our country's resumption of tariff autonomy), which contains an econometric analysis of the effects of tariff changes enacted under conditions of tariff autonomy and an assessment of the government's success in protecting domestic industries, required exact statistics. Those figures were supplied by the Maritime Customs.[33] Quantitative analysis of this kind made comparison with other countries possible.

The sophistication of Maritime Customs statistics attracted the attention of some critical observers, especially those concerned about the relative priorities of the Nationalist government. Lu Xun wrote: "When the ancients said, 'The man is not grinding the ink, but the ink is grinding the man,' they were lamenting the amount of time wasted in writing, and the fountain-pen was invented to make good this loss. But it can exist only in places where they value time and human lives.

31. Eberhard-Bréard, "Robert Hart and China's Statistical Revolution," pp. 607–8.
32. Zhao Fengtian, *Wanqing wushinian jingji sixiang shi*, pp. 88–89.
33. Zheng Youkui, *Woguo guanshui zizhu hou jinkou shuilü zhi bianqian*.

As China is not such a place, it cannot be a Chinese product. China has records of imports and exports, but no record of the population."[34]

A historian wishing to study Chinese economic history before 1949 must contend with a disconcerting array of widely differing local weights, measures, and currencies, evidence of China's separation into both regional economies and polities controlled by different power holders. For Chinese merchants, consumers, and revenue-collecting agencies, this plethora of different units was not merely a source of intellectual strain; it had a very real presence in their economic lives in that it contributed to containing consumption within local boundaries. The impact of the Maritime Customs on Chinese economic life, in providing national standards for weights and measures and establishing a currency that first was a unit of account before it eventually became fiat money, was therefore very significant. Certainly, Maritime Customs standards were frequently ignored or disputed; weights and measures were manipulated and currencies sabotaged. However, their existence created a criterion of uniformity and a tool for economic integration that reached beyond the boundaries of regional economies.

On the basis of these standardized weights and measures, and expressed in terms of its notional currency, the Maritime Customs compiled and published statistics that became the empirical basis for the work of many economists, both in China and abroad. What is particularly meaningful in this respect is that economists who argued against foreign economic penetration of China were using statistics compiled by foreigners to make that argument. This, apparently, was not a problem for Chinese scholars, or if it was, they were prepared to ignore it. More likely, they did not object to the foreign status of those preparing the statistics; the objectionable element was their remaining outside Chinese control while employed in a Chinese government agency. This suggests that Chinese scholars thought of the Maritime Customs, despite all its foreign influences, as a Chinese institution controlled by foreigners, while foreigners thought of it as an inherently foreign institution.

34. Lu Xun, "Prohibition and Manufacture," in *Selected Works*, vol. 3, p. 363.

The publication of nationwide trade statistics, or rather, trade statistics covering the trade registered at all custom houses, which covered most of China's foreign trade, did much to change the way Chinese scholars perceived China's economy. The concept of the modern national economy goes back to the writings of the mercantilist school and was adapted and developed by theorists like Adam Smith and Friedrich List. In economic history, the term "modern economy" applies to economies that combine sustained growth in per capita income and productivity; in the Western world, the earliest example of this phenomenon was seen in the Netherlands in the sixteenth and seventeenth centuries.[35] The Maritime Customs did much to domesticate the concept of an integrated, national Chinese economy, as different from the premodern regional economies described by G. William Skinner.[36] Westerners serving in the Maritime Customs and familiar with the national economies of their countries of origin brought to their work in China the sense that China, too, must possess a national economy. Thus Paul Barentzen, the tariff secretary, wrote in a letter to the inspector general in 1933 that "the market of this country, only just recovering from its own troubles and as yet on the fringe of advancing industrialism, did not participate to any great extent [in this trade boom]."[37]

Maritime Customs statistics were based on reports from port commissioners, the officials in charge of Maritime Customs offices in ports open to trade. The process of collecting statistics became more complicated as the number of items imported into and exported from China and, after tariff autonomy in 1929, the number of different tariff rates increased. The compilation of trade statistics collected from individual ports for publication was the responsibility of the Statistical Secretariat within the Inspectorate General of Customs, headed by a senior commissioner with the title of statistical secretary. The Statistical Secretariat was equal in rank to the departments administering, respectively, personnel, loan service, correspondence with Chinese authorities, tariff policy, and the enforcement of revenue protection.

35. Vries and van der Woude, *The First Modern Economy*, pp. 695–96, 717.
36. Skinner, "Marketing and Social Structure in Rural China."
37. SHAC 679/31798, P. G. S. Barentzen, Tariff Secretary, to IG of Customs, S/O No. 32, 15 January 1933.

One of the reasons for the relative importance of the Statistical Secretariat within the Inspectorate General was the fact that its published trade reports, running to three volumes by the 1930s and distributed in every country in which China maintained foreign obligations, served to reassure foreign creditors that the revenue collected by the Maritime Customs was sufficient for China to continue to meet its international obligations. Proof of this ability was essential to preserving the price of China's financial obligations traded on financial markets abroad, as evidenced in the fall in price of those financial instruments in the aftermath of the 1911 Chinese Revolution. In turn, stable prices for those obligations, together with published proof of China's revenue-gathering capability, were necessary for China to be able to secure further international loans.

Through the work of the Tariff Secretariat of the Inspectorate General of Customs, statistics also became the empirical basis for determining future tariff policy. Karl Gerth points out that trade statistics were "used iconically to convey a perceived truth" by the National Products Movement.[38] While it is certainly true that trade statistics were used by both the Chinese government and the National Products Movement in a discourse that identified China's annual trade deficit as an embodiment of China's lack of sovereignty, considering them as "an illustration," as Gerth describes them, rather than as straightforward statistical tables does not capture their full empirical potential.

The statistics published by the Inspectorate General of Customs were virtual statistics, insofar as they gave commodity values in the notional currency on which duties were based, not in the local currencies in which duties were paid. The notional currency, at various times, was the Haiguan (customs) tael, the customs gold unit, and the Chinese dollar. A more accurate picture of local trade necessitates converting the notional currencies used in the published trade reports into local currencies. This is possible only in cases where the exchange rate is known. It is also potentially misleading with regard to localities where several currencies circulated and were accepted as tender, such as most of the upriver Yangzi ports. In such cases, reconverting accumulated trade figures into one of the local currencies can yield fictitious figures,

38. Gerth, *China Made*, p. 45.

since it is often impossible to determine in which currency the commodities were paid for originally. In general, the larger the treaty port and the closer to the coast it was located, the likelier it is that one local currency was prominent compared with others, to the point that it can safely be considered the local currency from an empirical point of view. The best example, from the view of currency, is Shanghai.

The shortcoming of this example is that many of the commodities on which duty was paid in Shanghai were destined for onward shipment to ports in the interior of China, and they were shipped under exemption certificates. This system was based on the principle that imported commodities should have to pay duty only once. Converting Shanghai commodity values into Shanghai taels implies, incorrectly, that goods that were shipped to and paid for in the interior were consumed and paid for in Shanghai. The same applies to Hankou, which served as a distribution center for Hubei and Hunan.

Defining Commodity Values
in the Chinese Economy

One of the questions confronting the Maritime Customs in the process of assessing and recording the value of imported and exported commodities was how to establish uniform valuation practices across China. David Faure, among others, has pointed out that the problem with using Maritime Customs commodity values over long time periods was that the Maritime Customs changed from using free on board (FOB) values to cost, insurance, and freight (CIF) values in the late nineteenth century.[39] Assessing the value of imported commodities is central to determining the rate at which they are taxed. For this reason, values assessed by the Maritime Customs were frequently disputed by merchants, who correctly saw this as a successful way of protesting against the amount of tax they were required to pay without fundamentally disputing the right of the state to collect taxes.

The Maritime Customs developed an increasingly complex procedure for dealing with complaints about valuation. By the 1930s, a

39. Faure, *The Rural Economy of Pre-Liberation China*, p. 30.

merchant could appeal in the first instance to the local commissioner of customs; in the second, to the inspector general of customs; and in the third and final case, to the Tariff Board of Inquiry and Appeal, which consisted of two members representing the Office of Customs Affairs and three members representing the Inspectorate General of Customs. In a deviation from this regularized procedure, merchants also commonly lodged complaints through powerful allies, such as government officials and military officers in the case of Chinese merchants, and consular representatives and foreign ministries in the case of foreign merchants.

For reasons of both equity and efficiency, the method of assessment needed to be standardized. Market values, and hence duty-paying values, fluctuated according to transportation costs. In 1930, Carl Neprud, the director of the Maritime Customs Appraising Department in Shanghai, described how the Maritime Customs kept a record of wholesale market values: "What actually happens is that these invoice prices are compared with the values obtainable by the Chief Appraiser, through enquiries in the market, from records of previous importations, or from such other information—market reports, etc.—at his command. Discussions between the Chief Appraiser and the importer usually result in valuation agreeable to both parties, and it is seldom that a complete deadlock occurs."[40]

Because it was more feasible to do so, the Maritime Customs collected duties based on wholesale market values rather than retail values, chiefly because importers, rather than retail merchants or consumers, paid import duties. Assessing duties based on retail prices would have been logistically impossible, since the margin of profit a retail merchant added to his costs was subject to personal consideration. When the Maritime Customs was unable to establish wholesale market values, it used a hypothetical wholesale market value based on the retail value declared by the importer and checked against Maritime Customs price data. In Shanghai, individual arrangements for

---

40. SHAC 679/30590, Report on Shanghai Appraising Department, in Neprud to Bos, S/O, 2 May 1930.

reaching this value existed for each major importing firm.[41] As J. A. Dick, the technical adviser to the Shanghai Appraising Department, wrote in 1936:

> It may be argued that we ought to take the sale price of the dealer who buys from the importer, and who usually does carry some stock [as the basis of assessing tariff rates], but to take the figure of a second, or possibly third hand sale is unsatisfactory for the following reasons: —The Customs can only recognize importers of goods, we lay upon them the responsibility of making the correct declaration of value, and as it is often impossible for them to know the figure their buyer will sell at, it becomes impossible for them to make a declaration of another seller's price. The sale price of a dealer is not a very reliable guide to true wholesale values. The greater part of dealers' trade is the supply in fairly small lots to direct consumers, and much of this trade is done at very varied prices depending upon factors such as credit of buyer; need for cash, etc. The Customs cannot always verify the sales price of a "dealer," as if he refuses to supply the required information, we have no standing to make investigation [sic] into his trade, as he does not import, or come into contact with the Customs.[42]

Also in 1936, Financial Secretary A. C. E. Braud of the Inspectorate General, on behalf of the absent tariff secretary, wrote to the commissioner of customs in Xiamen (Amoy) that "the wholesale market value on which the duty paying values of imports is based is not a value peculiar to or fixed by the Customs":[43]

> It is the value at which the goods in question are actually bought and sold by merchants and it therefore stands to reason that the importer who actually owns and/or is dealing in the goods is in a better position to know and quote the wholesale market value of his own property than the Customs.

41. SHAC 679/17560, Report on the Shanghai Customs Appraising Department, in Lowder to IG of Customs, No. 16,827, 2 April 1921.
42. SHAC 679/9 6562, "Valuation," J. A. Dick, Technical Advisor, 9 March 1936.
43. SHAC 679/30468, A. C. E. Braud, Financial Secretary, for Tariff Secretary, to Commissioner, Amoy, Tariff Dossier No. 35, 23 July 1936.

It is for this reason that it is the general Customs principle as enunciated in Sections 2, 3 and 8 of Rule I of the Import Tariff Provisional Rules, that importers must first declare the value of their goods and support their declaration with all available evidence such as invoices, contracts etc., and that the Customs will then proceed to verify the declaration.

It is most important that this principle shall be strictly maintained, for if once the Customs assumes the responsibility of assessing values without insisting upon accurate declarations or evidence from the owners of the cargo (or their representatives, the importers) in the first place, merchants would be quick to feign ignorance of values and suppress documents in the hope that the Customs values, assessed in the dark and without access to the most important and natural sources of information[,] would be lower than the duty paying value based on the actual selling price of the goods. It would not then be long before the Customs lost touch entirely with actual market conditions and Customs figures would degenerate into arbitrary figures with but little relation to actual prices at which the goods were being bought and sold. It is therefore essential to insist on a declaration of value from importers before the assessments are undertaken.[44]

Based on a decision of the Tariff Board of Inquiry and Appeal in 1929, the Maritime Customs was required to take as the basis of valuation, in order of precedence, the wholesale market value at the port of importation, the wholesale market value at the principal markets in China (presumably as published by Maritime Customs), the CIF value as declared by the importer, and the value as appraised by the Maritime Customs.[45] In other words, the Maritime Customs "[accepted] declared values unless [it had] reason to raise them because they [did] not agree with [its] finding or estimate of the wholesale market value."[46]

44. SHAC 679/30468, A. C. E. Braud, Financial Secretary, for Tariff Secretary, to Commissioner, Amoy, Tariff Dossier No. 35, 23 July 1936.

45. SHAC 679/27229, Minutes, 33rd Meeting of the Tariff Board, 1929, in "The Making of Import Tariff Rule I and Its Sections." SHAC 679/27229, Yeh Yu Chun, "Tentative Code of Import Valuation Bases," in Tariff Secretary's Printed Note No. 91, 15 January 1949.

46. SHAC 679/27229, Yeh Yu Chun, "Tentative Code of Import Valuation Bases," in Tariff Secretary's Printed Note No. 91, 15 January 1949.

Table 3.1.
Scott Harding schedule of importers' costs

Cost for importer	Percent of item's value
Commission	2.5%
Interest (6.0% for four months)	2.0%
Fire insurance and storage (including landing charges, conservancy, and wharfage duties)	1.0%
Brokerage fee	1.0%
Telegrams, and interest on duty	0.5%

Source: From SHAC 679/27229, "The Making of Import Tariff Rule I and Its Sections."

When no wholesale market value was available, the Maritime Customs used the contracts between importers and trading partners overseas to establish the "cost" element of the "cost-insurance-freight" formula used to assess values. The allowances made for insurance and freight were based on the Scott Harding schedule, a list of importing costs put forward by a Shanghai importing firm of that name in 1909. The British legation, in a communication to the Chinese Ministry of Foreign Affairs, supported the position of Scott Harding and Company, that costs accruing to the importing merchant should be deducted from the wholesale market value in calculating the duty-paying value. The Scott Harding schedule of costs to be deducted (see table 3.1) was adopted by the Inspectorate General in 1913 with the concurrence of the Shuiwu chu (the central government organ then dealing with Maritime Customs affairs), after the schedule had been accepted by the four foreign chambers of commerce in Shanghai.[47]

In calculating duty-paying values, Maritime Customs officials used two set formulas, depending on whether a wholesale market value could be established or they had to rely on invoice values (see figure 3.1). The reasoning behind the use of these formulas was that wholesale market values, whether recorded by the Maritime Customs or declared by merchants, already included all duties paid on those commodities. Charging duties based on wholesale market values would have meant taxing the same commodity twice. For commodities for which the

47. SHAC 679/27229, "The Making of Import Tariff Rule I and Its Sections."

Formula for goods with established wholesale market value:

$$\frac{\text{Wholesale Market Value} \quad \times \quad 100}{100 + \text{Duty rate} + \text{Surtax rate} \quad + \quad 7 \text{ (Scott Harding allowance)}}$$

Example: Goods with an established wholesale market value of $3,000, taxed at 25% ad valorem

Duty-paying value: $\dfrac{3,000 \times 100}{100 + 25 + 2.5 + 7} = \dfrac{3000}{1.345} = \$2,230.48$

Duty amount: $2,230.48 × 0.25 (25% duty) = $557.62

Formula when the Maritime Customs had to rely on invoice values:

(CIF value + 5%) x duty rate (%)

Example: Goods worth £500 according to the covering invoice and taxed at 25%

Invoice value: £500.00
Duty-paying value: £525.00 = CGU3,858.72 (@ £1 = CGU7.35)
Duty amount: CGU3,858.72 × .25 (25% tax) = CGU964.69 [*sic*]

Plus: 5% of duty amount for revenue surtax
                        5% of duty amount for flood relief surtax
                        3% of duty amount for conservancy dues
                        1% of duty amount for wharfage dues

Total duty rate: 14% of duty: CGU964.69 × .14 = CGU135.06

Total duty amount: CGU964.69 + CGU135.06 = CGU1,099.75

Figure 3.1. Calculation of duty-paying values under the Scott Harding schedule. *Source*: Calculations and examples from SHAC 679/30468, Barentzen to Macoun, 12 January 1935.

Maritime Customs maintained records of wholesale market values, the duty-paying value was calculated according to the first formula in figure 3.1.

The Maritime Customs retained value lists—compilations of local price data—for both imported and exported commodities to serve as an empirical basis on which to challenge declared commodity values thought to be too low. While custom houses were required to maintain and publish statistics concerning commodity values, "the system of periodical value lists for certain commodities was adopted merely as a mutual convenience to the Customs and the public to avoid repeated delay and discussions over shipments from day to day of articles which may vary slightly in value," as Tariff Secretary E. N. Ensor wrote to the Chongqing commissioner in 1936.[48] "The fundamental basis of Customs tariffs on exports is the wholesale market value at the time of shipment according to Rule I of the Export (and Interport) Tariff Provisional Rules which cannot be replaced or overruled by the system of periodical value lists." By 1946, Wu Yaoqi, the acting commissioner of customs at Shanghai, stated that "by practice of long-standing, the wholesale market value has been taken to mean the various importers' average selling price of the goods in the ordinary course of trade."[49]

The Maritime Customs also faced the problem of establishing equitable nationwide values for the same commodities. This was done initially through examiners' conferences, in which the commodity experts of a district, usually as large an area as was practical for traveling purposes, were brought together to discuss authoritative commodity values, or, more likely, to be instructed in assessing values decreed authoritative by their superiors. This system, however, proved to be impracticable and was replaced by a system of correspondence in which values assessed in Shanghai became the standards on which to base valuations elsewhere. This was because Shanghai, being the port with the greatest amount of trade, also had the biggest Appraising Department, which contained both experts and technical equipment to assist in valuation decisions.

China was one of the last countries in the world to retain a silver-based currency; it was not abolished and replaced by a managed currency until 1935. The effect of fluctuations in the price of silver relative to that of gold is not immediately apparent from trade statistics in which values were expressed in a notional currency, the customs gold unit, until 1933. The achievement of the CGU lay in establishing a notional

---

48. SHAC 679/30470, E. N. Ensor to Commissioner of Customs, Chongqing, 23 January 1936.

49. SHAC/30649, Woo Yao-tchi, Acting Commissioner, Appraising Department, Appraising Department Order No. 1589, 11 May 1946.

national currency that, in turn, advanced the notion that China possessed a national economy. The CGU did not bring about monetary uniformity throughout China; that was left to the Communists, who achieved it in the early 1950s. Also, the CGU was initially designed to be a unit of account rather than fiat money, even though CGU-denominated notes were issued from 1931 to make paying Maritime Customs duties easier and less dependent on prevailing exchange rates.

Even after the 1935 currency reform, the fiat money issued by the Nationalist government was less widely used than the CGU. As a fiat currency, the customs gold unit was flawed by its sensitivity to gold-silver exchange rate fluctuations. Most importers had to purchase CGU notes with silver, since they did not have sufficient gold reserves. Purchasing CGU notes therefore meant gambling that the gold-silver exchange rate would remain stable or the silver price of gold would rise. A falling silver price in terms of gold would mean losses for the importer. Because of this uncertainty, the CGU's role as fiat money was limited. Also, importers typically paid large tariff dues by cheque or from CGU bank accounts.[50]

The gold-silver exchange rate fluctuations to which the customs gold unit was so susceptible from the merchants' point of view were largely irrelevant to the problem that the CGU had originally been introduced to address. With an increasing number of Western economies abandoning the silver standard, and an increase in US silver production, the gold price of silver suffered a secular decline in the 1920s. China's foreign obligations were payable in foreign currencies, most of which were gold-based by the late 1920s, at a time when China's own currency was still silver-based. This meant that while it cost the Chinese government $51,515,911 to meet foreign obligations of £7,526,151 in 1928, meeting virtually the same obligations (£7,762,280) cost $82,113,419 in 1929.[51] In other words, the cost of meeting the same amount of gold-denominated foreign obligations in consecutive years increased by 60 percent. Since foreign obligations were largely serviced with Maritime Customs revenue, the potentially disastrous implications of a further decline in the gold price of silver were obviated

50. King, *A Concise Economic History of Modern China*, p. 137.
51. Inspectorate General of China, *Trade of China: 1938*, p. 110.

by restating duties in the CGU, thus introducing a gold-based unit of account.

The significance of the CGU lies in the fact that it established a unit of account in which Maritime Customs duties were payable throughout China; map 3.1 shows the distribution of treaty ports, each of which had a custom house to administer revenue collection. Beth Notar has argued for the importance of Republican-era currencies as propagandistic tools.[52] The CGU note had a portrait of Sun Yat-sen on one side and a view of the Shanghai Custom House on the other, thus making visual reference both to nationalism as a political ideology and Guomindang rule, and to administrative modernity and competence. Since the CGU was largely a unit of account, its function as visual propaganda was limited. However, even in Yunnan, Sichuan, and, until 1931, the Manchurian provinces, Maritime Customs duties were stated in CGUs at all custom houses, projecting the alleged capacity of the Nationalist government to collect duties even into those areas of China over which it had no political and military control.

The failure of Nationalist currency reform to displace local currencies by introducing the Standard Dollar in 1935 accentuates the achievement of the CGU as a countrywide unit of account. When analyzing Maritime Customs trade statistics, we should recall that Chinese importers had to pay for their imports in gold-based currencies while earning profits in silver-based currencies. The degree to which values assessed by the Maritime Customs were based on estimates indicates the limits on the use to which they can be put. As Thomas Lyons points out, Maritime Customs statistics are "generally reliable," though they are to be used carefully because of issues of coverage and definition, variations in coverage and nomenclature, changing methods of valuation (such as those described in this chapter), problems of aggregation, and gaps in Maritime Customs data.[53] Thus, Maritime Customs statistics are best viewed as approximations that support the analysis of trends. However, these approximations allowed Chinese economists to analyze government tariff policy according to the methods of Western economics.

52. Notar, "Viewing Currency Chaos," p. 124.
53. Lyons, *China Maritime Customs*, pp. 69–71.

Conclusion

On the performative level, the act of collecting and publishing statistics was a practice of modern states. On a substantive level, the statistics collected by the Maritime Customs were used for policy making. When the Maritime Customs published trade and revenue statistics abroad in English to assure foreign bondholders of the stability of China's government finances, performative and substantive considerations both played a role. Chinese economists also used these statistics as an empirical basis on which to criticize the Nationalist government's tariff policy for not being effective enough in defending China's nascent industry from foreign competition.

The use of modern technology, too, could be understood in multiple ways. In the case of sugar, for example, the increased sophistication in the classification of imported sugar that underlay increased import tariffs was made possible by the introduction of chemical analysis using the polarimeter, a chemical measuring device that replaced the visual measuring aids formerly used by the Maritime Customs. The resulting increase in tariff revenue could have been achieved by increasing tariff rates on the basis of the old valuation system. However, the Nationalist government decided instead to increase its tariff revenue through the introduction of a more complex measuring device, which lent the move the rhetorical gloss of modernity.

Designing tariffs to promote the growth of domestic industries required Maritime Customs to collect nationwide trade data in order to analyze China's trade and measure the effect of tariff changes. Compiling the data necessitated the use of standardized valuation procedures and standard units of account in all Chinese treaty ports. Through these data sets, which were widely used by Chinese economists, the Maritime Customs contributed much to the way the modern Chinese economy was viewed in China and abroad, including the very notion that China possessed a national economy.

FOUR

Nationalist Tariff Policy
and the Import Trade

Nationalist tariff policy was primarily orientated toward producing central government revenue. In the course of achieving that aim, it created patterns of consumption that privileged some domestic consumers and some domestic producers at the cost of others. Eastman has pointed out that peasants bore a heavy weight of taxation as a result of the land tax and the salt monopoly.[1] They also bore the brunt of increases in commercial taxation, particularly on articles such as sugar, cotton, kerosene, and chemical fertilizer. A protectionist tariff policy was attempted where it was fiscally and politically possible, but the government's efforts to shape consumption according to its own vision were substantially constrained by external factors, such as Japanese political, military, and economic aggression, and by internal factors such as revenue considerations. Importantly, Nationalist tariff policy was sustainable in the midterm. While fiscal stability was pursued at the cost of economic growth, tariffs were never so high as to lead to a collapse in government revenue. Because import tariff revenue accounted for the greatest share of total tariff revenue during most of this period, as is demonstrated by fig 4.1, the analysis in this chapter focuses on the effects of changes in import tariff rates.

China's first tariff after regaining tariff autonomy was promulgated on 7 December 1928 and implemented from 1 February 1929. Figure 4.2 shows the values of import tariffs as a percentage of total

1. Eastman, *The Abortive Revolution*, pp. 205–8.

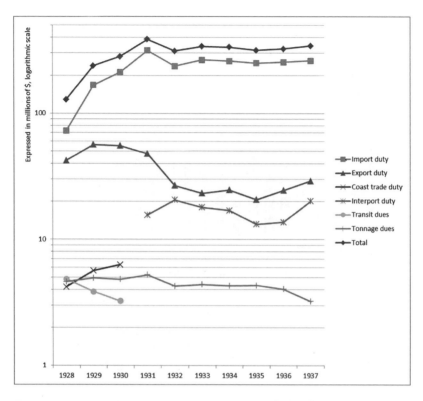

Figure 4.1. Maritime Customs revenue, 1928–37, in Standard Dollars. Source: Inspectorate General of Customs, *Trade of China, 1937*, vol. 1, p. 115.

import values. This amount, which is the average of import tariffs in percentage, is a rough indicator of the heaviness of import taxation. The first bar in each pair in the graph (for years 1928–35) shows the values arrived at by Frank Kai-Ming Su and Alvin Barber in 1936. Su and Barber did not explain their choice of totals for import value and import tariff value.[2] Recalculating their indicator with the respective values provided in Hsiao Liang-lin's (1974) statistical compilation, I arrived at values that are only slightly different for all years except 1931 and 1933, as I demonstrate with the second set of bars.[3] This indicator shows that from 1929, the first year of tariff autonomy, China's imports

2. Su and Barber, "China's Tariff Autonomy," p. 119.
3. Hsiao, *China's Foreign Trade Statistics*, pp. 23–24, 133.

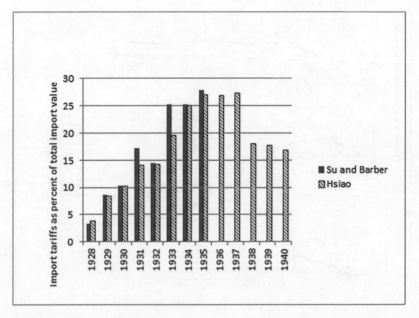

Figure 4.2. Value of import tariffs as a percentage of total import value, 1928–40.
Source: Data from Su and Barber, "China's Tariff Autonomy," and Hsiao, *China's Foreign Trade Statistics*.

were taxed increasingly heavily until the beginning of the Second Sino-Japanese War in 1937; from 1939 onward, imports were taxed more lightly once more.

By increasing import tariffs, the Nationalist government sought to achieve two objectives: to increase its revenue and to extend tariff protection to reflect Chinese economic interests.[4] These twin objectives were frequently at variance with each other. From the point of view of maximizing revenue, the optimum rate of taxation is the highest point of a Gaussian distribution; lowering or raising the rate of taxation will lead to lower taxation revenue. This means that the tax rate and revenue are positively correlated up to the optimum rate of taxation, and negatively correlated beyond that point. Frederick Maze, then commissioner of customs in Shanghai, warned the Nationalist government in 1927 against raising tonnage dues, pointing out that increasing the cost of

4. Kong Xiangxi, "Caizhengbu niju 1934 niandu," pp. 576–77.

landing goods at Shanghai would drive importers to land their goods elsewhere. According to a Western proverb, Maze told Finance Minister Song Ziwen, it was "unwise to strangle the goose that lays golden eggs."[5]

At the same time, the optimum rate of import taxation from a protectionist point of view is not the highest point on a bell curve; rather, it is the highest rate that is politically possible. From a protectionist point of view, the less foreign competition for domestic goods, the better. This objective is best achieved through high rates of taxation; hence the 70 percent rate on "lace trimmings, embroideries, plushes, velvets, silk piece goods, natural and artificial" in the 1929 tariff.[6] Besides protectionist considerations, these high rates were also influenced by revenue goals and prescriptive visions for Chinese consumption.

Given the basic contradiction between revenue considerations and protectionist interests, how did the Guomindang use the tariff schedule to further its political aims? At the time that the first autonomous tariff was implemented in 1929, the government announced that it would use its newly gained tariff autonomy not only to increase tariff revenue but also to protect and further the growth of domestic industries. Subsequent tariff schedules until 1938 were affected by this basic contradiction, while the international repercussions from tariff changes became another important factor affecting tariff policy. Figure 4.3, which shows the values of total Maritime Customs revenue and import tariff revenue at the port of Shanghai, demonstrates that the Guomindang did not strangle the goose that laid golden eggs by introducing higher tariff rates. Instead, it shows a long-term rise from 1926 to 1933, with the Northern Expedition accounting for a drop in trade volume and consequently tariff revenue in 1927, and the world economic depression, as well as the annexation of Manchuria, accounting for a second drop in 1932.

The development of the Chinese import tariff may be observed through the tariff rates imposed on four imported commodities: sugar,

---

5. Foreign Office [FO]: Political Departments: General Correspondence 1906–66, FO 371, National Archives of the UK [hereafter cited as FO 371], FO 371/12414 Frederick Maze, "Remarks on Imposition of Surtax on Tonnage" (translation), 23 July 1927, in Sir Sidney Barton to Sir Miles Lampson, No. 43, 28 July 1927.

6. "Customs Import Tariff of the Republic of China," in Woodhead, *China Yearbook: 1929–1930*, pp. 238–66.

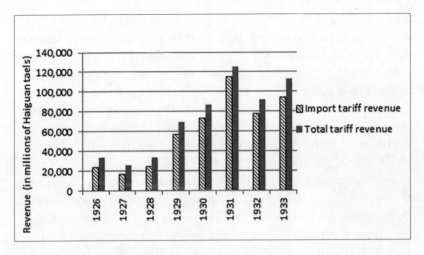

Figure 4.3. Shanghai customs revenue, 1926–33. *Source*: Data from Ministry of Industry, *Statistics of China's Foreign Trade by Ports*, pp. 168, 251.

chemical fertilizer, kerosene, and cigarettes. I have chosen to focus, for the most part, on the prewar period, when Nationalist tariff policy was as free from external constraints as it was ever going to be. Figure 4.4 shows the percentage shares of Maritime Customs revenue represented by tariffs from Shanghai and Hankou; this explains why the reporting from these two ports is so prominent in my analysis. By looking at imported goods that had different levels of competition from domestically manufactured goods, we can avoid attributing to protectionism tariff increases that were in fact the result of revenue concerns. Sugar, kerosene, and cigarettes had varying degrees of competition from domestic manufacturers; chemical fertilizer had no direct competition, but instead competed with natural fertilizers. I also elected to study imported goods associated with different countries. Legitimate sugar imports came to China from Cuba, the Dutch East Indies, and Hong Kong. When sugar smuggling increased in scale, Japan's stake in the sugar trade increased. Imports of kerosene were primarily British and American, and those of chemical fertilizer came from Germany, Japan, and Great Britain. Cigarettes, a luxury good, are included because the taxation on imported cigarettes offers an example of the Guomindang vision for nationalist consumption as it was put into practice. Sugar, kerosene, and cigarettes also were heavily smuggled in

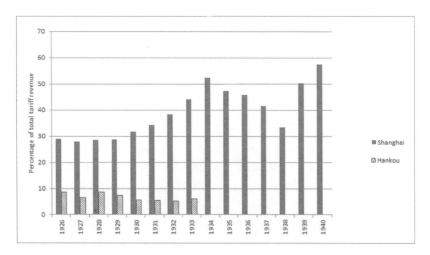

Figure 4.4. The Shanghai and Hankou shares of total tariff revenue, 1926–40. *Source*: Data from Ministry of Industry, *Statistics of China's Foreign Trade by Ports*, pp. 168, 251 (1926–33); Shanghai haiguanzhi bianji weiyuanhui, *Shanghai haiguanzhi*, p. 334 (1934–40).

the 1930s; all four commodities were subject to rival commodity taxation from local power holders in locales outside the Nationalist government's control.

The inclusion of the ports of Shanghai and Hankou in the volumes of trade statistics published by the Ministry of Industry facilitates my choice of other sites for tracing the impact of tariffs on consumption. For this I have looked at the ports grouped in Maritime Customs returns as Yangzi ports (Chongqing, Wanxian, Yichang, Shashi, Changsha, Yuezhou [now Yueyang], Hankou, Jiujiang, Wuhu, Nanjing, and Zhenjiang), Central Coast ports (Shanghai, Hangzhou, Suzhou, Ningbo, and Wenzhou), and northern China ports (Tianjin, Qinhuangdao, and Yantai [Chefoo]). The Yangzi River, China's most important inland waterway, provides a powerful image of both China's different regional economies and the reach of the Maritime Customs Service as a collection agency for the Nationalist government in Nanjing. Added to the Maritime Customs groups of Yangzi river ports should be Shanghai, which also served as a distribution center for the Yangzi Delta economy, and Suzhou. Tianjin, in Hebei Province, and Wenzhou, in Zhejiang Province, provide opportunities to study the impact of Japanese trade, both legal and illegal, as those ports are adjacent to Manchuria and Taiwan, respectively. In addition, throughout the time of this study Shanghai and Tianjin were the two ports with the largest shares of trade and tariff revenue. To ensure the statistical uniformity of the tables and graphs, I have converted post-1933 figures from national dollars into Haiguan taels.[7]

In the context of early twentieth-century Chinese nationalism, consuming foreign goods was fraught with complications. Consumption in Republican China has been the subject of several major works in recent years. Karl Gerth has demonstrated the degree to which consumer culture was politicized.[8] On the other hand, Frank Dikötter, having traced "everyday changes in the material landscape of China" from the mid-1800s to the mid-1900s, concludes that "worship of the foreign . . . could be fraught with ambivalence. In China, for instance, political elites gradually identified 'foreign' with 'imperialist' in the first decades of the twentieth century. Many ordinary people, on the other hand, were pragmatic enough to differentiate between the practical borrowings of things foreign and the rhetorical denunciations of imperialist powers."[9]

We may also conceptualize these two constituencies as being overlapping—as making choices about politics and consumption that were informed by different sets of values, political on the one hand and economic on the other. Ordinary people could and frequently did decide not to consume foreign goods, as is evidenced by the debilitating effect of anti-British and anti-Japanese boycotts on the import trade with those countries. While boycotts were often instigated by political elites, they were effective only because of the large-scale participation of ordinary consumers. Members of the political and intellectual elites, on the other hand, were perfectly capable and willing, despite nationalist sentiment, to consume foreign goods.

Besides the question of whether to consume goods imported from foreign powers that had encroached on Chinese sovereignty, Chinese

7. 1 Haiguan tael = 1.55 national dollars; see SHAC 679/1/26912, IG Circular No. 4588, 2nd ser., March 1933.
8. Gerth, China Made, pp. 101–5.
9. Dikötter, Things Modern, p. 2.

consumers were also faced with the problem of relating the consumption of imported modern goods to traditional Chinese material culture. In a newspaper column ridiculing the decision of local authorities in North China to prohibit the import of foreign fountain pens, the author Lu Xun wrote that "when a good thing is not a national product, China prohibits it, whereas Japan learns how to manufacture it." For him, this was "where our two countries differ."[10]

Within this framework of two ambivalences—national goods versus imperialist goods and modern goods versus traditional ones—imported goods were widely consumed throughout Republican China and certainly beyond the treaty ports. In his short story "Spring Silkworms," Mao Dun provides a literary reflection of this phenomenon when he describes an old peasant reflecting on the impact of foreign goods in his village. Of course, the old man does not speak with the authentic voice of a Chinese peasant but instead articulates Mao Dun's view on what ordinary Chinese citizens ought to have thought of the Nationalist government. Even so, this work is inspired by familiarity with the conditions in the Chinese countryside, and despite Mao Dun's political motives in writing the story, he provides a useful critique of Nationalist tariff policy: "From the time foreign goods—cambric, cloth, oil—appeared in the market town, from the time the foreign river boats increased on the canal, what he produced brought a lower price in the market every day, while what he had to buy became more and more expensive."[11]

Sugar

In Republican China, sugar was a necessity, used both as a sweetener and as a preservative in the preparation of food. Refined sugar was one of the most important imported goods; as such, it attracted steadily increasing import tariffs, which in turn significantly reduced the importation of sugar throughout the 1930s. Domestic consumers were driven either to use domestically produced raw sugar or to purchase

10. Lu Xun, "Prohibition and Manufacture," in *Selected Works*, vol. 3, p. 363.
11. Mao Dun, "Spring Silkworms," in *Spring Silkworms and Other Stories*, p. 4.

smuggled refined sugar. Refined sugar became the commodity most widely smuggled into China in the 1930s.[12]

Sugar cane was introduced into southern China from South Asia in the third century BC; however, sugar did not become a staple food in China until the eighteenth century, when its status changed from an item consumed on special occasions to a commodity for everyday use.[13] Advances in manufacturing technology, new trade networks, and changing tastes made sugar more popular. Cane sugar was an important source of tax revenue for the Qing government; according to one estimate, it produced the third highest amount of revenue, after salt and tea.[14] Until the 1890s, China was a net exporter of sugar.[15] But the establishment of two sugar refineries in Hong Kong, and Japan's development of the Taiwanese sugar industry after China ceded Taiwan to Japan under the provisions of the Treaty of Shimonoseki in 1895, destabilized the Chinese native sugar industry, both through purchases of sugar beet and through the large-scale importing of white sugar.[16] Around the turn of the century, sugar imports multiplied and exports declined, as China's domestic sugar production declined. Sugar production in Sichuan Province dropped off by one-half between the latter half of the nineteenth century and the 1930s; the amount of land cultivated for sugar production in Jiangxi Province was reduced by two-thirds between 1900 and 1934.[17] In Fujian, sugar production fell by 93 percent between 1900 and 1931: "Owing to the use of old methods of planting, harvesting, crushing and refining, the cost of production [was] high, and it [was] for this reason that native sugar . . . failed to compete with

12. Hanson, "Smuggler, Soldier and Diplomat," p. 544; Inlow, "Japan's 'Special Trade' in North China," p. 143.

13. Mazumdar, *Sugar and Society in China*, p. 15; Zhou Zhengqing, *Zhongguo tangye de fazhan yu shehui shenghuo*, p. 302; Qu Dajun, *Guangdong xinyu*, 14: 20b–22a, in Pomeranz, "Issues in the History of Consumption in China," p. 5.

14. Ji Xianlin, *Zhonghua zhetang shi*, p. 530, cited in Zhou Zhengqing, *Zhongguo tangye de fazhan*, p. 300.

15. Qing gongye bu ganzhe tangye yanjiusuo, Guangdong sheng nongye kexue-yuan, *Zhongguo ganzhe caipei xue*, p. 8.

16. Qing gongye bu ganzhe tangye yanjiusuo, Guangdong sheng nongye kexue-yuan, *Zhongguo ganzhe caipei xue*, p. 8.

17. Zhu Boneng, "Zhongguo zhi tangye ji qi tongzhi," pp. 59–65; Zhang Youyi, *Zhongguo jindai nongyeshi ziliao*, p. 661.

its foreign rival."[18] In the 1920s and 1930s, only half of China's sugar demand was being met by domestic production. China thus formed an important market, particularly for sugar imported from Java, in the Dutch East Indies.

The decline of the Chinese domestic sugar industry has much to do with the process of sugar production. Table sugar (sucrose) comes chiefly from two plant sources, sugar cane and sugar beets. Sugar cane grows in warm, subtropical regions; sugar beets grow in regions with cooler climates. Most domestically produced Chinese sugar was derived from sugar cane; the sugar beet was not introduced in northeastern China until 1903.[19] To produce sugar from sugar canes, the canes are crushed and the resulting juice is purified and boiled. Sugar crystals formed during the cooling process can then be sold as raw sugar or be processed further.[20] Crucially, raw sugar can be produced with simple machinery and human and animal labor. Refining raw sugar requires chemicals, advanced machinery, and specialized labor.[21]

Various factors account for the decline in China's domestic sugar production. Once sugar was imported into China in large quantities, it became less economical to transport domestic sugar from China's southern sugar-growing regions to the eastern seaboard and to the North China Plain. Imported sugar benefited from economies of scale in terms of transportation and production. It also benefited from the nimbus of modernity, especially in the case of imported refined sugar. Another factor was the state of war and upheaval that prevailed in China in the early twentieth century relative to the late nineteenth; peace had favored sugar production in the former period, compared with the latter.

After regaining tariff autonomy, import tariffs on sugar were increased in four main stages, which became effective in 1929, 1930, 1931, and 1933, respectively. Taking refined sugar, the most expensive kind of imported sugar, as an example, import tariff rates increased from

18. SHAC 679/18830, Tan Woon Chai to Commissioner, Amoy, 28 May 1931, in C. N. Holwill to IG of Customs, Amoy, No. 8,083, 29 May 1931.

19. Zhou Zhengqing, *Zhongguo tangye de fazhan*, p. 12.

20. Heriot, *The Manufacture of Sugar*, p. 159.

21. Heriot, *The Manufacture of Sugar*, pp. 159–200.

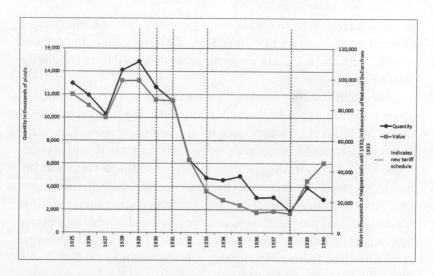

Figure 4.5. Quantity and nominal value of imported sugar, 1925–40.

CGU 0.79 per 100 kilograms in 1922 to CGU 1.98 per 100 kilograms in 1929, CGU 4.80 per 100 kilograms in 1930, and CGU 9.60 per 100 kilograms in 1933.[22] For the purpose of comparison in this instance, I have converted the 1929 figure from Haiguan taels into customs gold units at the 1930 exchange rate, the CGU having been introduced in 1930. Also, I have converted Chinese piculs into kilograms.[23] Again converted at 1930 exchange rates, the 1928 import tariff is equivalent to 0.70 US$ per kg, the 1930 rate to 1.90 US$ per kg, and the 1933 rate to 3.84 US$ per kg. In 1931, Maritime Customs changed its method of classifying white and brown sugar from the Dutch standard, a visual examining aid, to a chemical procedure that entailed measuring the polarization of sugar dissolved in water. This change led to a much more differentiated import tariff scale for sugar. While I have no disaggregated figures for different kinds of sugar, figure 4.5 shows the trends in the volume and value of imported sugar for the period under consideration.

22. Woodhead, *China Year Book: 1925*, p. 477; *China Year Book: 1929–1930*, p. 250; *China Year Book: 1931*, p. 683; *China Year Book: 1933*, p. 755.

23. 1 picul = 60.479 kilograms. Ministry of Information, *China Handbook, 1937–1945*, p. ix.

In Shanghai, China's biggest trade port, Commissioner of Customs Lancelot Lawford described a greatly increased sugar trade during the 1920s: "During the period under review the quantity of sugar imported into Shanghai has increased by approximately 100 per cent." This increase he ascribed to both "population increase and, to a lesser extent, an improvement in the standard of living." The majority of the increase was accounted for by white sugar, and the fact that the increased demand was for that variety of sugar, Lawford said, "may be attributed to the combined influence of steadily declining prices and regular improvement in the quality offered by Java, whence comes practically the whole of the plantation sugar sold to China." For the same reasons, imports of brown sugar had declined, and the sale of refined varieties was limited to a specialized market that had not shared in the general increase in sugar consumption. Sugar cane was imported into Shanghai primarily for use as a "sweetmeat by the poorer classes," since "the production in China [was] not sufficient to constitute a source of supply for sugar on [a] modern industrial scale." Imports and consumption of sugar cane showed sharp variations over time.[24]

In Tianjin, too, foreign sugar dominated the market. Foreign sugar imports into Tianjin averaged 1.2 million piculs a year; native sugar imports—that is, shipments of sugar from elsewhere in China—averaged just 95,000 piculs a year over the decade from 1922 to 1931, a difference that illustrates the decline of the native sugar industry and the market dominance of foreign firms. Sugar imports from Java, on account of their lower price, displaced imports from Hong Kong, only to be challenged by Japanese sugar imports toward the end of the decade.[25] In Chongqing, Commissioner of Customs Li Guiyong recorded that "white and refined sugar, being superior in quality to the sugar produced in the province, [was] in greater demand"; in Wanxian, refined sugar was one of only two commodities to show an appreciable increase over the decade, going from 944 piculs in 1921 to 68,353 piculs in 1931.[26] As table 4.1 indicates, prices increased twofold in terms of national dollars, and sixfold in terms of copper cash.

24. Inspectorate General of Customs, *Decennial Reports*, vol. 2, pp. 3–4.
25. Inspectorate General of Customs, *Decennial Reports*, vol. 1, p. 344.
26. Inspectorate General of Customs, *Decennial Reports*, vol. 1, pp. 474, 493.

Table 4.1.
Wanxian sugar prices, 1922 and 1931

	1922		1931	
	National dollars	Copper cash	National dollars	Copper cash
Value of sugar (1 catty)[a]	$0.09	200	$0.19	1,200

Source: Data from Inspectorate General of Customs, Decennial Reports: 1922–1931, p. 493.
[a] 1 catty = 0.60479 kg (Ministry of Information, China Handbook, 1937–1945, p. ix).

In Changsha, the trade in imported sugar suffered, like all foreign trade, from multiple boycotts of foreign goods throughout the 1920s and from the town being sacked by the Communists in 1930.[27] Surprisingly, no particular mention is made of sugar imports in Hankou, the largest upriver Yangzi port, but statistics published by the Ministry of Industry in 1935 show significant growth in sugar imports in the late 1920s, with a fall to only 93 percent of its previous value in 1927, a recovery lasting until 1931, and a subsequent sharp decline in early 1932.[28] The decline in 1927 can be explained by reference to Hankou's overall trade figures for that year, which show a decline that is explained in the *Decennial Reports* as due to anti-foreign riots, boycotts, and general unrest. Similarly, the increase in sugar imports in 1928 can be explained as an effort by importers to replenish their stocks. In Wuhu, sugar imports showed a long-term advance throughout the decade, averaging 250,000 piculs. A particularly good rice harvest in 1925 led to a decade high of 325,000 piculs of sugar imported in 1926.[29] In Nanjing, sugar remained one of the most important commodities imported over the decade; in Ningbo, it was a staple commodity, the import of which showed a long-term decline over the decade.[30]

Sugar imports also responded to international trends. In 1932, sugar imports for the whole country fell because of price agreements

27. Inspectorate General of Customs, *Decennial Reports*, vol. 1, p. 524.
28. Ministry of Industry, *Statistics of China's Foreign Trade by Ports*, p. 180.
29. Inspectorate General of Customs, *Decennial Reports*, vol. 1, p. 599.
30. Inspectorate General of Customs, *Decennial Reports*, vol. 1, p. 620; vol. 2, p. 85.

among the international sugar cartels. At the International Sugar Convention of 9 May 1931, eight sugar-producing countries accounting for 60 percent of sugar exports agreed to limit exports in the interest of preserving price stability on the international sugar market.[31] The sugar trade was also disrupted by the Japanese attack on Shanghai, while China's purchasing power was diminished because of the 1931 floods.[32] In 1933, Chinese consumers began to feel the effect of import duties assessed using the polarization technique rather than the Dutch Sugar Standard. The increased import duty "priced imported sugar out of the range of most consumers," with two consequences: both the smuggling of foreign sugar into China and the domestic cane sugar industry experienced a period of growth.[33] In 1934, import tariffs averaging 222.25 percent of the CIF (cost, insurance, freight) price of imported sugar contributed to a continued increase in smuggling. The Maritime Customs Service's Chinese secretary, Ding Guitang, reported from Guangdong in 1934 that "the present import tariff on sugar is so high and the market price of sugar so low that no legitimate trade in sugar can exist."[34] The Maritime Customs claimed to have asserted some control in Hebei and Shandong Provinces and forced imported sugar back on the legal market. Overall, though, there was a decline in imports of sugar because of the depressed state of China's domestic economy.[35] The currency reform of 1935 increased the purchasing power of Chinese consumers abroad and led to a slight increase in sugar imports, particularly from Japan and Taiwan. At the same time, the Nationalist government attempted to develop the domestic sugar industry.[36] In 1936, international suppliers of sugar lowered their wholesale price in order to recover the China market, but markets remained depressed, particularly because importers did not

---

31. Crespo, "Trade Regimes and the International Sugar Market," p. 163.

32. Inspectorate General of Customs, *Trade of China: 1932*, vol. 1, p. 50.

33. Inspectorate General of Customs, *Trade of China: 1933*, vol. 1, p. 46.

34. SHAC 679/14715, K.T. Ting to IG of Customs, Special No. 1304, 30 January 1934. See also Hill, *Smokeless Sugar*, pp. 225–42.

35. Inspectorate General of Customs, *Trade of China: 1934*, vol. 1, p. 52.

36. Inspectorate General of Customs, *Trade of China: 1935*, vol. 1, p. 58.

have sufficient confidence in the market to make forward purchases of imported sugar.[37]

In keeping with the overall trends in import trade and economic development, the imported sugar trade increased in 1937 until the Japanese invaded the North China Plain and renewed attacks on Shanghai. After the outbreak of hostilities, sugar imports declined rapidly. The increase in imported sugar had been at least partly due to speculative buying in advance of new sugar production quotas being determined by the major international sugar producers at the London Sugar Conference. Because of the Japanese attack on Shanghai, however, the stocks intended for onward shipment to Yangzi ports stayed in Shanghai and the inland ports remained unsupplied.[38] Owing to the war, sugar imports declined overall in 1938 at the same time that domestic sugar refineries were being destroyed. The high cost of transportation meant that imported sugar could not be sold economically on inland markets, even when it was possible to get it to those markets. On the other hand, as a result of the Japanese occupation, smuggling in North China decreased significantly; the amount of duty-paid sugar shipped into Tianjin increased tenfold between 1936 and 1938. The Japanese naval blockade of Guangdong Province reduced smuggling from Hong Kong into South China as well.[39] In 1939, the world market supply of sugar decreased after September because of the outbreak of the Second World War in Europe; however, both the quantity and the value of sugar imported into China increased, with the shares of Japanese and Taiwanese sugar imports increasing even further. Expecting a new sugar production quota from the international sugar cartel in September, importers of sugar had sold their stocks at discounted prices because they counted on being able to replace them cheaply. Instead, the outbreak of war in Europe led to increased sugar prices, which the Maritime Customs expected to rise further in 1940 because of the increased costs of production and freight. However, price controls were already in place to prevent sugar prices from fluctuating too widely.

37. Inspectorate General of Customs, *Trade of China: 1936*, vol. 1, p. 69.
38. Inspectorate General of Customs, *Trade of China: 1937*, vol. 1, p. 75.
39. Inspectorate General of Customs, *Trade of China: 1938*, vol. 1, p. 95.

The Maritime Customs also acknowledged that the domestic Chinese sugar industry had been badly damaged, particularly the sugar refining industry in South China.[40] In 1940, sugar imports to China increased in value but decreased in quantity, reflecting higher wholesale prices owing to wartime shortages as well as a poor sugar crop in Taiwan and Japan's restricting of sugar exports to preserve food supplies for the war effort.[41] In 1941, sugar imports increased both in quantity and value, with the Dutch East Indies contributing most of the increase.[42]

Summing up the effect of tariffs on the sugar trade, increased import tariffs in 1929, 1930, 1931, and 1933 caused a significant decline in both the quantity and value of legally imported sugar. The effect of rising tariffs in driving up the price of imported sugar was compounded by the supply policy of international sugar cartels in the early 1930s. Furthermore, sugar was smuggled into China both from Taiwan and, after 1931, from the Japanese-controlled Manchurian provinces as part of measures to destabilize the Chinese economy. Sugar imports increased again after 1937, when tariffs on imported sugar were lowered in Japanese-controlled areas and smuggling was curbed by the Japanese military authorities.

Kerosene

In China, kerosene, a distillate of crude petroleum, was mainly burned in lamps as an illuminant and used for cleaning purposes. In a purified and deodorized form, it was also used as a basis for medicines and hair tonic and as an insect repellent in malaria-prone regions. While kerosene was not as important an imported commodity as sugar, the trade in imported kerosene was significant enough to attract increased import tariffs, which, as in the case of imported sugar, drove Chinese consumers either to use cheaper domestically produced substitutes, such as vegetable oils, or to purchase smuggled kerosene. *Oil for the Lamps of China*, a 1933 novel written by the wife of an employee of

---

40. Inspectorate General of Customs, *Trade of China: 1939*, vol. 1, p. 93.
41. Inspectorate General of Customs, *Trade of China: 1940*, vol. 1, p. 81.
42. Inspectorate General of Customs, *Trade of China: 1946*, vol. 1, p. 52.

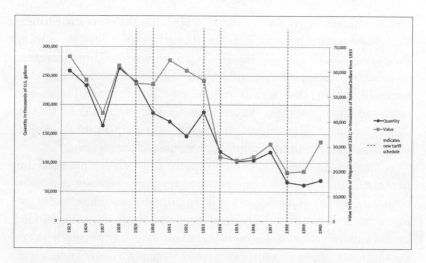

Figure 4.6. Quantity and nominal value of imported kerosene, 1925–40. *Source*: Data from Hsiao, *China's Foreign Trade Statistics*, p. 44.

the Asiatic Petroleum Company stationed in Nanjing, offered striking testimony of the extent to which lamp fuels were a commodity that Chinese and foreign companies competed to sell throughout China in the 1920s and 1930s; the novel describes a marriage that almost breaks down under the strain of the husband's devotion to his job selling kerosene to Chinese consumers.[43] Kerosene was transported to regional distribution centers by tanker ships and then commonly sold in cases containing two tins that held five American gallons each, the case weighing sixty-five pounds. By the early 1930s "practically all of the kerosene imported [came] from the United States of America or from Sumatra" whereas previously, "large amounts of kerosene [had been] imported from [the Soviet Union]."[44]

Figure 4.6 shows the general trends in the value and quantity of kerosene imported into China during the relevant period. Import tariffs were assessed either on the basis of a case of two tins of kerosene, containing five US gallons (18.93 liters) each, or on bulk imports. For cases of kerosene, tariff rates increased from CGU 0.21 in 1922 to CGU 1.32 in

43. Hobart, *Oil for the Lamps of China*.
44. Watson, *The Principal Articles of Chinese Commerce*, p. 125.

1929 and CGU 1.50 in 1930, before being lowered to CGU 1.43 in 1933 and raised again to CGU 1.80 in 1934. For bulk imports, the rate for ten US gallons rose from CGU 0.18 in 1922 to CGU 1.27 in 1929 and CGU 1.45 in 1930, fell to CGU 0.35 per liter (equivalent to CGU 1.33 for ten US gallons) in 1933, and rose again to CGU 0.45 per liter (CGU 1.70 for ten US gallons) in 1934.[45] No particular comments are recorded for Shanghai kerosene importation in the Maritime Customs *Decennial Reports*. Statistics recorded by the Ministry of Industry reveal two striking differences between Shanghai and upriver Yangzi ports. First, for Shanghai, no decline is recorded for 1927, a year marked by boycotts and uncertain local power structures at many inland ports. Second, far from declining in the early 1930s, kerosene imports into Shanghai increased threefold in terms of volume and value in the early 1930s compared with 1926, despite the decline in silver prices.[46] Luigi de Luca recorded in Tianjin that the local importation of kerosene oil had "reached the climax of 44 million American gallons in 1925." Thereafter it declined, and "in 1931 only 22 million were recorded, undoubtedly due to the abnormally high price"; however, annual imports of kerosene into Tianjin averaged 33 million gallons a year in the decade from 1922 to 1931 compared with 25.5 million a year in the previous decade.[47] It seems hardly surprising that 1925 saw the lowest and 1931 the highest average price for kerosene in the decade 1922–31: $0.08 and $0.16 per catty, respectively. In Chongqing, Li Guiyong reported that "there was an increasing tendency among the rural population to use seed and wood oil for illuminating purposes." Furthermore, he wrote, "the free use of kerosene in the hinterland is impeded as [its] price has been enhanced—partly by the slump in silver and partly by the imposition of numerous taxes at Chongqing and en route to the interior."[48]

Like trade in other imported commodities, kerosene importation into Changsha fluctuated according to political circumstances, rising

45. Woodhead, *China Year Book: 1922*, p. 481; *China Year Book: 1929–1930*, p. 254; *China Year Book: 1931*, p. 686; *China Year Book: 1933*, p. 758; *China Year Book: 1934*, p. 437. Haiguan taels and piculs converted into CGU and kilograms for ease of reference.

46. Ministry of Industry, *Statistics of China's Foreign Trade by Ports*, p. 174.

47. Inspectorate General of Customs, *Decennial Reports*, vol. 1, pp. 344, 368.

48. Inspectorate General of Customs, *Decennial Reports*, vol. 1, p. 473.

from 4.75 million US gallons in 1925 to 13 million in US gallons in 1926, falling dramatically in 1927 (no figures provided), recovering in 1928 and 1929 to the mid-1920s' levels, and falling again in 1930 and 1931.[49] In Yuezhou "the demand for kerosene had remained fairly steady in the neighbourhood of 2,500,000 American gallons per year." Like Changsha, the main problem affecting the local kerosene trade was political unrest: "In 1926 a large stock [of kerosene oil] was imported owing to the completion of an oil installation built by the Standard Oil Company in Chengling, but in the year 1927 there was an excess of re-exports over imports owing to political disturbances and unrest. In 1928 nearly 6.5 million gallons were brought in to replenish stocks, but the year 1930 showed a big drop to 333,000 gallons owing again to unsettled conditions."[50]

From Hankou, E. G. Lebas reported that "the demand for kerosene oil has remained practically unchanged, this commodity having been firmly established as a means of lighting as compared with the crude vegetable oils previously in use."[51] According to his report, kerosene imports dropped only when "sudden disaster, such as flood and famine, [struck] the country" and even then the drop was only temporary.

Kerosene oil imports into Wuhu followed the pattern set at Changsha and Yuezhou, with an advance until 1926, a fall in 1927, a recovery in 1928 and 1929, and another fall in 1930 and 1931.[52] Average import levels rose compared with the previous decade. In Zhenjiang, kerosene importation remained constant across the decade: 10,088,456 US gallons were imported in 1922 and 10,756,327 US gallons in 1931, making it the principal article imported from abroad and yielding 80 percent of the import tariff revenue in 1931. Two-thirds of all kerosene oil imported to Zhenjiang originated in the United States, with the remainder coming from the Dutch East Indies. In Hangzhou, He Zhihui noted that kerosene had "long been a favourite illuminant of the farmers, to whom it [was] no longer a luxury."[53] However, the decline in silver

49. Inspectorate General of Customs, *Decennial Reports*, vol. 1, p. 524.
50. Inspectorate General of Customs, *Decennial Reports*, vol. 1, p. 543.
51. Inspectorate General of Customs, *Decennial Reports*, vol. 1, p. 554.
52. Inspectorate General of Customs, *Decennial Reports*, vol. 1, p. 600.
53. Inspectorate General of Customs, *Decennial Reports*, vol. 2, p. 66.

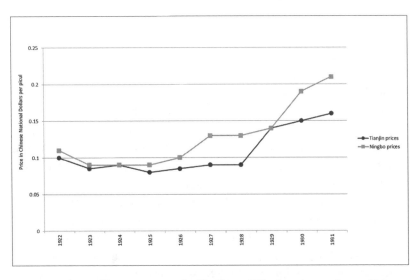

Figure 4.7. Nominal kerosene prices for Tianjin and Ningbo, 1922–31. *Source*: Data from Inspectorate General of Customs, *Decennial Reports: 1922–1931*, pp. 368, 645.

prices that began in the late 1920s had adversely affected the importation of kerosene and forced consumers to find substitutes for kerosene oil because of its high price. Similarly, in Wenzhou, the "importation of kerosene oil, more especially of the American variety [which had] gradually displaced vegetable oil throughout the hinterland [and supplemented] the deficiencies in the local electric-light service, . . . increased steadily."[54] But rising gold prices in relation to silver had rendered its price "almost prohibitive to the rural populace." Local price data for individual commodities are difficult to find for this period. The Maritime Customs publication *Decennial Reports* is one source of such data, even if the 1922–1931 issue provides price data only for two ports, Tianjin and Ningbo; these are graphed in figure 4.7.

While both the value and the quantity of kerosene imported into Shanghai and Hankou increased in 1932 compared with 1931, overall, imports of kerosene nationwide fell in both categories. The Maritime Customs recorded that there was little change in actual consumption, but because of the lower tariff on fuel oil, local manufacturers began

54. Inspectorate General of Customs, *Decennial Reports*, vol. 2, p. 100.

to refine and sell fuel oil as an illuminant.[55] Inspector General Frederick Maze addressed the Ministry of Finance directly about this in 1933: "[Does] the Government desire, and have they sufficient power, to abolish the distilleries recently established, and being established, throughout China—especially in the South?"[56] Maze spelled out the situation facing the Nationalist government (always provided that it had enough power to assert its policy): distillation of kerosene from fuel oil was "spreading with rapidity and [afforded] employment and profit for . . . an increasingly large number of people, and a result will be that Kerosene Oil will soon be available at cheap rates," he wrote.[57] However, this new mode of production would, over the course of a few years, destroy the kerosene import trade and hence the government tax revenue collected therefrom. As the tariff increase on fuel oil in 1936 showed, the Nationalist government chose to support the interests of foreign oil companies in the kerosene import trade. One may assume that this was because the government wanted both to protect its own revenue and to deprive the Guangdong provincial government of the tax it was collecting on distilled fuel oil. Still, for a government that had asserted its intention of improving the people's livelihood, making illuminants more expensive was a somewhat contradictory measure.

In 1933, kerosene increased in quantity consumed and decreased in value; a wholesale unit of 10 US gallons fell in price from $9.65 to $5.40 in Shanghai and from $11.00 to $5.40 in Hunan.[58] In the area around Hankou, speculative buying and price wars led to the increased use of kerosene as an illuminant among the poorer population, while China as a whole increased its importation of oil from the Soviet Union.[59] In 1934, kerosene imports declined for several reasons: because of earlier speculative buying in anticipation of a tariff increase, because of the actual tariff increase itself, and because of the spread of the use of distilled fuel oil.[60] In 1935, kerosene imports decreased slightly in value and increased in quantity according to the Inspectorate General's report, although this is contradicted by Hsiao's figures in fig. 4.6; owing to the

55. Inspectorate General of Customs, Trade of China: 1932, vol. 1, p. 52.
56. SHAC 679/28345, IG of Customs to Minister of Finance, 4 February 1933.
57. SHAC 679/28345, IG of Customs to Minister of Finance, 4 February 1933.
58. Inspectorate General of Customs, Trade of China: 1933, vol. 1, p. 47.
59. Inspectorate General of Customs, Trade of China: 1933, vol. 1, p. 14.
60. Inspectorate General of Customs, Trade of China: 1934, vol. 1, pp. 53–54.

low price of kerosene, the distillation of fuel oil did not develop much further. Kerosene smuggled from Taiwan had a further lowering effect on market prices. While floods and droughts in northern and central China diminished the purchasing power of many consumers, prices for kerosene averaged $8.60 per wholesale unit of 10 US gallons.[61] They remained at that level when a tariff increase on fuel oil made its distillation into an illuminant less profitable. A subsequent overall increase in kerosene imports was mainly the result of an increase in imports from the Dutch East Indies, while kerosene imports from the United States, the USSR, and Japan declined. The decline of the latter was at least partly due to the fact that Japanese kerosene was being smuggled into the North China Plain in large quantities: the Maritime Customs estimated 16 million liters (4.2 million US gallons) for the year 1936. The overall increase in kerosene importation also took place despite an increase in local kerosene taxation in both Sichuan and Shanxi Provinces, neither of which were controlled by the Nationalist government.[62]

Overall, in the calendar year 1937, kerosene importation increased by 10 percent because of favorable economic conditions and a general increase in consumption. However, after the onset of hostilities in the Second Sino-Japanese War in July 1937, trade in kerosene collapsed as shipping and rail transport were disrupted and both merchants and capital fled from the front line, particularly from North China and the Yangzi Valley; large-scale tariff evasions in North China continued.[63] Because of the breakdown in transport, currency fluctuations, and the disruption of prewar remittance networks between inland merchants and Shanghai wholesale importers, kerosene imports for the entire country declined from 448 million liters in 1937 to 253 million liters in 1938; as of October 1938, when the Japanese army occupied Guangzhou, kerosene could no longer be shipped to Hankou by rail.[64] As with sugar, smuggling from Manchuria and the Guandong Leased Territory into the North China Plain declined sharply as a result of the Japanese occupation; instead, the Maritime Customs recorded an increase in

61. Inspectorate General of Customs, *Trade of China: 1935*, vol. 1, p. 60.
62. Inspectorate General of Customs, *Trade of China: 1936*, vol. 1, p. 71.
63. Inspectorate General of Customs, *Trade of China: 1937*, vol. 1, p. 78.
64. Inspectorate General of Customs, *Trade of China: 1939*, vol. 1, p. 95.

duty-paid kerosene imports from Japan and Korea.[65] Both the overall decline in the trade and the increase in kerosene imports from Japan and Korea continued in 1939. Consumption in Shanghai and the Lower Yangzi area, behind the Japanese front line, increased slightly; because of a tightening of the economic blockade of Nationalist China, wholesale kerosene prices in Nationalist-controlled areas rose as high as $65 per unit of ten US gallons.[66] In upriver ports like Wanxian, kerosene became scarce even during the early years of the war; by June 1939, a municipal catty of kerosene retailed at $1.20.[67] However, prices varied greatly depending on local supply and market confidence: "The retail price [of kerosene oil] was $1.20 per municipal catty two days ago, but is $0.95 to-day; because a consignment of a few hundred tins is said to be arriving from [Yichang]." In general, commodities were "being imported in insignificant quantities, and at exorbitant prices"; "market prices (retail prices) for certain commodities have gone up by 200 to 300 per cent of what they were before the present hostilities due to speculation on the part of the dealers concerned."[68] During the early stages of the Second Sino-Japanese War, kerosene oil was traded across the front line. Carl Neprud, tariff secretary at the Inspectorate General, quotes Bei Zuyi of the Bank of China as saying that "kerosene oil and other products landed at Wuhu were carried on the backs of coolies into the unoccupied territories."[69] When Neprud protested that, if that were the case, they would be detected by Chinese soldiers, Bei suggested that smugglers bribed their way past the soldiers. In 1940 the kerosene trade declined further, accelerated by rapidly increasing local taxation and the decline in the value of the Chinese dollar relative to other currencies.[70] The decline continued in 1941, and the import trade in kerosene came to a complete standstill after the outbreak of war in

65. Inspectorate General of Customs, *Trade of China: 1938*, vol. 1, p. 97.

66. Inspectorate General of Customs, *Trade of China: 1939*, vol. 1, p. 95.

67. SHAC 679/30470, Chan Pak Hong to Lu Shou Wen, 16 June 1939, in Maze to Lu Shou Wen, 22 July 1939.

68. SHAC 679/30470, Chan Pak Hong to Lu Shou Wen, 16 June 1939, in Maze to Lu Shou Wen, 22 July 1939.

69. SHAC 679/31674, C. Neprud, Tariff Secretary, to IG of Customs, Confidential, 4 April 1939.

70. Inspectorate General of Customs, *Trade of China: 1940*, vol. 1, p. 83.

the Pacific in the Second World War following the Japanese attack on Pearl Harbor on 7 December.[71]

Thus increases in the tariff on imported kerosene in both 1929 and 1931 led to a significant decline in the quantity of imported kerosene. Because of the tariff increase, the value of imported kerosene first remained constant and then increased before eventually following the downward trend in quantity. A tariff reduction in 1933 produced a short-lived increase in both the quantity and value of imported kerosene, while a tariff increase in 1934, beyond even the levels of the 1931 tariff rate, produced another decline in both categories. Favorable economic conditions in early 1937 produced an increase in both the quantity and value of imported kerosene that was reversed with the beginning of the Second Sino-Japanese War, even though kerosene smuggling was curbed to a certain extent in Japanese-controlled areas.

Chemical Fertilizer

The Nationalists' taxation of imported chemical fertilizer demonstrates how revenue considerations, supported by nationalist ideology, superseded protectionist concerns in determining Guomindang tariff policy. Many agronomists held chemical fertilizer to be more effective than traditional Chinese fertilizers in increasing agricultural yields, and yet the high cost of imported chemical fertilizer prohibited its widespread use. The Nationalists increased import tariffs on chemical fertilizer in 1929 and then again in 1930, even though the number of Chinese farmers who would have benefited from increased yields achieved through the use of chemical fertilizer was much higher than the number of farmers subsisting on the profits from growing beans for producing traditional bean-cake fertilizer. This points to the predominance of revenue concerns in determining Nationalist tariff policy.

For centuries Chinese farmers had relied on human and animal manure for fertilizers, as well as green manures—crops grown solely

71. Inspectorate General of Customs, *Trade of China: 1946*, vol. 1, p. 53.

for the purpose of improving the soil for the following crop.[72] During the Song and Ming dynasties other forms of fertilization, including the use of farm and industrial by-products such as hemp waste, compost, oil cakes, and bean cakes, were added to the traditional range of fertilizers. The latter two types of fertilizer, plus other forms made of lime, mollusk shells, river mud, silkworm waste, and human manure, were traded as commercial commodities.[73] Francesca Bray claims: "The Chinese had a fine empirical grasp of the practical principles of fertilization, and understood that the addition of organic manures improved the soil structure and increased water retention as well as nourishing the crop. Deeper than this their knowledge could not go, for only with the development of botanical science and analytical chemistry in the last two centuries have we come to understand the processes of plant nutrition and the chemical composition of soils."[74]

Synthetic fertilizers, which relied on the industrial synthesis of ammonia compounds and superphosphates, as pioneered by the German chemist Fritz Haber between 1894 and 1911, were introduced in China in the 1920s; they are recorded as an individual product category for the first time in the trade returns for 1924.[75] Synthetic fertilizers contain larger amounts of nitrogen, potassium, and phosphorus than organic fertilizers and can therefore ameliorate the effects of soil deterioration through intensive cultivation more effectively than organic fertilizers. While there were many varieties of chemical fertilizers, the most common was ammonium sulphate, which had the largest share of the market in imported chemical fertilizers; for this reason I focus on ammonium sulphate in this chapter. Imported ammonium sulphate was manufactured chiefly by I. G. Farben and Imperial Chemical Industries Ltd. (hereafter ICI), a German and a British company, respectively, and sold in China through import firms and agents (I. G. Farben) and traveling salesmen (ICI).[76]

72. Bray, "Agriculture," pp. 290–93.
73. Bray, "Agriculture," pp. 294–95.
74. Bray, "Agriculture," p. 297.
75. Hsiao, *China's Foreign Trade Statistics*, p. 35.
76. Osterhammel, *Britischer Imperialismus im Fernen Osten*, pp. 167–72; Brodie, *Crescent over Cathay*, pp. 68–174.

T. H. Shen states that chemical fertilizers quickly became popular in China.[77] This assessment contrasts with the positions taken in many recent studies of China's rural economy during the Republican period. In his study of Hebei and Shandong villages, Ramon Myers shows that, based on Japanese surveys undertaken in the 1930s, chemical fertilizer was used in none of the communities he examined; instead, they predominantly relied on human and animal manure, sometimes enhanced by an admixture of bean cakes.[78] David Faure, who has studied the rural economy of Jiangsu and Guangdong Provinces in the late imperial and Republican eras, shows that chemical fertilizer was used in the mulberry-growing areas of the Pearl River Delta as early as 1922.[79] This difference in the use of chemical fertilizer reflects the difference between villages predominantly growing food crops, as in the communities surveyed by Myers, and villages growing cash crops—for example, mulberries—as in the communities cited by Faure; it is important to note that Faure's point applies only to cash-crop-growing villages. The difference in the use of chemical fertilizers can therefore be explained by the availability of funds. For the Hebei and Shandong villages studied by Myers, even bean-cake fertilizer was usually too expensive, let alone chemical fertilizer, while Guangdong villages relying on cash crops could better afford such an investment.

Once again, it is Mao Dun who gives literary expression to what Chinese intellectuals saw as the distrustful attitude of China's farmers toward chemical fertilizer. In his short story "Autumn Harvest," a peasant argues with his son over the use of chemical fertilizer: "That chemical stuff! Poison! Poison made by the foreign devils to kill people! I only know the bean-cake fertilizer our ancestors used. Fine, strong! That chemical powder ruins the land. Tomorrow, we will buy bean cake!"[80]

However, preferences in the use of synthetic fertilizer were also influenced by the propagandistic efforts of the domestic competitors of imported chemical fertilizer, of which the bean-cake producers were the best organized. Using the ideology of the National Products Movement,

---

77. Shen, *Agricultural Resources of China*, pp. 32–39.
78. Myers, *The Chinese Peasant Economy*, pp. 46, 74, 90, 109.
79. Faure, *The Rural Economy of Pre-Liberation China*, p. 37.
80. Mao Dun, "Autumn Harvest," in *Spring Silkworms, and Other Stories*, p. 48.

the bean-cake industry agitated against the use of imported chemical fertilizers in rural communities. In a letter of complaint to the German consul general in Guangzhou, a traveling salesman for the Deutsche Stickstoff Handelsgesellschaft (German Nitrogen Trading Company) complains of having been beaten up, as he explains, by toughs hired by the local bean-cake merchants when he was in rural Jiangsu. Furthermore, he complains that the local Guomindang official refused him redress and only very reluctantly offered protection.[81]

John Buck, who conducted the largest survey of Chinese farmers undertaken in the 1930s, claimed that an average of 3 percent of all farmers he surveyed (on 9,134 farms in 91 localities across 20 provinces in China) had begun using commercial fertilizers, which in his definition excluded organic fertilizers of any sort, during the period in question (1929–33). Broken down by agricultural macroregions, Buck's survey suggests that this increase occurred in the rice-growing rather than the wheat-growing regions of China, and that the increase was at its largest in what he termed the rice-tea region (southern Anhui, Zhejiang, Fujian, Jiangxi, and Hunan) and the Yangzi rice-wheat area (Jiangsu, northern Anhui, and Hubei).[82]

Tariff rates on ammonium sulphate, one of the most commonly imported chemical fertilizers, increased from CGU 0.69 per 100 kilograms in 1922 to CGU 1.04 per 100 kilograms in 1929 and CGU 1.22 per 100 kilograms in 1930, before being lowered slightly, to CGU 1.20 per 100 kilograms, in February 1934, when weights were assessed on a metric basis.[83] The Maritime Customs *Decennial Reports* for the decade 1922 to 1931, like the studies by Myers, Faure, and Buck, focus on the difficulties surrounding the introduction of chemical fertilizer in Chinese agriculture. Commissioner of Customs Lawford in Shanghai noted that "the chief fertilizers used by farmers are liquid manure, bean-cake, rape seed-cake, paddy straw ash, canal mud and stable manure," as well as "numerous weeds of a clover-like nature, which cover

81. Bundesarchiv, R9208/2712 Sakowsky, Guangzhou; to Auswärtiges Amt, No. 488/30 2041, 10 September 1930.

82. Buck, *Land Utilization in China*.

83. Woodhead, *China Year Book: 1925*, p. 479; *China Year Book: 1929–1930*, p. 252; *China Year Book: 1931*, p. 685; *China Year Book: 1934*, p. 436. Haiguan taels and piculs converted to CGU and kilograms for ease of reference.

every fallow field during the spring and are ploughed into the soil."[84]
With respect to ammonium sulphate, Lawford wrote that "this fertilizer has proved very suitable for the majority of crops in China, and
its growing popularity has not been without effect on the bean-cake
trade." Other chemical fertilizers imported into Shanghai, but so far
without success on the local market, included "nitrate of soda, superphosphate, potash fertilizers, . . . concentrated complete fertilizers
mixed in China from imported raw materials," and "ammonium phosphate fertilizers." Lawford also noted that local authorities had made
efforts to stop the importation of "harmful fertilizers."

Chongqing commissioner of customs Li Guiyong reported that
"artificial fertilizer [had] recently been introduced and [was] growing
in favour among the farmers."[85] To promote the use of chemical fertilizers, ICI had dispatched traveling salesmen to the Sichuan countryside to demonstrate the use of ammonium sulphate. Similarly, the
Tianjin commissioner, Luigi de Luca, reported that "as the application
of organic animal refuse [was] both costly and elaborate in process, the
inorganic chemical fertilizer [had] stepped into the farming field."[86]
However, he also stated that "whether or not it is a boon to the agricultural community [could not] be ascertained, for there still [existed] a
divergence of opinions among the users." At any rate, according to the
same report the volume of ammonium sulphate imported into Tianjin
increased more than tenfold, from 13,782 piculs in 1925 to 174,482 piculs
in 1931. What de Luca termed a "divergence of opinions among the users"
was commented on more sharply by other commissioners of customs.
H. Dawson-Grove, at Shashi, wrote that "the methods of farming in
the districts round Shashi [were] still primitive"; he added that "a
fairly considerable quantity of German fertilizer, known as ammonium sulphate, was imported, but had to be re-exported on account
of the farmers' refusal to employ such highly expensive manure."[87] At
the neighboring port, Changsha, Commissioner H. C. Morgan wrote
that "foreign fertilizers were introduced into Hunan in 1924 but were

84. Inspectorate General of Customs, *Decennial Reports*, vol. 2, p. 20.
85. Inspectorate General of Customs, *Decennial Reports*, vol. 1, p. 495.
86. Inspectorate General of Customs, *Decennial Reports*, vol. 1, p. 355.
87. Inspectorate General of Customs, *Decennial Reports*, vol. 1, p. 514.

found to be quite generally unsuited to the local soil, farmers alleging that their use rendered it quite unproductive after a few years."[88] E. G. Lebas reported for Yuezhou that "notable progress or development of agriculture can hardly be said to have taken place during the decade," a fact he attributed at least partly to "the Chinese farmer's traditional conservatism against change and innovation," since "the intelligent use of artificial fertilizer would without doubt improve the yield of the fields and thus advance the farmer's economic position."[89] From Hankou, Lebas reported that "the Chinese peasant, who represents approximately 75 per cent of the total population, remains strictly conservative in his methods of cultivation and tilling the soil."[90] However, he noted, "It would appear ... that the farmer is very slowly beginning to make use of [artificial fertilizers] but is hampered by the high costs." In both reports, Lebas drew attention to the difficulty of trading an expensive product in a rural hinterland notorious for banditry, because local agents were expected to provide financial guarantees for goods delivered for onward sale. In Wuhu, Hu Yaoqing reported that "more attention seems to have been paid by local farmers to fertilization": "While night-soil, bean-cake, pond and creek mud, and manures are still the principal fertilizers, chemical fertilizers were introduced into Anhui [in 1924] and they seem to be becoming increasingly popular. That ammonium sulphate can be used as a fertilizer is now well known throughout the province, and its consumption increased from 400 piculs in 1925 to 10 times as much in 1930."[91] In Wenzhou, Zhou Ziheng stated that "sulphate of ammonia, which made its first appearance in the trade statistics in 1924, created an extensive demand, as its value as a fertilizer became more and more appreciated, threatening to oust its native rival, bean-cake, completely from the market."[92] Organic fertilizers in use locally consisted of "night-soil, stable manure, canal mud, paddy-straw ash, burned soil, bean and rape seed cakes," plus "lime and gypsum." The "ever-

88. Inspectorate General of Customs, *Decennial Reports*, vol. 1, p. 529.
89. Inspectorate General of Customs, *Decennial Reports*, vol. 1, p. 545.
90. Inspectorate General of Customs, *Decennial Reports*, vol. 1, p. 561.
91. Inspectorate General of Customs, *Decennial Reports*, vol. 1, p. 604.
92. Inspectorate General of Customs, *Decennial Reports*, vol. 2, p. 100.

increasing expansion" of ammonium sulphate served as an "undeniable indication of the general preference for the foreign fertilizer, though more expensive, to the native article."[93] This confirms Buck's analysis, mentioned earlier.

Because the high import tax and provincial taxation added 40 percent of the purchasing price, on average, to the cost of chemical fertilizer, and thanks to the weak exchange rate of the Chinese silver dollar, imports of ammonium sulphate went into a mid-term decline beginning in 1930.[94] The decline continued in 1933 because of droughts in South China, the area that consumed by far the greatest share of chemical fertilizer, and a drop in agricultural prices elsewhere, both factors that decreased the farmers' purchasing power.[95] In 1934, further droughts, continued low prices for agricultural produce, the Fujian insurrection, and provincial restrictions on importing chemical fertilizer in Guangdong, Zhejiang, and Jiangsu—where the German traveling salesman experienced one of the restrictions' more violent manifestations—caused a further decline.[96] Overall, imports of chemical fertilizer decreased further in 1935 because of competition from domestic fertilizers and the poor economic circumstances of farmers; however, imports of ammonium sulphate increased.[97] In 1936, increased prices for agricultural goods led to greater prosperity and hence greater sales of chemical fertilizer, particularly in Guangdong and Fujian Provinces but also in the provinces of Zhejiang, Jiangsu, Shandong, and Hebei.[98] This trend continued in 1937, thanks to good harvests, stabilized exchange rates, a climate of economic confidence, and the increasing popularity of ammonium sulphate among farmers.[99]

Imports of ammonium sulphate declined by a third in 1938; however, domestic demand increased, particularly in South China, where the shortage of bean cakes, previously imported from Manchuria, was keenly felt. Also, merchants were attempting to preempt an anticipated

93. Inspectorate General of Customs, *Decennial Reports*, vol. 2, p. 104.
94. Inspectorate General of Customs, *Trade of China: 1932*, vol. 1, p. 51.
95. Inspectorate General of Customs, *Trade of China: 1933*, vol. 1, p. 46.
96. Inspectorate General of Customs, *Trade of China: 1934*, vol. 1, p. 53.
97. Inspectorate General of Customs, *Trade of China: 1935*, vol. 1, p. 59.
98. Inspectorate General of Customs, *Trade of China: 1936*, vol. 1, p. 70.
99. Inspectorate General of Customs, *Trade of China: 1937*, vol. 1, p. 78.

fall in the value of Chinese currency, which subsequently restricted trade because of high prices. Trade in northern and central China behind the Japanese front lines was hindered by the previous disruption of transport facilities. Transport of chemical fertilizer into Nationalist-controlled China by the end of 1938 was possible only through Shantou, in Guangdong Province, and even there it was disrupted by air raids.[100] Imports of chemical fertilizer into the whole of China increased in 1939, most of the increase being in the form of imports from Germany; prices in local currency increased toward the end of the year as the exchange value of the Chinese dollar fell. Increased consumption of chemical fertilizer in North China offset the decreased sales in South China due to continued hostilities; however, supplies from Europe were no longer obtainable after September 1939.[101] In 1940, imports declined by 80 percent, both because of a lack of supply and because the falling exchange value of the Chinese dollar made chemical fertilizer imported from Japan too expensive. Rural purchasing power was further weakened by severe droughts in Hebei and Shandong.[102] Imports of ammonium sulphate declined by a further 60 percent in 1941.[103] The trends in the value and quantity of imported ammonium sulphate are shown in figure 4.8.

The German agronomist Wilhelm Wagner, writing about findings from studies undertaken between 1911 and 1914, opined that the reason for the infrequent use of chemical fertilizer lay in the lack of "enlightenment" among Chinese farmers, for which he blamed the Chinese government.[104] Wagner was convinced of the potential usefulness of bean cakes as a fertilizer because of their high nitrate content, but noted that most of them were being produced for export, particularly to Japan.[105] Wagner's experiments with chemical fertilizer, undertaken in the years 1912–13 and 1913–14 while he was serving as professor of agriculture at the Deutsch-Chinesische Hochschule (German-Chinese University) in Qingdao, resulted in increased yields for winter grain

100. Inspectorate General of Customs, *Trade of China: 1938*, vol. 1, p. 96.
101. Inspectorate General of Customs, *Trade of China: 1939*, vol. 1, p. 94.
102. Inspectorate General of Customs, *Trade of China: 1940*, vol. 1, p. 82.
103. Inspectorate General of Customs, *Trade of China: 1941*, vol. 1, p. 53.
104. Wagner, *Die Chinesische Landwirtschaft*, p. 239.
105. Wagner, *Die Chinesische Landwirtschaft*, pp. 243–44.

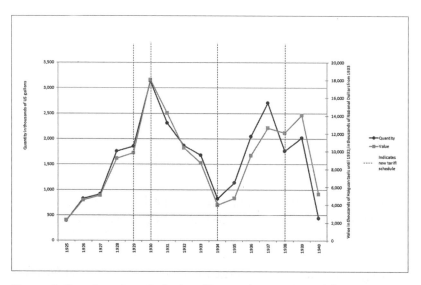

Figure 4.8. Quantity and nominal value of imported ammonium sulphate, 1925–40.
Source: Data from Hsiao, China's Foreign Trade Statistics, pp. 35–36.

(wheat and barley), as shown in table 4.2. A 1948 study by China's National Agricultural Research Bureau found that the widespread use of chemical fertilizers (ammonium sulphate, calcium superphosphate, and potassium sulphate) would increase the national output of rice, wheat, cotton, and rape by an average of 27 percent.[106]

On the other hand, John Reisner, a Cornell graduate who was teaching in the Nanjing University Department of Agriculture, wrote in 1921 that "practically speaking, [the advantages of chemical fertilizer] over night soil had not been demonstrated."[107] Reisner claimed that since human waste was in constant supply, it was cheap, and its use long established, Chinese farmers would be unwilling to pay for a commercial fertilizer and give up the use of night soil, which provided the same results at a fraction of the cost.[108]

106. Shen, Agricultural Resources of China, p. 38.
107. Stross, The Stubborn Earth, p. 119.
108. Reisner, "Modern Commercial Fertilizers in China," p. 54, in Stross, The Stubborn Earth, p. 119.

Table 4.2.
Wagner's fertilizer experiments

Artificial fertilizer used (1 kg)	Additional grain yield per hectare (kg)	Additional straw yield per hectare (kg)
Nitrate	30	50
Phosphoric acid	4	7
Potash	3	9

Source: Data from Wagner, Chinesische Landwirtschaft, p. 242.

By increasing tariffs on imported chemical fertilizer, the National-ist government may have been trying to protect the domestic green-fertilizer industry, but the same case cannot be made with regard to domestically produced synthetic fertilizers, since there was hardly any industry to protect. The domestic manufacture of chemical fertilizer was neither particularly encouraged nor undertaken by government enterprises; in 1949, there were only two chemical fertilizer plants in China. The Dairen Chemical Company in Dalian was formerly owned by a subcorporation of the Manchuria Railway Company; the Yong-lining plant near Nanjing was privately owned but enjoyed close rela-tions with the Nationalist government, receiving preferential tax treat-ment, for example, and government-backed loans.[109] While the Dairen Chemical Company's fertilizer plant had a productive capacity of 180,000 metric tons per year by 1935, producing mostly ammonium sulphate fertilizer, the Yonglining plant had a productive capacity of just 18,000 metric tons.[110]

The importation of ammonium sulphate depended on China's domestic economic conditions even more than sugar and kerosene imports did. Chinese farmers earned enough cash income to purchase chemical fertilizers only in years with good harvests. Figure 4.8 dem-onstrates the impact of increased tariff rates after tariff autonomy on imports of ammonium sulphate. Despite the first tariff increase in 1929, both the quantity and value of imported ammonium sulphate in-creased initially. A further tariff increase in 1930 and poor agricultural

109. Liu, China's Fertilizer Economy, pp. 7–8.
110. Manshu no shigen to kagaku kogyo, in Liu, China's Fertilizer Economy, p. 9.

yields led to a decline from 1930 onwards. A slight tariff reduction in 1934, and good harvests in 1936 and 1937 led to another increase in importation, but this was reversed by the onset of the Second Sino-Japanese War in July 1937. Overall, the evidence suggests that in determining tariffs on imported chemical fertilizer, either the Nationalist government's revenue concerns or its desire to appease the domestic green-fertilizer industry took priority over efforts to improve agricultural yields, with detrimental effects on China's agricultural output.

Cigarettes

Sugar, kerosene, and chemical fertilizer were all necessities of daily life in Republican China. By taxing these goods at a high rate, the Nationalists demonstrated their commitment to fiscal stability—at the expense of economic hardship for Chinese consumers. For comparison, the effect of Nationalist tariff policy on imported cigarettes offers an example of the Nationalists' taxation of luxury goods. The Guomindang presented itself as a rational, scientific, puritanical regime, and this image encompassed Nationalist visions of consumption. As part of its tariff reforms, the Guomindang promulgated a schedule of luxury taxes, based on an earlier draft schedule arrived at with the treaty powers at the 1925 Beijing Tariff Conference. As figure 4.9 demonstrates, the Nationalists brought legal cigarette importation virtually to an end by imposing two tariff increases in 1929 and 1930, respectively.

Chinese merchants had introduced tobacco to the Chinese market in the seventeenth century; by the end of the nineteenth century, pipe tobacco was distributed widely throughout China, and in the first decade of the twentieth century, anti-opium campaigns created a market that was particularly receptive to tobacco smoking. In the cigarette market, imported cigarettes accounted for half of Chinese cigarette consumption in 1910.[111] However, by 1936 they accounted for less than 1 percent of the cigarettes smoked in China, owing to increases in both domestic cigarette production and tariffs on imported cigarettes.

111. Cochran, *Big Business in China*, pp. 27–28.

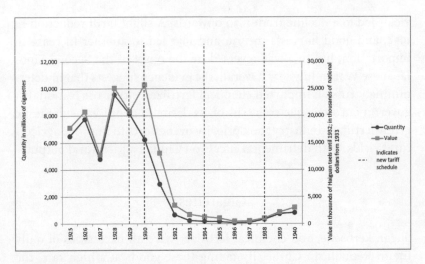

Figure 4.9. Quantity and nominal value of imported cigarettes, 1925–40. *Source*: Data from Hsiao, *China's Foreign Trade Statistics*, p. 53.

Although cigarette imports declined, cigarette consumption increased from 8,165 metric tons in 1910 to 22,680 metric tons in 1920 and 81,647 metric tons in 1930; it then remained stable at that level until 1937.[112]

Taking the most and the least expensive imported cigarettes as examples, tariffs on the most expensive imported cigarettes increased from CGU 1.245 per 1,000 cigarettes in 1922 to CGU 1.868 in 1929 and CGU 16.00 per 1,000 in 1930, and then to a rate of 80 percent ad valorem in 1934. For the least expensive imported cigarettes, tariffs increased from CGU 0.09 per 1,000 cigarettes in 1922 to CGU 0.14 per 1,000 cigarettes in 1929, CGU 1.30 in 1930, and CGU 1.40 per 1,000 cigarettes in 1934.[113] In Tianjin, the average number of foreign-made cigarettes imported in the decade 1922–31 was 800 million per year, valued at 2.6 million taels, and the average quantity of native-made cigarettes moving through the port in those years amounted to 62,000 piculs, valued at 6.4 million taels. Unfortunately, no formula to convert thousands of

112. Shen, *Agricultural Resources of China*, pp. 285–86.
113. Woodhead, *China Year Book: 1925*, pp. 478–79; *China Year Book: 1929–1930*, p. 252; *China Year Book: 1931*, p. 684; *China Year Book: 1933*, p. 756; *China Year Book: 1936*, p. 390. Haiguan taels converted to CGU for ease of reference.

cigarettes into piculs is provided in the report, but the Tianjin customs commissioner, Luigi de Luca, stated that "the cheapest varieties [were] always able to find a ready market."[114] He attributed a decline in the shipments of both foreign and native cigarettes to "high taxation." In the years under review, local cigarette production grew because of the "burden of increased tariff[s] and [the] high cost of taxation."[115] While prior to 1922 most of the cigarettes consumed locally were shipped to Tianjin from elsewhere in China or from abroad, de Luca noted that, as a result of higher import tariffs, the "four local cigarette companies, viz., the Karatzas Bros., the Tientsin Tobacco Company, the Toa Tobacco Company and the British Tobacco Company [sic] have increased their production and greatly extended their manufacturing plant."

In Chongqing, by the 1920s "the smoking of cigarettes [had] become popular and both foreign and native brands of all qualities [found] favour."[116] In Wanxian, native cigarette imports—that is, shipments of cigarettes from elsewhere in China—increased from 66 piculs in 1922 to 8,199 piculs in 1931, "practically eliminating their foreign rivals from the market."[117] In Changsha, H. C. Morgan, the commissioner of customs, observed that most of the cigarettes arriving in Changsha were transported by railway. However, he stated that the estimated total consumption of cigarettes in Hunan had increased from 300 million in 1922 to 1.288 billion in 1931, while the proportion of native cigarettes to total cigarette consumption rose from 95 percent to 98 percent.[118] Morgan attributed this latter change to both the improved quality of native products and antiforeign agitation; he did not comment on the fourfold increase in cigarette consumption, which must be attributed to other causes, such as the increasing popularity of smoking, as described by Li Guiyong for Chongqing and its surroundings.

The decennial reports lack an analysis of the cigarette trade for both Shanghai and Hankou. The Ministry of Industry figures indicate that tobacco imports into Shanghai dipped to 72 percent of their

114. Inspectorate General of Customs, *Decennial Reports*, vol. 1, p. 344.
115. Inspectorate General of Customs, *Decennial Reports*, vol. 1, p. 361.
116. Inspectorate General of Customs, *Decennial Reports*, vol. 1, p. 473.
117. Inspectorate General of Customs, *Decennial Reports*, vol. 1, p. 493.
118. Inspectorate General of Customs, *Decennial Reports*, vol. 1, p. 525.

previous value in 1927, followed by a recovery that peaked at 170 percent in 1931, and then a drop to 75 percent in 1933, the last year for which values are provided. As an inland port that was thus more exposed to the effects of boycotts, Hankou saw a decline in tobacco imports in 1927 to 7 percent of the trade's previous value. An initial recovery toward a peak of 171 percent of its previous value in 1929 was followed by a collapse of tobacco imports, to 1.2 percent, in 1932.[119]

Taxes on luxury goods are a more impressive measure than they are important; while they have a deterrent effect on consumers, they do not deliver as much revenue as taxes on necessities, since by definition they are levied on commodities less frequently purchased. Nationalist tariff policy proved demand for legally imported cigarettes to be highly elastic; because of that elastic demand and the availability of domestic substitutes of similar quality, as well as smuggled imported cigarettes, increased tariffs on imported cigarettes proved highly effective as a protectionist measure against legal cigarette imports. As both the quantity and the value of imported cigarettes declined dramatically, so too did the revenue from their import tariffs.

Conclusion

Nationalist tariff policy was guided by the government's determination to raise the revenue necessary for successful public debt management and to support its governance agenda. Because of this, it imposed tariffs that had an adverse impact on the consumption of imported goods. From 1928 to 1940, various other factors also accounted for the long-term decline in the quantity and value of imported goods—in particular, sugar, kerosene, chemical fertilizer (ammonium sulphate), and cigarettes. As one of the last countries in the world to retain a silver-based currency, which it did not abolish until 1935, China suffered from declining purchasing power abroad. Also, the ideologies of both the Guomindang campaign known as the New Life Movement and the National Products Movement, a popular movement closely monitored and often orchestrated by the Guomindang, emphasized the virtue of

119. Ministry of Industry, *Statistics of China's Foreign Trade by Ports*, pp. 173, 180.

consuming domestic products rather than foreign goods. In addition, post-1931 statistics lack figures for goods imported into the three Manchurian provinces, as these were not listed in the trade returns published by the Maritime Customs after the Japanese annexation of Manchuria in 1931. Imports into the three Manchurian provinces had accounted for 17 percent of China's import trade in 1931.

The Chinese import trade was also affected by international economic factors entirely outside the Nationalist government's control, as the following Maritime Customs report on trade conditions in 1933 suggests:

> Although the appended figures indicate considerably declining importations throughout the period of 3 or 4 years, as the case may be, the cause does not altogether lie with the increased Tariff rates. The year 1929, as will be remembered, saw the Western countries at the height of a trade boom in which the market of this country, only just recovering from its own troubles and as yet on the fringe of advancing industrialism, did not participate to any great extent. But with the declining purchasing powers of the former through the year 1930, witnessing at the same time China's growth of industrialism and increasing prosperity, attention was being drawn towards her markets as an outlet for surplus goods which could not be disposed of in the already overstocked markets of Europe and America. The year 1931[,] which witnessed the catastrophic slump in trade and finance in these countries[,] should have found in the markets of China depository for such surplus stocks. That they did so in many lines of goods is evidenced by the fact that 1931 produced a record revenue which could not have been due entirely to increased duties, but also to a genuine demand for goods from abroad, particularly throughout the sections of the Tariff where the rates had been retained at a low level for various reasons.[120]

With respect to the impact of economic nationalism on consumption, Dikötter notes that "the majority of the working people may simply have ignored the movement for national goods" since "advantageous prices rather than economic nationalism were the key factors in

---

120. SHAC 679/31798, P. G. S. Barentzen, Tariff Secretary, to IG of Customs, S/O No. 32, 15 January 1933.

substituting local equivalents for imported goods." He concludes that "boycotts in particular, and economic nationalism in general, no doubt contributed to the price differentials between foreign and local goods, the introduction of higher import tariffs in 1931 being a good example, but long-term factors, such as a constant supply of cheap labour, labour-intensive manufacturing methods, and above all a willingness to adapt foreign designs closely to local purposes, were ultimately far more decisive."[121] This negative assessment of the societal impact of the National Products Movement and economic nationalism in general is supported by the fact that a flourishing illicit economy existed on the borders of the Nationalist government's area of political and economic control, for example on the North China Plain and along the Fujian coastline. As we will see in chapter 5, many Chinese and foreign observers attribute this trade to official Japanese sponsorship, but it could not have flourished to the extent that it did without the willingness of Chinese consumers to purchase smuggled goods.

The impact of international economic factors may have been beyond the Nationalist government's control, but increased import tariffs in a difficult economic climate were not. Demand for imported goods proved to be highly price-elastic in all the examples studied; hence, increased tariffs led to a decline in the quantity and value of imports. Tariff incidence lay first with retail merchants, who then passed it on to individual consumers. According to the Maritime Customs, it was common for importers to pass the duty on to retail merchants: "By including in the sales contract a clause that duty is payable by the purchaser[,] a wholesale importer of foreign goods into China is in a position to protect himself against a sudden and unexpected rise in the amount of duty, whether caused by a change in the tariff rate or an increase in the duty-paying value."[122]

Nor was Nationalist tariff policy very effective as a protectionist policy, in most cases. The economist Chen Hansheng claimed that the falloff in imports in 1934 compared with 1931 had occurred despite the fact that China was "a country without a protectionist policy"; he at-

---

121. Dikötter, *Things Modern*, pp. 43–44.
122. SHAC 679/30470, IG of Customs Draft Despatch to Guanwu shu, 6 February 1937, in Maze to Myers, 9 February 1937.

tributed this drop to the decreased purchasing power of farmers.[123] Tariff Secretary Paul Barentzen, on the other hand, stated in a report in 1934 that "local manufacturers have naturally taken advantage of the protective nature of these higher duties whenever possible and are increasingly doing so to-day."[124]

In their statements about the aims of Nationalist tariff policy, Guomindang leaders stressed the importance of both increasing government revenue and promoting the growth of the national economy. And yet the authors of one contemporary piece of analysis noted with regard to the 1934 import tariff that "the effect of such [tariff] increases has been to put many necessary articles of life beyond the reach of the common people," and that the increased import tariffs acted as "an oppressive sales tax on the poor."[125] The evidence surveyed indicates that of these two aims, revenue and growth, increasing government revenue to finance expenditures and manage public debt was the more important one and was pursued by the Nationalist government at the cost of economic growth as well as socioeconomic hardship for Chinese consumers. In the cases of imported white sugar and cigarettes, higher import tariffs had a dual effect. On the one hand, China's domestic industries, which produced near substitutes for both products, received a stimulus. On the other, because not all consumers wanted to switch to domestically produced substitutes, a flourishing market emerged for smuggled goods. The implications of raised import tariffs on kerosene were different, since there was no close domestic substitute; here, too, higher import tariffs led to both a demand for smuggled goods and a return to the use of traditional substitutes. Finally, in the case of chemical fertilizer, public welfare in China may have suffered considerably from the Nationalists' preference for increased tariff revenue over the increased agricultural yields that the systematic use of chemical fertilizer would very likely have produced in Chinese agriculture. In all of these cases, maximizing the economic welfare of Chinese consumers through international trade thus was not the goal

123. Ch'en, *Agrarian Problems in Southernmost China*, p. 37.
124. SHAC 679/31798, P. G. S. Barentzen to L. H. Lawford, Officiating IG of Customs, S/O No. 44, 22 August 1934.
125. Su and Barber, "China's Tariff Autonomy," p. 121.

the Guomindang chose to pursue; rather, the Nationalist government relied on the growth of domestic industry to improve economic welfare, and used tariffs primarily to generate revenue and only secondarily, where feasible, to protect domestic industries. As Coble points out, Song Ziwen's efforts to enact a protective tariff had failed.[126]

126. Coble, *The Shanghai Capitalists*, p. 267.

FIVE

Trade, Tariffs, and Governance

If protection rackets represent organized crime at its smoothest, then war making and state making—quintessential protection rackets with the advantage of legitimacy—qualify as our largest example of organized crime.... A portrait of war makers and state makers as coercive and self-seeking entrepreneurs bears a far greater resemblance to the facts than do its chief alternatives: the idea of a social contract, the idea of an open market in which operators of armies and states offer services to willing consumers, the idea of a society whose shared norms and expectations call forth a certain kind of government.[1]

By increasing tariffs, the Nationalists also increased the incentives for smuggling. How they dealt with this challenge reveals both the divided nature of the Nationalist polity and the success of Nationalist fiscal policy in the face of formidable odds, when measured in terms of extraction and sustainability, at least in the midterm. To understand the attempts by the Nationalist state to police trade and suppress smuggling, it is helpful to ask, first of all, whether the Nationalists had any right to police China's trade. Through the analogy of organized crime, Charles Tilly has drawn attention to the degree to which state making and the use of force to protect governmental interests can be understood in terms of "the logic of expanding power," rather than as "an awesome, noble, prescient enterprise, destined to bring peace to a

1. Tilly, "War Making and State Making as Organized Crime," p. 169.

people."[2] While Tilly's argument is based on his research on early modern Europe, it can also be employed to understand the rise of the Chinese Nationalist state during the Republican period, particularly in the context of the Nationalists' attempts to police trade in regions bordering the Japanese colonial empire and in areas in which control was disputed between the Nationalist government in Nanjing and local political and military competitors. Challenges to the Nationalist government's authority in matters of tariff policy certainly had performative elements; that is, they were mounted partly as an act of protest against the Nationalist government as a whole. More commonly, however, challenges occurred for economic reasons—for example, Chinese consumers bought smuggled goods because of their low prices—or with the aim of inflicting fiscal damage, such as when the Japanese military backed smuggling into the North China Plain in the 1930s.

Many of the struggles described in this chapter can be partly explained by the fragmented nature of the Nationalist polity. While the Nationalist government was recognized internationally as the legitimate government of the Republic of China, its political and military control extended over a mere fraction of the territory that it claimed to govern. Between 1927 and 1937, the Nationalist government directly controlled the provinces of Jiangsu, Zhejiang, Anhui, and Jiangxi (with the exception of the Communist soviets in Jiangxi until 1934). Guangdong and Guangxi Provinces were controlled by a separatist Nationalist faction in 1931–32 and Fujian Province briefly seceded from the Nationalist government in 1935.[3] More established regional power holders beyond the control of the Nationalist government in Nanjing included Yan Xishan in Shanxi Province; Zhang Xueliang in Hebei and the three Manchurian provinces (until 1931), of Liaoning, Jilin, and Heilongjiang; and Feng Yuxiang in Shaanxi Province. These regional power holders had nominally pledged allegiance to the Nationalist government in Nanjing but in practice retained administrative control of the areas under their military domination. Other provinces, such as Sichuan and Shandong, were variously controlled by more short-lived military regimes. In this context, asserting fiscal control

2. Tilly, "War Making and State Making as Organized Crime," p. 175.
3. Domes, *Vertagte Revolution*, pp. 680–81.

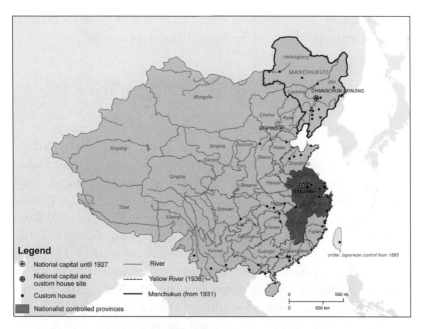

Map 5.1. Nationalist-controlled areas, 1928–37.

was a way for the Nationalist government to project its power into areas it did not control militarily. Besides viewing tariffs as revenue-generating tools, the Nationalists saw them as a means for creating a modern national economy by declaring some regional economies illegal and by enforcing distinctions between legitimate and illegitimate trade and between domestic and foreign products. Map 5.1 illustrates the extent of Nationalist political control and the much wider distribution of custom houses throughout China.

An investigation of the challenge that smuggling presented for the Nationalist government in the arena of tariff policy reveals that, until 1937, the Nationalist government succeeded in imposing its fiscal authority in terms of extractive capacity and medium-term sustainability, despite a variety of challenges. Smuggling was the most serious challenge to the Nationalists' fiscal authority; however, the Maritime Customs developed a Preventive Service that enjoyed some success in containing small-scale smuggling. Also, despite extensive smuggling, the Maritime Customs also delivered sufficient amounts of revenue to the Nationalist government for China to be able to meet its external financial obligations—until the Second Sino-Japanese War.

The Political Context for Policing Trade

Increased revenue extraction after the regaining of tariff autonomy in 1929 went against older patterns of tax collection in which compliance was set against low taxation rates or low collection rates, despite higher taxation rates. As L. H. Lawford, the officiating inspector general, noted in 1934, while China had "for centuries... been a happy hunting ground for smugglers," "the inducement of smuggling, so far as imports from abroad were concerned, was not so much the evasion of duty, as duties were not repressive, but the getting in of contraband goods."[4] After 1929, the margin of profit for smugglers increased considerably, owing to raised import duties on legitimate imports. The Nationalist government's policy to increase its extractive capacity from the late 1920s onward also met with resistance from chambers of commerce, individual merchants, and foreign bodies in China, and efforts to increase the share of locally collected revenue submitted to the Nationalist government also met with resistance from local power holders.

Through tariffs, the Nationalists declared some regional economies illegal and attempted to enforce distinctions between legitimate and illegitimate trade. To establish the boundaries of the government's fiscal regime, it is necessary to address, first, the question of its right to levy taxes, police trade, and enforce its vision for trade. As discussed in the first chapter, Yau-Pik Chau, in his study of Nationalist tax reforms, suggests that the notion of a social contract on the basis of which a government is entitled to levy taxes in exchange for ensuring public order and providing services, did not emerge in China until the 1930s.[5] Chau's analysis confirms Tilly's argument regarding state making as the activity of self-seeking and coercive entrepreneurs rather than the result of a social contract.

---

4. IG Circular No. 4913, 2nd ser., 4 August 1934, Inspectorate General of Customs, *Documents Illustrative*, vol. 4, p. 407.

5. Chau, "Taxation Reforms of the Chinese National Government."

Chinese commentators writing at the time accepted the rights of the government with respect to local commerce and did not question the Nationalist government's basic right to levy taxes. Local governments were more concerned with preserving their power to levy taxation in contravention of the government's single taxation principle, a stance that both gave them the appearance of governments devoted to furthering commerce and denied revenue to the Nationalist government's local competitors. It is important to distinguish between taxation and the policing of trade in this respect. While there were instances of local governments complaining to the central government about the heaviness of central government taxation, there are no records of complaints that the central government, by policing trade, was destroying local trade. On the contrary, local governments in many cases set up their own trade-policing institutions. This indicates that the crucial criterion in distinguishing legal from illegal trade was whether such trade paid taxes to whichever government was collecting them. When the term "smuggling" is defined in relation to the Nationalist government's sanctioning of trade, it can therefore be understood to include unlicensed trade in commodities very similar to those traded with government approval, such as imported sugar, as well as trade in banned commodities, such as opium.

The Nationalist government's right to police trade was also questioned through several local insurrections in the 1930s. One of these, carried out by the Guangdong Nationalist government, led by Chen Jitang, lasted from 1929 until 1936. Chen's claim to political legitimacy was founded on his commitment to "safeguarding Guangdong and providing reassurance to the Guangdong people."[6] The Guangdong Nationalist government erected "tariff barriers between Guangdong and the world at large, and between Guangdong and the rest of China," partly to shield Guangdong from the effects of the Great Depression and partly to deny revenue to the Nationalist government in Nanjing.[7] From 1933, the Guangdong Nationalist government also implemented a three-year plan for the economic reconstruction of Guangdong Province that included forming a provincial sugar monopoly. This sugar

6. Lin, "Building and Funding a Warlord Regime," p. 178.
7. Fitzgerald, "Increased Disunity," pp. 767–68.

monopoly was at variance with the Nanjing Nationalist government's import tariff regulations, since it provided that sugar could be imported into Guangdong Province only under government license and had to be sold by licensed sugar traders.[8] Faced with the potential loss of an important market, sugar importers like the Taikoo Sugar Refinery (which belonged to the British company Butterfield and Swire Ltd.) imported sugar to the provincial capital, Guangzhou, under license, thus evading Maritime Customs import tariffs. This trade finally came to an end when the Guangdong and Nanjing Nationalist governments negotiated an arrangement whereby sugar imported under license into Guangdong Province had to pay only half the Maritime Customs import tariff levied on sugar imports into other parts of China.[9]

During the Guangdong Nationalist government's tenure, local merchants had to distinguish between the claims of local and national revenue-collection agencies. In 1934 Ding Guitang, the Chinese secretary in the Inspectorate General of Customs, was sent to Guangzhou to determine on what terms the provincial separatist government was willing to accept the Nationalist government's authority in tariff matters. He reported that "the smugglers [had] been willing to pay the local tax on their smuggled sugar and asked the [Guangdong Provincial] Preventive Bureau not to seize their goods when they only attempt to evade the Customs duty."[10] This request on the part of the smugglers—that is, importers and exporters who did not pay Maritime Customs duties on their goods—comes close to expressing the notion of a quid pro quo contained within a social contract. The Guangzhou smugglers were prepared to pay taxes to the Guangdong Provincial Preventive Bureau, a trade-policing organization set up to rival the Maritime Customs Preventive Service, but they were not willing to pay taxes to the Maritime Customs itself, which served the Nationalist central government. This offer could have been reported to an emissary of the Maritime Customs only under the circumstances prevailing in 1934–35, which saw the Guangdong and Guangxi insurrections against the Nationalist government. Once an end to the insurrections had been

8. Hill, *Smokeless Sugar*, p. 148.

9. Osterhammel, *Britischer Imperialismus im Fernen Osten*, pp. 333–36.

10. SHAC 679/14715, K. T. Ting to IG of Customs, Special No. 1304, 30 January 1934.

negotiated in 1936, smugglers may still have paid off local patrols in order not to have to pay Maritime Customs duties. It is much less likely, however, that such arrangements would have been discussed with the inspector general's representative.

By the summer of 1936, the central government in Nanjing had come to a political accommodation with the provincial authorities in Guangdong; since the latter had run their own trade regime during their virtual independence from Nanjing, this move had repercussions for local trade. In December 1936, Sir Frederick Maze wrote in a draft letter to Minister of Finance Kong Xiangxi that "the collection for the July–December period recorded an advance of some million dollars over the figure for the corresponding period of 1935. This may be attributed in part to the liquidation of the political situation in the South, in part to the general progress made in the suppression of smuggling in the North, and in part to a growing revival of trade during the closing months of the year."[11] This demonstrates, once again, the importance of definitions of smuggling.

Defining Smuggling

After tariff autonomy, increasing import and export duty rates increased the incentives for smuggling as the smugglers' margin of profit—the difference between cost and freight, on the one hand, and cost, freight, and duties, on the other hand—rose. Smuggling became an even greater problem for the Chinese government after 1931, when the Japanese military authorities in Northeast China began tolerating, if not actively encouraging, smuggling into China as a means of destabilizing the Chinese economy. The increase in smuggling necessitated costly antismuggling operations that raised the cost of revenue collection. Smuggling was one way to evade the new taxation regime or indeed to make a profit from the price difference between legally imported and smuggled goods.

11. SHAC 679/9/3462 Suggested Confidential Letter to Minister, 31 December 1936.

In recent years, smuggling has received increasing attention as a political act, among scholars interested in consumption and in imperial and economic history. In *Secret Trades, Porous Borders*, Eric Tagliacozzo analyzes the history of colonial state making and transgressions on the frontier between the Dutch and British spheres in Southeast Asia. He describes the reciprocal relationship between the anxieties of the colonial state and the actions of peoples living in or passing through border regions. As the two colonial states' fears regarding threats to their security and revenue led them to construct an increasingly solid border, a variety of challenges arose. Smugglers, traders, pirates, traffickers, local rulers, and the state's own officers pursued their interests along and across the frontier, simultaneously penetrating and manipulating the border. As the border-making project developed, challenges to state authority were gradually worn down through the deployment of new material and administrative technologies, but state authority remained fragile and contested in the region well into the twentieth century.[12]

Also stressing the political dimension of smuggling, Amar Farooqui, in *Smuggling as Subversion*, describes the role of the Malwa opium trade in challenging the dominant position of the East India Company (EIC) in the import of opium into China in the early nineteenth century. Farooqui argues that while the EIC was substantially involved in the production of Bengal opium, the production of Malwa opium was financed by local Malwa entrepreneurs and Rajasthani and Gujarati merchants and thus undermined the EIC's position in the opium trade. Profits from the opium trade, in turn, enabled Parsi artisans and petty traders to participate in primitive capitalist accumulation, as a prerequisite for their emergence as an industrial capitalist class. The Malwa opium export trade was largely a product of Indian initiative; unlike Bengal opium, the trade in Malwa opium was not promoted by the EIC but instead was the target of EIC efforts to establish a monopoly of Bengal opium in western and central India. Against these heavy odds, Malwa opium became a tool that indigenous groups in western and central India used to carve out a niche for themselves within the political and economic system imposed by

12. Tagliacozzo, *Secret Trades, Porous Borders*, p. 3.

colonialism. For Farooqui, the production, export, and marketing of Malwa opium is a success story in as much as it demonstrates the resilience of native capitalism when confronted with an external model of opium manufacturing. Farooqui, too, distinguishes between licensed and unlicensed trade. It is important to note that he regards the classification of Malwa opium as "smuggled" as reflecting an arbitrary distinction between legal and illegal commodities imposed by the colonial state, the opium trade itself being legal at the time.[13] Transferred to the North China Plain in the 1930s, the arbitrary nature of this distinction between legal and illegal goods goes some way toward explaining the readiness of Chinese people to consume smuggled Japanese goods, if the East India Company in Farooqui's model is equated with the Nanjing Nationalist government. If consumers in the North China Plain are conceptualized as self-aware citizens of the Nationalist Chinese state and self-aware consumers within the framework of the Chinese economy, this model has less explanatory power. Efforts to convince Chinese consumers that the distinction between legally and illegally imported goods was anything but arbitrary were an important part of Nationalist fiscal policy. These efforts were complicated by the Nationalist government's patent "ambivalence towards opium, [which it expressed] by certifying that poppy growing was not entirely criminal, and by presenting users as victims rather than criminals, and by [the fact that it brought] the government substantial revenue [that] implicated the government in the trade and that the government was reluctant to give up."[14] Throughout their rule on the Chinese mainland, the Nationalists relied on revenue from licensed trade in opium as well as on their political ties with opium producers and merchants.[15]

That leaves the question of the extent to which Chinese consumers were aware of the political dimension of their consumption choices. Karl Gerth has described the political aspects of consumption in Republican China in the context of Japanese political and economic aggression and the Guomindang's efforts to shape Chinese consumption

13. Farooqui, *Smuggling as Subversion*, pp. 1–10.
14. Baumler, "Opium Control versus Opium Suppression," p. 272.
15. Marshall, "Opium and the Politics of Gangsterism in Nationalist China," p. 19.

according to its own vision.[16] While Gerth points out that the activities of the National Products Movement extended beyond the metropoles into the countryside, Dikötter argues that since "price ruled the market in China . . . the majority of working people may simply have ignored the movement for national goods."[17] I contend, however, that in the North China Plain in the 1930s smuggled goods were primarily consumed because they were cheaper than taxed goods. Given the low cash income in rural areas, opposing the Japanese occupation in principle but consuming smuggled goods because of their cheap price may have been not a contradiction but a necessity for many inhabitants of the region.

Motivations for Smuggling

Why did people engage in unlicensed trade? A case from the Pearl River Estuary illustrates the limited reach of Nationalist governance, the role of the Maritime Customs in extending it, and the economic motivation behind smuggling. This case, involving fishermen from the Pearl River Estuary, is one of the rare instances in which complaints about tariff rates on the grounds of individual economic deprivation were successful. In 1933 and 1934, the import tariff on salted fish was first raised, from CGU 0.55 per picul to CGU 1.40 per picul, and then slightly lowered, to CGU 2.30 per 100 kilograms (equivalent to CGU 1.38 per picul). The tariff increase threatened the livelihood of Hong Kong and Macao fishermen, who sold their produce in Guangzhou and other ports in the Pearl River Delta. The commissioner of customs at Lappa, J. M. H. Osborne, wrote to the inspector general as follows: "The ill effects of the present Tariff are dual in that, by causing trade depression, the revenue suffers direct and total loss, while indirect loss also occurs from the fishing fleet being deprived of their legitimate means of livelihood and being driven to smuggle."[18]

16. Gerth, *China Made*, pp. 101–5.
17. Gerth, *China Made*, pp. 222, 232; Dikötter, *Things Modern*, p. 43.
18. SHAC 679/28522, J. M. H. Osborne, Commissioner, Lappa, to IG, Lappa No. 7044/IG, 9 March 1934.

The raised import tariff on salted fish was one of many tariffs that had an adverse effect on producers' or consumers' livelihoods (see chapter 4 for a discussion of the impact of Nationalist tariff policy on Chinese consumers). As distinct from other such tariffs, however, the import tariff on salted fish was subsequently lowered to a 20 percent ad valorem duty. This occurred, first, because the fishermen whose livelihood had been adversely affected by the tariff increase and who had taken to smuggling were demonstrably outside the Nationalist government's control, owing to their status as British and Portuguese colonial subjects, and second, because the fishermen's case had also been taken up by the British and Portuguese colonial authorities, who promised support for Nationalist government antismuggling operations if the tariff was lowered.[19] In 1934, Ding Guitang reported from Guangzhou that

> before the import duty on salted fish was raised there were more than 1000 fishing junks in Macao district[,] but at present there are only about 400 fishing junks still engaging in [the] fishery industry at Macao. Those fishing junks which have lost their business in [the] fishery have nearly all been driven to smuggling, because they could do nothing else. This has been one of the factors responsible for the increased smuggling activities in both Lappa and Kowloon Districts. As the salted fish industry was vitally important to the prosperity of Macao, the Macao Authorities may be willing to help the Lappa Customs in their preventive work if the Custom tariff on salted fish can be reduced.[20]

The tariff was lowered, therefore, because of the foreign-policy complications involved in stopping the smuggling brought about by its original increase, and the Chinese fishermen who benefited from the lowered tariff owed the relief to their status as colonial subjects.

Smuggling was also difficult to suppress when it was undertaken by those charged with its suppression. One of the issues that Ding Guitang was meant to settle by negotiation with the Guangzhou provincial government was whether Guangzhou would continue to maintain its

19. SHAC 679/28522, E. N. Ensor, Commissioner, Jiulong [Kowloon], to António José Bernardes da Miranda, Governor, Macao, No. 820/FO, 11 April 1934.

20. SHAC 679/14715, K. T. Ting to IG of Customs, Special No. 1304, 30 January 1934.

own preventive bureau, with its cruisers operating separately from the Maritime Customs preventive fleet. Ding reported to the inspector general that "the Preventive Bureau [had] been established for the purpose of protecting the local tax collection, and that they have no confidence in [the] Customs preventive fleet because they said they have private information that some of the Customs preventive vessels have been working in collusion with some privately organized smuggling concerns."[21] In addition to Maritime Customs preventive vessels, Chinese naval vessels and vessels of the Inspectorate General of the Salt Monopoly were also alleged by the Guangzhou provincial government to be engaged in smuggling.

The official perception of smuggling, or illegal trading, was framed in terms of race. Maritime Customs reports often refer to smuggling undertaken by Japanese and Korean traders but do not discuss the roles of Chinese importers as well as Chinese smugglers. Apportioning blame along racial lines may have led the Maritime Customs to ascribe smuggling into the North China Plain to "the Japanese" when it may well have been undertaken by ronin operating without the encouragement of the Japanese military authorities. The Maritime Customs, however, thought otherwise, as B. E. F. Hall recalled later: "Their [i.e. the Japanese's] purpose [in annexing the East Hebei Autonomous Area], which they carried out for some six or seven years, was to attack China's morale and economy by mass smuggling of drugs and highly dutiable articles such as sugar, artificial silk yarn etc into China with the assistance of the Japanese army and navy, and gangs of Korean and Japanese hoodlums who were well armed for the purpose."[22]

The Geographic Distribution of Smuggling

Smuggling chiefly occurred in three geographical areas: the Pearl River Delta (coming from Hong Kong and Macao), the Fujian coastline (from Taiwan), and North China. After the Japanese invasion of Manchuria in

21. SHAC 679/14715, K. T. Ting to IG of Customs, Special No. 1304, 30 January 1934.
22. B. E. F. Hall, foreword to "Chinese Maritime Customs, Chefoo Saga, 1935–1937," B. E. F. Hall Papers, Bristol University Customs Collections.

1931, the smuggling in that region moved to the border region between Liaoning Province and the northernmost province of China proper, Hebei. While this chapter focuses mostly on smuggling into the North China Plain, smuggling into the other two regions was also significant. An unsigned Maritime Customs memorandum from 1933 noted:

> Sugar is smuggled wholesale: the only sugar which pays duty in Hainan is sugar which has been seized by the Customs. Smuggled sugar comes mostly from the Straits and Java by junk and from Kwangchowwan. Sugar is shipped in large quantities from Hongkong to Kwangchowwan and Macao by steamers over which we have no control, and thence distributed by junks, snake boats, carriers and by any means of conveyance throughout Kwangtung: the quantities thus smuggled cannot be estimated since Hongkong Trade Statistics are very incomplete, the cargoes of many small steamers, junks, etc, being listed as sundries. Formosa is a great smuggling run for sugar; the greater part of the sugar is shipped by Japanese steamers from Java for Formosan ports in transit. . . . Nearly 4,000 tons were so shipped by three Japanese steamers between 20th November and 31st December, 1932. Sugar is distributed from Formosa to various parts of the Fukien and Chekiang coasts by "puff-puff" boats and junks. The latter frequently load from steamers outside Formosan port limits. We are seizing huge quantities of this sugar and have even forced some legitimate imports into Amoy and Foochow, but smuggling continues. Sugar leaves Dairen in junk loads and "puff-puff" boat loads for the Shantung and Kiangsu coasts; smuggling has increased by leaps and bounds since we lost control at Dairen.[23]

To combat smuggling from Taiwan—then part of the Japanese colonial empire—the Maritime Customs stationed an ethnically Chinese employee on Taiwan, disguised as an attaché to the Chinese consulate in Taibei, to gather information about smuggling. The employee, Wang Wenju, reported to Maze in 1937 on smuggling from Taiwan to Fujian Province:

23. SHAC 679/30609, Unsigned Memorandum, Confidential, dated Shanghai, 23 October 1933. A "puff-puff boat" was a vessel twenty to twenty-five meters long that was powered by an early form of a diesel engine. See van de Ven, *Breaking with the Past*, p. 243.

Taking Formosa as a base, junks to smuggle dutiable foreign goods and/ or other contrabands are thought to have been in existence before a National Tariff was adopted by China, or probably when or after Formosa was ceded to Japan. The problem, nevertheless, remained insignificant from the revenue point of view until a tariff of higher duties was introduced. The enormous difference of duties had given to junks a great impetus to grow rapidly in number. Power craft followed suit with a rather humble beginning, and not until the year 1932, when the boycott agitation militated against Chinese junks, developed vehemently into a formidable force.[24]

Because of a mass reporting exercise carried out in the 1930s, we have an unusual perspective on smuggling in various locations in China. In spring 1936, newspapers such as *Shenbao* and journals including *Funü shenghuo* (Women's life), *Yong sheng* (Everlasting life), and *Shijie zhishi* (World knowledge) published announcements from the Literary Society and the editorial board of *One Day in China* for the submission of textual and visual material from all over China, all originating on or relating to 21 May 1936, in order to "reveal the entire face of China during one day."[25] A contributor from the island of Jinmen [Quemoy] drew attention to the involvement of Chinese people in smuggling: "The truth is that Jinmen is merely a warehouse for [Japan]. [Japan's] goods are transshipped to Xiamen [previously transliterated as Amoy] and other places from here. Since Jinmen is an island with ocean on all sides, any village—especially the ones on Lie Island between Jinmen and Xiamen—can be used as a warehouse for [Japan], and has loyal distributors of evil [i.e., Japanese] goods."[26] The same contributor was highly critical of the Maritime Customs' preventive efforts on Jinmen:

Although the Maritime Customs has antismuggling boats which are effective, [Japan's] goods flow in freely, day and night, without the least bit of interference. The smugglers have made deals in advance with the

24. SHAC 679/31726, Wang Wenju to IG of Customs, 1 April 1937.
25. Cochran and Hsieh, with Cochran, *One Day in China*, pp. 265–66.
26. Cochran and Hsieh, with Cochran, *One Day in China*, p. 236.

authorities who could have interfered with goods that are flowing in. Not long ago, because bribes were not equally distributed among the Maritime Customs authorities, there was a falling out between the Maritime Customs authorities and the smugglers, which resulted in the Maritime Customs authorities coming once to Jinmen to crack down. But very soon they again became friendly.[27]

Maritime Customs records show that smuggling from occupied Manchuria into the North China Plain was tolerated and protected by the Japanese military authorities.[28] Whether they actually encouraged it is more difficult to establish, not least because, from the 1920s onward, the Guandong Army had a foreign-policy agenda quite different from that of successive imperial governments in Tokyo. In the opinion of the Nationalist government, it was clear that the smuggling was a form of officially sponsored Japanese economic aggression, not just something predominantly undertaken by Japanese nationals.[29] Equally, the American academic Haldore Hanson, writing in *Pacific Affairs* in 1936, squarely identified the Guandong Army as responsible for the smuggling.[30] The most direct admission of Japan's unwillingness to curb smuggling from Manchukuo, the Japanese client state in Manchuria, into the North China Plain was made by a Japanese official identified only by his surname, Sumi, to the British commercial counselor in Tokyo in April 1936. Sumi stated that "he had for some time been pressing the [Nanjing] Government to reduce tariffs, but without success; ... meanwhile, Japan could not agree to assist in suppressing smuggling."[31]

However, smuggling into the North China Plain did not begin with the Japanese invasion of Manchuria. In August 1931, just before the Manchurian Incident, Luigi de Luca, the Tianjin commissioner, wrote

27. Cochran and Hsieh, with Cochran, *One Day in China*, p. 236.
28. SHAC 67/27756, "Preventive Secretaries, Handing-Over Charges Memoranda," Mr. A. H. Forbes to Mr. E. A. Pritchard, 20 April 1936.
29. "Xingzhengyuan zhi shiye bu xunling," 11 March 1936, No. 1552, in Zhongyang dang'anguan, *Huabei jingji lüeduo*, pp. 127–28.
30. Hanson, "Smuggler, Soldier and Diplomat," p. 544.
31. Mr. D. J. Cowan (Tokyo) to Mr. Eden, 4 May 1936, Telegram No. 234 [F 2548/991/10], *BDFA*, vol. 44.

to the inspector general that "the cheapness on the Tientsin market of Japanese Sugar and the fact that there [appeared] to be larger stocks of this commodity than the Customs Returns [could] account for" had induced him to suspect "that along the coast of the Gulf of Pohai [Beihai] there must be places where smuggling can easily be effected."[32]

An investigation undertaken by Maritime Customs official Yao Dingxin in 1931 showed that "most of the sugar sent by rail [arrived] from Weihaiwei." Having checked the railway freight statistics at Luanxian and Changli, which recorded the transport of more than 2,000 tons of sugar during 1930, Yao judged that "most of the cargoes thus shipped... will be brought to T'angshan and/or Hsuk'ouchuang to be subsequently embarked on small boats and carried by way of an inland river to Tientsin or places farther west, in the same manner as cotton and groundnut are concentrated to the market. . . . There is no doubt that the Lower Luanho districts absorb goods from outside for their supply. Their consumption, nevertheless, is limited and small. The greater part of such imports, chiefly foreign goods, will go to the richer and more densely populated hinterland lying beyond Tientsin." Yao also reported that "though Ch'angli and Luanhsien are interior places and are not open to foreign residence and trade, there are Japanese merchants dwelling and trading in the eyes of local authorities; even in the petty Luanhsien village town of Pencheng. . . . Their residing in these places means not only constant influx of narcotics for those fallen victims but also inexhaustible resources of military supplies to the re-enforcement of banditry. This is not restricted to that part of the country. Actually the whole of North China is open to the invasion of dangerous matters from this direction."[33] The Tianjin region is depicted in map 5.2.

Japanese importers in Tianjin were quick to take advantage of the Maritime Customs' diminished ability to enforce the levy of tariffs after September 1931. The importer, Baifu Company (百福), Japanese-owned despite its Chinese name, advertised its services to Tianjin

32. SHAC 679/1/20385, L. de Luca to Maze, 22 August 1931, Tientsin No. 9,414.
33. SHAC 679/1/20385, Yao Ting-hsin, Memorandum for Commissioner, Report on Tour of Inspection in Lower Luanho Valley, 8 August 1931, in L. de Luca to Maze, 22 August 1931, Tientsin No. 9,414.

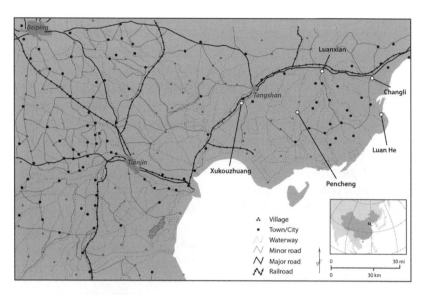

Map 5.2. Smuggling routes in the Tianjin area.

merchants with an English-language printed circular in 1936: "Don't you aware [*sic*] that if you import your cargo through Chitung district via Dairen you can save three quarters on the import duty as compared with the Tientsin Maritime Customs? In other words, it means to save you considerably on the cost of goods, and, consequently, it will enable you to meet the competitive price of the market."[34]

Maritime Customs officials mostly viewed smuggling into the North China Plain as part of Japan's undeclared war against China. As B. E. F. Hall recalled later, "The Japanese were encouraging and giving protection to smugglers of every description and they were also running drugs into China to debilitate the country folk."[35] Japanese economic aggression needs to be put into local context, however. The protests against smuggling were also taken up by the Japanese Chamber of Commerce in Tianjin, whose secretary, Y. Kobayashi, wrote to the commissioner of customs in Tianjin as early as July 1932 to point

34. SHAC 679/1/20833, W. R. Myers to Maze, 12 December 1936, Tientsin No. 10762.
35. Hall, "My Life and Work in China, 1913–1943," in B. E. F. Hall Papers, Bristol University Customs Collections.

out that "for three months or more, righteous importers of sugar [had] been suffering a heavy loss by unjust lower price [sic] in the market caused by smuggling on a large scale."[36] At the request of the Tianjin commissioner of customs, the Tianjin Japanese Chamber of Commerce also forwarded a copy of its correspondence to the authorities of the Guandong Leased Territory in an effort to enlist their support in suppressing smuggling by junks sailing from the territory, in which the Customs Preventive Service was not allowed to function.[37] In 1936, Japanese merchants in Tianjin complained to their local consul that the influx of smuggled goods was damaging to legitimate Japanese commercial interests in China. These examples demonstrate that the notion of a concerted Japanese onslaught on China in the 1930s needs to be modified; Japanese subjects were asking the Chinese state to defend its border against smugglers, who, even from the most cursory attention to a daily newspaper, they must have learned were Japanese, or were Korean subjects of the Japanese colonial empire. And these requests were not solely from small firms; rather, the protests emanated from the Tianjin offices of Mitsui and Mitsubishi, two of the largest Japanese corporations.[38]

So what was smuggled into the North China Plain in the 1930s? To be profitable, smuggled commodities had to be cheap in Japan or its dependent territories, easy to transport, and subject to high import duties in China. Frequently smuggled commodities included artificial silk yarn, white sugar, cotton piece goods, gasoline, kerosene, and cigarettes. By the 1930s, smuggling into the North China Plain was no longer only a clandestine undertaking. Commodities to be smuggled were transported by boat, train, or truck from Japanese-controlled territory into the North China Plain. Under the Tang'gu Truce between China and Japan on 31 May 1933, large parts of North China became a demilitarized zone. While the Maritime Customs nominally continued to function within this area, its guards were forbidden by

36. SHAC 679/1/20385, Japanese Chamber of Commerce to Commissioner of Customs, Tientsin, 5 July 1932, in L. de Luca to Maze, 14 July 1932, Tientsin No. 9599.

37. SHAC 679/1/20385, Japanese Chamber of Commerce to Commissioner of Customs, Tientsin, 13 July 1932, in L. de Luca to Maze, 14 July 1932, Tientsin No. 9599.

38. Hanson, "Smuggler, Soldier and Diplomat," p. 552.

the collaborationist government and the Japanese occupation forces to take effective action, on the threat of being entirely evicted from North China, and risked confrontation with Japanese troops if they tried to assert their jurisdiction over Japanese smugglers.

At the same time, smuggling by concealment continued; B. E. F. Hall recalled later a variety of ways in which contraband goods, or goods on which no duty had been paid, were hidden from customs officials:

> Merchandise in "hides" constructed in vessels; [p]ackets of sewing-needles in the ash of ships' cooking stoves; silk etc. underneath the coal in ships' bunkers; narcotics in tin drums, inserted into liquid pitch or chemicals in drums, so that when the stuff hardened, the drugs were successfully buried; opium made up into the shape of candles, with proper candle-ends protruding from either end of the packet; opium made up as kernels in groundnuts, opium made up as false calves in peoples' legs; opium made up behind the glass on mirrors; opium made up in hollowed-out firewood; opium made up in wheelbarrows, all the woodwork of which had been ingeniously hollowed out; opium sewn into carpets; gold bars carried in especially contrived trousers beneath the ordinary Chinese long gown; goldbars [sic] hidden in a saucepan of soup which a cook on a liner was stirring on the stove.[39]

The importance of the Japanese in this trade, and also the wide availability of smuggled goods, is documented in an entry submitted to *One Day in China* from Henan Province, in which a student described a conversation between two merchants he had overheard in the streets of Xuchang:

> "Shortage, there's no real shortage, but is the imported sugar coming or not?" "I heard a [Japanese] person say it will be coming again within three to five days." "Three to five days? You don't know whether it will arrive tomorrow?" "This is no easy matter! Making it through customs is a lot of trouble. You don't know how insistent the customs people are. If the [Japanese] people's soldiers weren't there as escorts, it wouldn't come through at all!" "How come it wouldn't make it through customs?

---

39. Hall, "My Life and Work in China, 1913–1943," in B. E. F. Hall Papers, Bristol University Customs Collections.

Didn't it go smoothly before?" "This is different than before! In days past, each time goods were imported, they had to declare dutiable goods at customs. But now they simply don't declare dutiable goods." "They don't declare dutiable goods? They are allowed to pass?" "How could they not be allowed to pass? A battalion of soldiers is guarding the train! Each man is armed with a pistol. If the train is not allowed to pass, the guns will open fire. So who would dare block their way! You think about that. Therefore nowadays wherever imported goods go, they are always priced more cheaply than local goods." "Oh, I see! That's why the price of each bag of sugar has dropped so much."[40]

Song Wuwei, a contributor to *One Day in China* from Tianjin, wrote that according to his estimates, on 21 May 1936 goods weighing 93,000 kilograms were smuggled into Tianjin Eastern Railway Station and 113,000 kilograms of goods were smuggled out from the same station (see tables 5.1 and 5.2). In 1933, smuggling expanded enormously because Maritime Customs officers in the demilitarized zone were no longer allowed to carry arms, and also because the East Hebei Autonomous Government, under the leadership of Yin Rugeng, began taxing smuggled goods, albeit at approximately one-fourth of the Maritime Customs tariffs, "thus giving these goods a claim to legality."[41]

Song also described in some detail the methods used to smuggle non-duty-paid commodities into Tianjin for onward distribution:

The smugglers' sources are several train stations located at the eastern terminal of the Beiping-Shenyang Railroad near the sea. Tianjin is an important place for selling smuggled goods and a center for redistribution. From Tianjin, goods are further transported on railroads such as the Beiping-Suiyuan, the Beiping-Hankou, the Tianjin-Pukou, the Lanzhou-Lianyun (Long Hai), and the Jiaozhou-Jinan, eventually finding their way into farming villages. They are well organized, systematic, and always have armed guards escorting them along the way. A huge quantity of goods is being smuggled in and out daily, and the value of [the] goods is impossible to calculate. The effect of the smugglers' tax evasion on

40. Cochran and Hsieh, with Cochran, *One Day in China*, pp. 242–43.
41. Cochran and Hsieh with Cochran, *One Day in China*, p. 239n3; Bisson, *Japan in China*, pp. 130–31.

Table 5.1.
Smuggled goods entering Tianjin Eastern Railway Station, 21 May 1936:
Song Wuwei's estimates

Place of origin	Type of goods	Number of trains used	Weight of goods (kg)
Qinhuangdao	white sugar	4	13,000
Qinhuangdao	kerosene	2	7,000
Nandasi	white sugar	9	29,000
Nandasi	artificial silk yarn	1	3,000
Liushouying	white sugar	11	35,000
Changli	white sugar	3	6,000
Totals	white sugar	27	83,000
	kerosene	2	7,000
	artificial silk yarn	1	3,000

Source: Data from Cochran and Hsieh, with Cochran, One Day in China, p. 240.

national tax revenue and the effects of competition from smuggled goods on domestic industries and commerce have created serious problems nowadays.[42]

Daily figures extrapolated from internal Maritime Customs figures reveal that either 21 May 1936 was not an especially busy day for smugglers in the North China Plain or Song Wuwei's estimates of smuggling for that day were much too low. In a report to the director general of the Office of Customs Affairs, the inspector general stated that during the period from 18 May to 31 May 1936, trains arrived at Tianjin Eastern Railway Station carrying 209,160 kilograms of artificial silk, 10,771,650 kilograms of white sugar, and 179,880 gallons of kerosene, on which the duty had not been paid.[43] Based on these numbers, the average daily smuggling figures would have been 14,940 kilograms of artificial silk yarn, 769,404 kilograms of white sugar, and 12,849 gallons of kerosene.

In terms of the fiscal impact of smuggling, the Maritime Customs estimated that in 1936, goods smuggled through East Hebei to Tianjin

42. Cochran and Hsieh, with Cochran, One Day in China, p. 239.
43. SHAC 679/6/1226, "Brief Sketch of Smuggling Situation in North China for Last Two Weeks of May 1936," in Maze to Loy Chang, 4 June 1936.

Table 5.2.
Smuggled goods leaving Tianjin Eastern Railway Station,
21 May 1936: Song Wuwei's estimates

Railroad line	Destination	Type of goods	Number of trains used	Weight of goods (kg)
Beiping-Shenyang	Beiping	white sugar	2	6,000
Tianjin-Pukou	Jinan	white sugar	4	13,000
Tianjin-Pukou	Botouzhen	white sugar	5	13,000
Tianjin-Pukou	Bangfo	white sugar	4	11,000
Tianjin-Pukou	Zaozhuang	white sugar	1	4,000
Tianjin-Pukou	Sangyuan	white sugar	1	4,000
Beiping-Suiyuan	Xuyuan	white sugar	1	3,000
Beiping-Suiyuan	Shahe	white sugar	1	2,000
Beiping-Suiyuan	Taiyuan	artificial silk yarn	1	1,500
Beiping-Suiyuan	Datong	artificial silk yarn	1	1,500
Beiping-Suiyuan	Baotou	artificial silk yarn	1	3,000
Beiping-Suiyuan	Baotou	white sugar	4	12,000
Beiping-Hankou	Handan	white sugar	1	4,000
Beiping-Hankou	Yancheng	white sugar	4	10,000
Beiping-Hankou	Shunde	white sugar	2	8,000
Beiping-Hankou	Shijiazhuang	white sugar	1	2,000
Beiping-Hankou	Yuzi	white sugar	1	4,000
Lanzhou-Lianyun	Xi'an	white sugar	1	2,000
Lanzhou-Lianyun	Xuchang	white sugar	2	6,000
Lanzhou-Lianyun	Qilicun	white sugar	1	3,000
Totals		white sugar	36	107,000
		artificial silk yarn	3	6,000

Source: Data from Cochran and Hsieh, with Cochran, One Day in China, p. 240.

evaded import duties totaling $50 million; the estimate was based on railway statistics on goods transported for which the Maritime Customs calculated hypothetical duty rates.[44] Maritime Customs had access to the freight statistics of the Beiping-Liaoning Railway Administration, under an agreement negotiated in July 1932.[45] The purported

44. SHAC 679/32746, IG of Customs to Minister of Finance, Confidential, 7 January 1937.
45. SHAC 679/1/20385, "Provisional Rules for the Control of Smuggling Goods at Railway Stations," in L. de Luca to Maze, 27 June 1932, Tientsin No. 9586.

accuracy of the statistics was based on the fact that for goods smuggled in bulk—as opposed to those concealed in passengers' baggage, for example—importers had mostly paid railway freight charges.

Assessing the fiscal effect of smuggling in the North China Plain involves analyzing counterfactual scenarios and extrapolations based on reports of intercepted smuggled goods. The difference between the cost of smuggled versus legally imported goods was considerable in the case of sugar. Hanson estimates that in 1935 the Tianjin price of smuggled sugar was about 40 percent of the price of legally imported sugar in Shanghai. Even though the base price might have been different, it is here that we recognize the importance of the smuggling into North China. According to Hanson, had all goods smuggled into the Tianjin region paid duty at the Tianjin Custom House, the weekly receipts of that custom house would have been $2 million, or $104 million annually. Instead, the annual collection of the Tianjin Custom House in 1935 was $41 million. In other words, through the addition of illegal trade, the value of goods traded in the Tianjin region almost tripled.[46] This assumption is counterfactual, however; had duties been levied on them, many of the smuggled goods would not have been imported in the first place, since there would not have been the same incentive to import them if the cost of importation to the merchant had been higher. Nevertheless, this estimate shows the seriousness of smuggling in the North China Plain.

The Maritime Customs' Response to Smuggling

In 1931, members of the Shanghai General Chamber of Commerce wrote to the inspector general of customs to complain about the Maritime Customs' policy of holding the master of a vessel responsible for unmanifested—that is, smuggled—goods, and its treatment of arrested smugglers:

> It is well known that such smugglers are engaged in this traffic, yet, when such smugglers are caught actually engaged upon their trade, no action

46. Hanson, "Smuggler, Soldier and Diplomat," pp. 545–56.

whatever is taken against them by the Maritime Customs, other than the confiscation of smuggled goods, which acts as a very small deterrent in view of the large profits to be made. . . . We shipping companies are willing and anxious to see this smuggling stopped; and we are willing to cooperate with Chinese Maritime Customs to this end to the best of our ability, but we consider that the duty of carrying out effective preventive measures lies primarily with the Customs and not with shipping companies, and we write to ask if representations could be made to the Customs requesting them to organize measures which will more effectively discourage smuggling.[47]

Drawing attention to what they regarded as the deficient trade policing of the Maritime Customs, the members wrote that

effective policing of harbours, and enforcement of harbour regulations, would largely restrict the movement of bad characters; at many treaty ports, gangs of smugglers are well known, and could be dealt with by the authorities had they the will to do so; and we would particularly request you to impress on the Customs how absolutely essential it is to deal with those caught in the act of smuggling, whether members of ships [sic] crews or not, who are now allowed to go about their business without fear and punishment, and that these should invariably be prosecuted for their offences.[48]

The present policy of the Maritime Customs, they continued, "[blamed] only the Shipping Companies." The measures they suggested were "measures which would be taken in almost any other country in the world and we consider that if the Customs cannot by such means deal with those responsible for smuggling, they cannot expect private traders to do so."[49]

47. SHAC 679/1/20362, Shanghai General Chamber of Commerce to IG of Customs, 25 September 1931, in IG Circular No. 4343.
48. SHAC 679/1/20362, Shanghai General Chamber of Commerce to IG of Customs, 25 September 1931, in IG Circular No. 4343.
49. SHAC 679/1/20362, Shanghai General Chamber of Commerce to IG of Customs, 25 September 1931, in IG Circular No. 4343.

This very critical perspective contrasts with the Maritime Customs Service's own rhetoric, which emphasized the Maritime Customs' efficient response under challenging circumstances, and of which the following dispatch from the inspector general in 1931 is but one example:

> Preventive work along the coast was thrust upon us without adequate preparation and the difficulties against which Commissioners have to contend are fully recognized. With stations scattered at wide intervals along a vast coastline where land communications are lacking and proper supervision impractical, with a staff accustomed to work on different lines, with inadequate control over junks, and without the support of a coast patrol, it is difficult to see how Commissioners are to prevent the clandestine landing in their district of merchandise smuggled over from Formosa.[50]

Enforcing the distinction between domestic and foreign commodities entailed either adjusting the definition of Chinese commodities or distinguishing between domestic and "foreign" Chinese goods. Taiwanese commodities, for example, were not counted as Chinese goods, that appellation being reserved for commodities produced in areas actually or nominally under the Nationalist government's control. Similarly, goods produced in Manchukuo were not counted as Chinese. The question of whether these goods were culturally Chinese was secondary to the fact that they were produced in areas outside the Chinese government's nominal control; Chinese products were defined as domestic products, in opposition to foreign products. Thus Taiwanese sugar, as well as Manchurian produce after 1931, were considered foreign commodities. This applied even more to imports from the Chinese diaspora communities in Southeast Asia. In the case of sugar, the decline in domestic production was paralleled by an increase in Taiwanese sugar production, which benefited from the large-scale smuggling of sugar into China from Manchuria in the 1930s.

The proclivity of members of other branches of the Chinese government, whether national or local, to see themselves as beyond the

---

50. SHAC 679/1/30609, IG to Commissioners Wenchow, Santuao, Foochow, Amoy, 21 August 1931.

purview of the Maritime Customs with regard to commodities imported by them is well attested in documents, such as the following memorandum on Maritime Customs preventive duties: "It has to be remembered that the proximity of Kwangchowwan, Macao, Hongkong, Formosa, the Leased Territory and now the so-called 'Manchukuo' render it a practical impossibility to completely suppress smuggling, and further, that in their efforts to control the menace[,] the Customs are faced with the difficulties of having their actions limited to the thin cordons of the land and sea frontiers and, in many cases, of meeting with active opposition, instead of the cooperation which should be expected, from local authorities and police."[51]

Attempts to evade taxation ranged in subtlety from letters written to local commissioners or the inspector general to request exemption from taxation to government troops threatening Maritime Customs personnel with armed force during attempted inspections. One such instance occurred within the area policed by the Great Wall Maritime Customs Station, where the acting deputy commissioner reported that members of the local militia (*baoweituan* 保衛團) were "working in collusion with smugglers and in addition to giving armed protection to them are supplying information to the smugglers whenever our Officers are out on patrols in order to enable them to escape from being caught by the Customs."[52] These evasion attempts, which are by no means particular to Republican China, are relevant here because at first glance they negate the Nationalist government's attempts to define the limits of legal trade by tax compliance. Hence commodities imported by members of government or government agents on which no duty had been paid should have been beyond the limits of legal trade.

In responding to the Nationalist government's policing of trade, rather than arguing for tariff revision or questioning the right of the Nationalist government to levy taxes, in most cases Chinese chambers of commerce and individual merchants complained about the dishonesty or incompetence of the Maritime Customs in administering

51. SHAC 679/30609, Unsigned Memorandum, Confidential, dated Shanghai, 23 October 1933.
52. SHAC 679/1/28122, "Report on Smuggling at the Great Wall Maritime Customs Station for May, 1935," 21 June 1935.

existing tariffs. This may be because the Chinese chambers of commerce felt the necessity of preserving ties to their political patrons, given that Republican China lacked the political stability necessary for establishing chambers of commerce as politically independent institutions.[53] Alternatively, it may have held out a greater chance of success. In the mid-Yangzi port of Shashi in 1938, the local Chinese chamber of commerce complained to the Office of Customs Affairs of the Ministry of Finance that "Customs procedure and practice in connection with application to pass cargo, levy of duty, examination of cargo and prevention of smuggling are altogether too complex and strict, that Customs officials abuse their power by arbitrary treatment of merchants and passengers, and that the Customs discriminate between Chinese and foreigners in their dealings with the public."[54] The Office of Customs Affairs, after administering a nominal reprimand to the Maritime Customs, chose to leave this matter, and many like it, in abeyance, presumably because the Maritime Customs had a presence on the ground outside the capital and they did not.

According to at least one commentator, by the summer of 1936 the North China smuggling problem had at least been alleviated, owing to the success of the Nationalist government's trade-policing measures.[55] While the Ministry of Finance could have collected more revenue if all trade had paid tariffs, even the widespread smuggling in the North China Plain did not interfere with China's ability to meet her financial obligations. The difficulties that even the Ministry of Finance experienced in achieving compliance from the Beiping-Liaoning Railway Administration shows, once more, the fragmented nature of the Nationalist polity against which Nationalist fiscal policy has to be seen. As late as 1936, the Maritime Customs found it necessary to ask, through the Office of Customs Affairs, for an Executive Yuan order to the Ministry of Railways to the effect that "the Pei-ning and Tsin-pu Railway Authorities [were] under no circumstances to prevent Customs officers from carrying out their duties on trains and at the various stations on

53. Fox, "Common Sense in Shanghai," p. 37.
54. SHAC 679/16905, IG Circular No. 4566, 2nd ser., 13 February 1933.
55. Inlow, "Japan's 'Special Trade' in North China," p. 164.

the railways."[56] Based on this order, the Maritime Customs was able to set up the Customs Chief Inspection Bureau for the Prevention of Smuggling by Rail, investing it with authority to operate, for the first time, on board trains.[57] However, in April 1937 the Beiping-Liaoning Railway Administration was still refusing to allow uniformed Maritime Customs officers to operate inside Tianjin Eastern Railway Station.[58] In June 1937, Myers, the commissioner of customs, reported from Tianjin that "the Pei-Ning Railway [continued] to assist smuggling by transporting smuggled goods to Tientsin East Station. . . . When the smuggled goods arrive at the Tientsin East Station, the Pei-Ning Railway Authorities place the wagons conveniently for the Japanese roughs, hired by the consignees of the smuggled goods, who remove the smuggled goods at their leisure. . . . The Railway authorities adopt the attitude that it is immaterial to them if the goods carried have paid duty to the Government or if they have not."[59] This illustrates the limits of the power of the Nationalist government.

While the Maritime Customs and the Ministry of Finance were unable to achieve full cooperation from the Beiping-Liaoning Railway Administration, the use of roadside barriers had begun to show effects by the summer of 1937 and made it more difficult for smugglers to move their goods onward from Tianjin:

No trucks with smuggled goods have passed the Customs barriers for the interior for some considerable time. The smuggled goods in the interior are gradually being rounded up by the Superintendent and the men under his orders, and smugglers are finding that they are now unable to find any regular buyers for their goods, which are accumulating in Tientsin, with no extensive market for them. The only free outlet for smuggled goods from Tientsin is by the Pei-Ning Railway to Peiping; but as the railways outwards from Peiping are now controlled by the Customs, and the control outwards by road is also gradually being tightened, the

56. SHAC 679/1/20388, Chief Secretary (Kishimoto) to Commissioner, Tientsin, 4 May 1936, 161221/106557.
57. SHAC 679/1/20388, Maze to Commissioners, 27 May 1936.
58. SHAC 679/1/20388, W. R. Myers to Maze, 26 April 1937, Tientsin No. 10908.
59. SHAC 679/1/20388, W. R. Myers to Maze, 7 June 1937, Tientsin No. 10952.

smugglers are finding themselves in the same position in Peiping as they are in Tientsin.[60]

At the same time, the Ministry of Finance, through the Maritime Customs, offered Tianjin merchants the opportunity to register imported goods on which the duty had not been paid, so as to co-opt local trade back into legitimate channels. Myers concluded his report by stating that "the smugglers [were] finding it more and more difficult to find Chinese buyers for their goods, which are thus being left on the hands of the smugglers." The result was "a very great decrease in the influx of smuggled goods." The chief remaining problem was the attitude of the railway authorities: "The Pei-Ning Railway can easily place the wagons with smuggled cargo in such positions that the smugglers cannot get at them. They refuse to do this, because they are hand-in-glove with the smugglers, and until some means is found to force them to obey the Government, the Pei-Ning Railway authorities will continue to supply Tientsin with smuggled goods and oblige the Government to spend large and unnecessary sums in providing means to fight the situation, which is kept alive entirely by their Railway, a Government Organization."

In the 1930s, local political secession was a threat far more serious than wide-scale smuggling. While the secessions of the 1930s were brought under control in each case by the Nationalist government, the virtual partition of the Maritime Customs after 1937 brought an end to the special position of the Maritime Customs, in terms of both revenue delivered and administration.

Conclusion

Smuggling necessitated an accommodation between the Guomindang's visions of taxation and consumption and what was possible in real terms. The Guomindang, aided by the Maritime Customs, was largely successful in negotiating this accommodation and managed to increase revenue extraction, despite regional military coups that

60. SHAC 679/1/20388, W. R. Myers to Maze, 7 June 1937, Tientsin No. 10952.

disrupted the Maritime Customs control of custom houses in, for instance, Guangzhou from 1929 until 1936, Tianjin in 1930, and Fuzhou in 1933. Fiscal authority was threatened most by the fragmented nature of the Nationalist polity; hence, secession threatened the Maritime Customs and the Nationalist government's fiscal authority more than wide-scale smuggling. Until the beginning of the Second Sino-Japanese War, local secessions were successfully ended through negotiated solutions. In Charles Tilly's phrase, the Nationalist government's "protection racket" worked smoothly so long as its rivals in the business of state making were only domestic rivals. As we will see in the next chapter, the challenge that led to the collapse of Nationalist fiscal policy was the Japanese invasion of China in July 1937.

The Nationalist government's ability to police trade by creating efficient and effective bureaucratic and enforcement structures was a measurement of the success of its state-building project. Therefore, the increase in smuggling that accompanied the rise in import tariffs was a test of the government's ability to govern—as was the continued existence of rival political regimes in China that often disputed Nanjing's right to collect tariffs. Until 1937 the Nationalists were largely successful in dealing with various challenges to their military-fiscal state; despite widespread consumption of smuggled goods, the fiscal losses in terms of tariff revenue were not catastrophic. We often think of the challenges to the authority of the Nationalist government in Nanjing from rival regional regimes as a more elevated concern than smuggling because of the political and statal nature of those challenges. But smuggling was a part of those challenges, as regional regimes set up competing tariffs and taxes. The problem of smuggling is therefore best thought of as a matter of the political labeling of trade by competing political regimes. As a national agency frequently based outside the areas under the Nationalist government's actual political control, the Maritime Customs often served as the test case for relations between Nanjing and rival regimes. The Nationalist government was able to negotiate tariff revenue-sharing arrangements with local political competitors, and as smuggling increased throughout the 1930s, so did the Maritime Customs' ability to police trade. All of this changed with the outbreak of war in 1937.

SIX

Trade, Tariffs, and War,
1937–1945

The Second World War changed the economies of all major belligerent states dramatically, affecting GDP growth, distribution
of national expenditure, labor relations, and the structure of public
finance, to name just a few areas. Whereas the United States and the
United Kingdom experienced real GDP growth, the Soviet Union,
Germany, and Japan experienced a decline in real GDP.[1] Comparative
figures for China are more difficult to locate, not least because the
borders of the Nationalist-controlled wartime state shifted constantly
with the course of military operations, and because of the lack of reliable statistical material for China compared with the other states.
Another complication is the conceptual issue of whether to include the
economies of the various Chinese collaborationist regimes within the
Japanese economy—on the grounds that they were Japanese client
regimes—or within a broader definition of the Chinese wartime economy, because the economic actors within them were predominantly
Chinese. Since this is a study of the tariff policy of the Chinese Nationalist party-state, which at this point was fighting for its survival against
Japan, it makes sense to use the economy of only Nationalist-controlled
China as the unit of comparison with the other WWII belligerents'
economies.

One major difference between China's economy and those of the
other major belligerents is seen in the area of public finance. From 1937

1. Howlett, "The War-Time Economy," p. 10.

until 1940, Guomindang fiscal policy managed to preserve a degree of relative stability, but the loss of the remaining central Chinese provinces in 1940 propelled Guomindang fiscal policy into a long-term collapse, leading to hyperinflation in the late 1940s. The first section of this chapter places Nationalist China's wartime fiscal policy in the context of policies of some of the other major combatants. We then explore how the Maritime Customs, as a revenue-collecting institution, adapted to the outbreak of war, and investigate the function of the two chief wartime fiscal instruments employed by the Maritime Customs, the revised Interport Duty and the Wartime Consumption Tax. Finally, we will see how the demise of the Maritime Customs as a foreign-led institution with wide-ranging independence from the Ministry of Finance was linked to both its diminishing importance in terms of revenue extraction and the intensifying hostility toward the Maritime Customs by elements within the Nationalist government.

Financing War

Like the United Kingdom, Nationalist China experienced a wartime transformation that moved it toward a centrally managed economy, reflected in the distribution of national expenditures; also like the UK, in Nationalist China the labor participation rate in 1945 was significantly higher than it had been at the beginning of the war. There was, however, a conspicuous difference between Britain's and Nationalist China's wartime public finances. In the UK, revenue from direct taxation quadrupled between 1939 and 1945. While the nominal revenue collected from direct taxation in Nationalist-controlled China increased fortyfold between 1937 and 1945, that increase becomes meaningless when adjusted for inflation. In addition, by 1945 direct taxation in the UK produced a greater amount of revenue than that collected from indirect taxation. In contrast, the revenue collected from indirect taxes in Nationalist-controlled China in 1945 was twenty-five times the amount of revenue collected from direct taxation. Table 6.1 shows the relative importance, among the major combatants, of personal income tax receipts (direct taxation) within central government receipts; table 6.2 shows the equivalent values for customs receipts.

Table 6.1.

Personal income tax receipts (nominal value) as a percentage of total
central government receipts, 1937–45

Year	China	US	UK	France	Italy	Japan
1936	0.6[a]	—	—	—	—	—
1937	0.9[b]	9.7	37.4	6.6	13.7	16.4
1938	0.7[c]	9.3	39.7/41.0[d]	8.1	13.8	20.4
1939	0.9	7.1	42.1	8.3	15.2	17.9
1940	0.8	6.7	43.3	6.3	13.8	23.1
1941	0.7	7.6	39.9	11.7	14.2	16.3
1942	0.7	13.1	38.9	14.2	12.7	24.3
1943	1.2	32.9	40.5	14.7	12.4	18.6
1944	0.6	33.6	42.0	17.5	14.9	19.2
1945	0.2	35.4	43.6	16.8	12.4	16.3

Sources: Data from Liesner, *One Hundred Years of Economic Statistics*, pp. 58–59, 112–13,
194–95, 244–45, 268–69; Young, *China's Wartime Finance and Inflation*, pp. 331–32.
[a] 1936–37, fiscal year ending 30 June 1937.
[b] 1937–38, fiscal year ending 30 June 1938.
[c] Second half of year only.
[d] First/second budget.

Nationalist-controlled China did not make use of direct taxation
to finance its war effort in the same way that the other belligerents did.
While it may be tempting to explain this fact by the absence of a
tradition of direct taxation in China—in Britain, after all, this fiscal
instrument was first adopted during the Napoleonic Wars—many Chinese economists had been calling for its introduction since before the
war, and the Ministry of Finance had long regarded direct taxation as
desirable, believing it to be a manifestation of administrative modernity and thus an appropriate tax for a modernizing regime such as the
Nationalist government.[2] The outcome of an attempt by the Nationalist
Ministry of Finance to introduce a personal income tax in 1936 illustrates why direct taxation did not play a greater role in Nationalist fiscal
policy. Having introduced the personal income tax, the government
realized that the tax was being paid only by government employees,
including the employees of the two largest commercial banks, which
had been partly nationalized in 1935. Private employers, on the whole,

2. Lin Meili, *Xiyang shuizhi*, p. 71.

Table 6.2.

Customs receipts (nominal value) as a percentage of total central government receipts, 1937–45

Year	China	US	UK	France	Italy	Japan
1936	30.3[a]	—	—	—	—	—
1937	11.4[b]	14.9	35.4	28.7	5.3	10.1
1938	10.8[c]	13.2	33.8/41.2[d]	25.5	5.0	9.0
1939	11.3	13.6	44.5	24.8	4.2	6.2
1940	0.7	13.5	40.1	19.2	3.9	4.6
1941	0.1	12.8	38.4	11.3	3.3	2.5
1942	2.1	11.3	37.4	6.5	2.8	2.2
1943	1.7	9.1	34.9	4.3	2.5	1.4
1944	1.3	10.9	34.5	3.6	1.1	0.4
1945	0.3	12.6	37.0	5.8	0.2	0.08

Sources: Data from Liesner, One Hundred Years of Economic Statistics, pp. 58–59, 112–13, 194–95, 244–45, 268–69; Young, China's Wartime Finance and Inflation, pp. 331–32.

Note: For China and Italy, percentages represent customs receipts; for other countries, percentages represent customs and excise receipts. For 1942–45, customs receipts for China include receipts from the Wartime Consumption Tax, collected by the Maritime Customs.

[a] 1936–37, fiscal year ending 30 June 1937.
[b] 1937–38, fiscal year ending 30 June 1938.
[c] Second half of year only.
[d] First/second budget.

refused to open their books to the bureaucracy of the Ministry of Finance.[3] While the Second World War brought an increase in the central government's enforcement capacity, direct taxation never became as important in the financing of the Nationalist Chinese war effort as it did in the British case, where it accounted for 35 percent of government revenue, excluding foreign borrowing, by 1945.[4]

The second issue that becomes apparent when comparing the structure of Nationalist China's wartime public finance with that of the other belligerents is the fact that the wartime government in Chongqing was far less able to rely on foreign loans than were the two other major allies of the United States, Britain and the USSR. During the Second World War, the United Kingdom (as opposed to the British Empire) received US$27 billion (equivalent to 62 percent of a total net

3. Young, China's Nation-Building Effort, p. 68.
4. Howlett, "The War-Time Economy," p. 14.

value of $43.6 billion) and the USSR, US$11 billion (equivalent to 25 percent) of the lend-lease financing provided by the United States.[5] The total value of US lend-lease received by the Chinese Nationalist government during the same period was just US$1.3 billion, equivalent to 3.06 percent or 2.68 percent of US lend-lease dollars, depending on the calculations used.[6] Another US$18 million in lend-lease was provided to China by Britain. One total for US aid given to the Nationalist government for the two periods 1937–41 and 1941–45 is US$1.55 billion.[7] The disparity in the amount of US aid given to different allies, especially in lend-lease, was not lost on Nationalist China's wartime leadership. It caused much friction between Nationalist China and its wartime allies—both British and US leaders thought that Chinese demands were importunate—and after the war it was used as a charge against the record of the Roosevelt administration by the China lobby in the United States.[8]

To understand the importance of international trade to the Nationalist government's finances, it is instructive to consider the measure of China's international trade as a share of GDP in 1936, the last prewar year. In Britain, by comparison, that share (total value of exports plus total value of imports) was approximately 18 percent in 1938.[9] Customs and excise combined contributed 33.8 percent of tax revenue to the British Exchequer in 1938 in the first budget and 41.2 percent in the second. In China, where tariffs contributed 43.7 percent of central government tax revenue to the Ministry of Finance in 1936, the last prewar year, trade accounted for approximately 5 percent of GDP.[10] The Nationalist government was therefore dependent on a much smaller trade to a much greater extent than the British government in terms of the relative GDP share of international trade in the two countries.

The Second Sino-Japanese War forced the Nationalist government to accelerate its existing project to widen its tax base. The war also

5. Howlett, "The War-time Economy," p. 19.

6. 3.06 percent, based on Howlett's total, and 2.68 percent according to Young, *China and the Helping Hand*, p. 350.

7. Young, *China and the Helping Hand*, p. 403.

8. Mitter, *China's War with Japan*, pp. 242–43, 245, 300.

9. Harley, "Trade, 1870–1939," p. 163.

10. See table 0.1 in the Introduction.

regularized many of the particularities of China's tariff system arising out of the unequal treaties concluded in the nineteenth century. Ultimately, Guomindang fiscal policy did not survive the Nationalist government's loss of control over Chinese seaports; by early 1938, the Nationalists had lost control of ports yielding 80 percent of Maritime Customs revenue. While the Maritime Customs countered the loss of tariff revenue from these ports by developing other revenue-collecting strategies, those alternative sources of revenue never compensated for the revenue lost from the seaports. The state of the Chinese economy was such that it could not sustain the expense of modern warfare, and the industrial output required for a modern war, for more than a short period of time.[11] This fact, and the collapse of Guomindang finance it engendered, contributed to a situation in which neither side was able to win the war, since China's inability to defeat Japan was matched by Japan's inability to occupy and consolidate its control over all of China. Only the Allied victory in the Pacific and Japan's unconditional surrender after the detonation of US nuclear bombs over Hiroshima and Nagasaki resolved the deadly stalemate in the Second Sino-Japanese War.

On the verge of war, Nationalist fiscal policy was still successful. Reporting on Maritime Customs net revenue, E. D. G. Hooper, the acting financial secretary, wrote to Kong Xiangxi in early 1937 that "now, finally ... it has reached the very considerable figure of 16 million dollars, ... a sum which constitutes the largest revenue surplus on record for any one month since the Inspector-General took control of the Customs revenue and of the foreign loans and Indemnity and Internal Loans Service."[12] Hooper attributed this increase to "a growing revival of world trade and general economic recovery, together with signs of returning prosperity in China fostered by successful currency reform, settlement of outstanding political differences in the South and bumper harvests and the amelioration of smuggling conditions throughout the country."[13] Similarly, the British embassy's country report for 1937 records an upward trend in trade:

11. Van de Ven, *War and Nationalism in China*, p. 295.
12. SHAC 679/9/3560, Hooper to Kung, 31 March 1937.
13. SHAC 679/9/3560, Hooper to Kung, 31 March 1937.

Had it not been for the hostilities, the trade figures for 1937 might well have approached those of the previous record year of 1931, before the world depression had begun to affect this country. By the end of July [1937], imports had gained 36.7 per cent and exports 45.5 per cent. In fact, in the summer of 1937, China's foreign trade was for the first time showing that it had almost completely recovered from the financial crisis of 1934–1935, which was caused largely by the exodus of silver owing to the high price of metal abroad. That crisis ended in the measure taken to stabilize the currency in November 1935, when China "went off" silver, since which date the foreign exchange value of the Chinese standard dollar has been successfully maintained at about 1s. 2½ d., with salutary effects on the trade position. The good results of this reform were aided by a bumper harvest in 1936, a factor in the life of this agricultural country which it is hard to exaggerate.[14]

The Maritime Customs and Foreign Interests, 1937–41

The Maritime Customs' position in the occupied territories was anomalous, insofar as it was protected by the treaty powers' interest in the security of the service as a source of revenue for the service of foreign obligations. When the Nationalist government suspended the service of its foreign loans and indemnities in January 1939, principal sums outstanding included £972,000 remaining unpaid on the Boxer Indemnity Loans, £190,264 on the Huai River Commission 1935 6-Percent Loan, and £441,868 on the 1936 Jing-Gan Railway Loan.[15] The final installments on the Boxer Indemnity Loans, to take but one example, were to be paid in 1945 (to Japan), 1946 (to Britain), and 1947 (to the United States), according to a payment schedule agreed to earlier in 1937.[16] While the service of foreign loans no longer took up the entire net Maritime Customs revenue, as it did before China regained tariff autonomy in 1929, these obligations constituted a significant midterm

14. "Annual Report on China for 1937," in Sir A. Clark Kerr to Viscount Halifax, 29 April 1938 [F 6312/6312/10], BDFA, vol. 21: China, 1932–1939, pp. 372–73.

15. King, "The Boxer Indemnity—'Nothing but Bad,'" p. 686.

16. Young, China's Wartime Finance and Inflation, p. 94.

drain on Nationalist government finances at a time of spiraling military expenditures. On the eve of the war, total foreign debt was equivalent to US$513 million, compared with the equivalent of US$646 million in 1928.[17] Foreign debt thus totaled approximately one-and-a-half times the last peacetime annual central government budget, which was equivalent to US$373 million.[18]

Paradoxically, this very drain on Nationalist government finances, and the constant reminder of China's political and military defeats in the late nineteenth century, ensured a modicum of stability for the Maritime Customs even during the initial phase of the Second Sino-Japanese War. This was because all foreign creditors—except those in Japan—were interested in preserving the Maritime Customs' function within the framework of the Nationalist government's constrained sovereignty.[19] Individual foreign staff members were also protected by their status as foreign nationals. Until the United States' declaration of war against Japan after the bombing of Pearl Harbor, that protection applied to foreign staff members who were nationals of Allied countries. For nationals of neutral or Axis countries during WWII, the protection lasted until 1945.

Britain's interest in preserving the Maritime Customs' status quo, and the lengths to which it was prepared to go diplomatically to ensure it, were demonstrated most clearly in the case of the British-Japanese Customs Agreement of 3 May 1938. This agreement specified that revenue collected in the occupied areas was to be deposited with the Yokohama Specie Bank, and that revenue already deposited in the Hong Kong and Shanghai Bank was to be transferred to the Yokohama Specie Bank. The Yokohama Specie Bank was then to remit full quotas for the service of foreign obligations to the inspector general of customs. The Chinese Nationalist government was to accept the financial burden of converting the quotas into foreign currency and to release the

---

17. Young, *China's Nation-Building Effort*, pp. 111–12.

18. Young, *China's Nation-Building Effort*, pp. 433–39; converted at June 1937 median exchange rates (1 Chinese dollar = US$0.2985), p. 473.

19. Lee, *Britain and the Sino-Japanese War*, pp. 113–21; Trotter, *Britain and East Asia*, pp. 19–20; Shai, *Origins of the War in the East*, pp. 174–75; Shai, *Britain and China*, pp. 20–21; Bickers, *Britain in China*, pp. 120–22.

Japanese portion of the Boxer Indemnity payments that it had suspended since autumn 1937.[20]

Britain and Japan concluded the agreement without consulting the Nationalist government. Additionally, the agreement did not provide for the release of revenue quotas from the occupied areas to service the domestic financial obligations of the Nationalist government. As a consequence, the Nationalist government refused to acknowledge the legality of the agreement, claiming that it violated the principle of noninterference of foreign powers in China's internal affairs, as guaranteed in the Washington Treaty of 1922.[21] The Ministry of Finance allowed the Maritime Customs to place revenue collected in the occupied areas in Yokohama Specie Bank accounts but refused all other arrangements suggested in the British-Japanese Customs Agreement. Following the position of the Nationalist government at the time, the British-Japanese Customs Agreement has usually been seen as unlawful in Chinese historiography of the Second Sino-Japanese War. This view is summed up best in the following extract from Chen Shiqi's history of the Maritime Customs:

> Japanese aggression against China severely threatened Britain's and the United States' interests in China, and deepened Japan's conflict with Britain and the United States. Britain and the United States were not willing to let Japan seize their interests in China. However, firstly, they hoped to involve the Soviet Union in the war so that they could let others do the fighting; and secondly, they were busy dealing with the tense situation induced by Hitler's aggression in the West so that they tried their best to alleviate Japan's threats toward their interests in the East. So as to avoid Japan attacking their interests in the East, Britain and the United States unceasingly and with all their efforts sought to compromise with Japan before the Pacific War broke out in 1941. Under these circumstances, to imagine that Britain and the United States might have interfered with Japan is simply a fruitless approach. In the end, Britain and the United States not only did not interfere, but, turning their backs toward China, sacrificed the sovereignty of the Chinese Customs so as to safeguard their

20. Lee, *Britain and the Sino-Japanese War*, p. 119.

21. SHAC 679/1/32745, K. K. Chen, "Customs Revenue in Occupied Areas," 23 March 1944, in L. K. Little to Dr. H. H. Kung, 28 March 1944.

own interests; for that reason, Britain and Japan concluded the unlawful agreement concerning the issue of the Chinese Customs.[22]

In English-language studies, the British-Japanese Customs Agreement is often judged by the standard of the Munich Agreement and the policy of appeasement in Europe, and is usually seen as not falling into the same category as the Munich Agreement—"If appeasement means buying off a potential aggressor at the sacrifice of principle, then the British stand acquitted in the case of Japan" since "they made no 'Munich Agreement' in the East."[23] Aron Shai, in a much more critical account of British policy in East Asia in the late 1930s, argues that "appeasement in the Far East gained strength without a Far Eastern Munich as such. No agreement marked the end of a policy and the beginning of a new one. The policy of accommodating Japan was practised not by a dramatic world-shaking agreement but by the gradual erosion of principles which Britain seemed to cherish."[24]

The instinctive comparison between the British-Japanese Customs Agreement and the Munich Agreement points to the limitations of British foreign policy at a time when British attention was focused on Europe and the threat of German aggression. In this situation, an accommodation with Japan, even at the cost of Chinese resentment, seemed preferable to involvement in a conflict in East Asia: "The deterioration of the European situation, only briefly alleviated by the hope of Munich, tended to discourage any strong policy in the Far East."[25] Adopting such a policy would also have been difficult, given the United States' isolationist stance.[26] Britain's strategic preoccupation with Western and Central Europe at this time also needs to be seen in the context of an earlier policy decision to reduce its commitments in East Asia.[27] Yoichi Kibata's suggestion that British policy in East Asia was motivated by a desire to protect British interests in China through

22. Chen Shiqi, *Zhongguo jindai haiguanshi*, p. 819.
23. Louis, *British Strategy in the Far East*, p. 238.
24. Shai, "Was There a Far Eastern Munich?" p. 169.
25. Clifford, "Britain, America and the Far East," p. 146.
26. Clifford, "Britain, America and the Far East," pp. 147–48.
27. Fung, *The Diplomacy of Imperial Retreat*, p. 9.

imperialistic cooperation with Japan has less explanatory value in this context, given what is known of this determination.[28] Shai has pointed out that, far from meeting its policy objective, "the sacrifice by Britain of Chinese interests meant the further erosion of the remaining British interests and principles," since Japan took British willingness to conclude the British-Japanese Customs Agreement, as well as the manifest lack of cooperation between Britain and the United States, as an indication of Western unwillingness to oppose Japanese aggression in China.[29]

The Maritime Customs as an institution thus played a major role in the breaking down of the rules-based international order of the interwar years in East Asia. At its most instrumental level, the demise of the Maritime Customs as the principal revenue-collecting institution of the Nationalist government was linked to the sharp decline in its contribution to central government revenue during the Second Sino-Japanese War. Although this demise would not have occurred had the Maritime Customs not been weakened as an institution by the reduction in revenue it delivered, a growing Nationalist hostility toward the Maritime Customs as "an agency in the British orbit" was also an important contributing factor.[30] This hostility, which had its origins in the Nationalist discourse on the unequal treaties of the nineteenth century and the Maritime Customs' role in upholding them, intensified because of what the Nationalists perceived as the weakness of Britain's international standing during the Second World War.

Losing Control

Most important, the course of the hostilities affected Maritime Customs revenue collection, since under the terms of the British-Japanese Customs Agreement that had been concluded in defiance of China's reclaimed tariff autonomy, revenue collected in Japanese-occupied territory had to be paid into reserve accounts at the local branch of the

28. Kibata, "Reasserting Imperial Power?" pp. 169–84.
29. Shai, "Was There a Far Eastern Munich?" p. 169.
30. Bickers, "The Chinese Maritime Customs at War," p. 301.

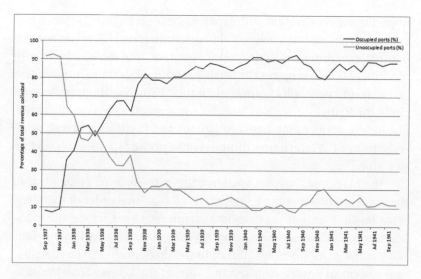

Figure 6.1. Share of Maritime Customs revenue collected in unoccupied China versus Japanese-occupied China, September 1937–September 1941. *Sources*: Data from SHAC 679/32750, F. W. Maze to P. T. Chen, Private and Confidential, 21 October 1939 (for September 1937–September 1939); SHAC 679/1/28980, "Financial Secretary's Correspondence with Ministry of Finance" (for September 1939–September 1941).

Yokohama Specie Bank and was no longer remitted to the Nationalist government. Figure 6.1 shows the relative shares of Maritime Customs revenue collected in unoccupied and Japanese-occupied territories, respectively; viewing unoccupied territory as Nationalist-controlled territory would overstate the extent of the Guomindang's political and military control.

The fall of Shanghai on 9 November 1937 and the Japanese conquest of the Lower Yangzi Delta by March 1938 resulted in a 45 percent decrease in the amount of revenue over which the Nationalists had control. Guangzhou and Hankou fell on 18 October and 25 October 1938, respectively. The fall of Hankou signified Japan's conquest of the geographic and economic macroregion of the middle reaches of the Yangzi River; this conquest, together with the fall of Guangzhou, reduced the portion of Maritime Customs revenue controlled by the Nationalist government to less than 20 percent. By the time the Nationalists suspended the service of foreign loans on 15 January 1939, they controlled only just over 20 percent of Maritime Customs revenue.[31] Calculated on a quarterly basis, the Nationalist government controlled 20.91 percent of Maritime Customs revenue in the last quarter of 1938, as compared with 82.77 percent in the last quarter of 1937.

Until the end of 1942, the revenue collected by the Maritime Customs in ports controlled by the Japanese military and by Chinese collaborationist governments was recorded as Nationalist government revenue; however, this revenue was paid into the revenue accounts opened by the Yokohama Specie Bank in each port, under the pretense that the money was being held in trust by the Japanese government until the end of the war. Chen Jingkun, who defected from the Wang Jingwei regime's Maritime Customs Service to the Nationalist government's Maritime Customs in Chongqing in 1944, described this arrangement in detail:

> Revenue collection at these ports, after payment of local office expenditure and statutory grants to certain local government organizations, [was] retained *in toto* and accumulated locally in the revenue accounts of the ports concerned[,] either with the Yokohama Specie Bank, or, in its absence, the Bank of Taiwan. Nominally, the balances so retained have always been regarded as still being held by the custodian banks, but, as a matter of fact, according to information gathered through informal sources, they are non-existent, having either been loaned to the bogus governments to meet administrative expenses or appropriated by the Japanese authorities for other purposes.[32]

More specifically, the "quotas for ... foreign loans and indemnities as due by each of the occupied ports before 1943, calculated in accordance with its revenue collection, [were] regarded as having been set aside locally in the ports' revenue accounts but included in their frozen balances"; in other words, the loan and indemnity service quotas, like the

31. SHAC 679/32750, F. W. Maze to P. T. Chen, Private and Confidential, 21 October 1939.

32. SHAC 679/1/32745, K. K. Chen, "Customs Revenue in Occupied Areas," 23 March 1944, in L. K. Little to Dr. H. H. Kung, 28 March 1944.

remainder of Maritime Customs revenue in the occupied areas, had in fact already been used up by the time of Japan's surrender in August 1945.[33]

Following the Japanese attack on Pearl Harbor on 7 December 1941 and the subsequent declaration of war against Japan by the United States and Britain, Japanese forces invaded the International Settlement in Shanghai, where the Inspectorate General of Maritime Customs was still located. On 11 December 1941, Sir Frederick Maze was dismissed as inspector general by Wang Jingwei's Nationalist government and replaced by Kishimoto Hirokichi, previously chief secretary (effectively second in command) within the Inspectorate General and a Japanese national. In response, the Ministry of Finance for Chiang Kai-shek's Nationalist government, by then based in Chongqing, ordered the local commissioner of customs to establish a new Inspectorate General of Customs in Chongqing. From then until September 1945, two Maritime Customs Services existed in China, both of which claimed legitimacy.[34] David Barrett has argued that Wang Jingwei's Nationalist government was characterized to a great degree by its continuity, rather than disjuncture, with Chiang Kai-shek's Nationalist government.[35] The Maritime Customs Service controlled by Kishimoto's Inspectorate General in Shanghai supports Barrett's argument, as it retained the majority of Maritime Customs staff, including the remaining neutral or Italian Axis nationals, and controlled the greater number of Maritime Customs stations.[36] Until the introduction of the Wartime Consumption Tax by Chiang Kai-shek's Nationalist government in 1942, it also collected the same kinds of duties, albeit at lower rates.

Like the Maritime Customs Service in Nationalist-held China, the Maritime Customs of Wang Jingwei's Nationalist government experienced a decrease in the importance of its import and export tariff receipts as a share of total Maritime Customs receipts. Import tariff receipts were replaced as the most important source of Maritime

33. SHAC 679/1/32745, K. K. Chen, "Customs Revenue in Occupied Areas," 23 March 1944, in L. K. Little to Dr. H. H. Kung, 28 March 1944.

34. Bickers, "The Chinese Maritime Customs at War," pp. 299–301.

35. Barrett, "The Wang Jingwei Regime," p. 115.

36. Bickers, "The Chinese Maritime Customs at War," p. 299.

Customs revenue by Interport Duty receipts. A report on revenue collection in occupied China compiled by the Chongqing Inspectorate General of Customs in 1944 noted that "the fact that most of the import and export trade [was] being carried on by military transports without passing through the Customs [had] reduced to insignificance the collection of import and export duties and therefore also the revenue and flood relief surtaxes."[37] Duties on imports from Japan and Manchukuo and on goods withdrawn from bonded warehouses accounted for only approximately 10 percent of revenue collection, and export duties accounted for another 5 to 10 percent. As a result of this decline, the Kishimoto Inspectorate General was forced to close some of its existing Maritime Customs stations.[38] The majority of Maritime Customs revenue in Japanese-held areas derived from the Interport Duty, the collection of this tax having increased through the establishment of additional collecting stations.[39]

Wartime Fiscal Instruments, 1937–45

The success of the Japanese military campaign, besides causing the Nationalist government's progressive loss of fiscal control over the territories that produced the majority of Maritime Customs revenue, also affected Nationalist fiscal policy in other ways. In particular, it fostered the development of wartime fiscal instruments designed to deliver revenue under changed revenue-collecting conditions. In April 1938 Maritime Customs revenue collected in unoccupied areas accounted for 25 percent of total Maritime Customs revenue.[40] The main drop in revenue occurred between April and November 1938, by which time revenue in the occupied areas accounted for more than 80 percent of total Maritime Customs revenue (see figure 6.1). Map 6.1 shows the

37. SHAC 679/1/32745, K. K. Chen, "Customs Revenue in Occupied Areas," 23 March 1944, in L. K. Little to Dr. H. H. Kung, 28 March 1944.
38. SHAC 679/9/481, "Outline of History of the Chinese Maritime Customs" (undated, ca.1942–45), in Bickers, "The Chinese Maritime Customs at War," p. 300.
39. SHAC 679/1/32745, K. K. Chen, "Customs Revenue in Occupied Areas," 23 March 1944, in L. K. Little to Dr. H. H. Kung, 28 March 1944.
40. SHAC 679/1/32747, Maze to Kung, Confidential, 11 June 1938.

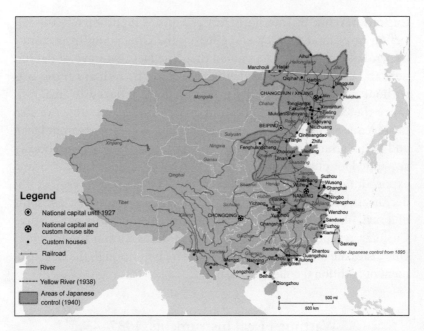

Map 6.1. Japanese-occupied area of China, 1940.

extent of Japanese military control by 1940; the fact that the majority of the custom houses were in occupied territory is especially noticeable. Meanwhile, between August 1937 and April 1938, the first nine months of hostilities, the value of import trade fell by 34 percent, and import tariff revenue fell by 58 percent compared with the same period in the previous year, owing to the increase in duty-free imports (particularly arms and army supplies). In reaction to low tariffs introduced in areas occupied by the Japanese and the collaborationist governments, the Nationalist government also implemented tariff cuts in unoccupied areas.[41] The collaborationist East Hebei Autonomous Government, for instance, charged tariff rates equivalent to only one-fourth of the Nationalist government's rates.[42] The combined effect of the loss of control over revenue-yielding territories, tariff cuts, and a

41. Young, *China's Wartime Finance and Inflation*, p. 34
42. Nakamura, "Japan's Economic Thrust into North China," p. 235.

decrease of tariff revenue, even when calculated at the notional nation-wide level, made the development of fiscal instruments suited to the new wartime conditions all the more imperative.

Once the Nationalist government had lost control of most of the Chinese seaports and the Maritime Customs had lost the capacity to pay the revenue collected at those ports to the Bank of China, the revised Interport Duty and the Wartime Consumption Tax became the two most important alternative sources of Maritime Customs revenue. Both were old taxes, presented in a slightly different form and billed as emergency fiscal measures. The term "Interport Duty" (Zhuankoushui), levied on native goods moved between two treaty ports, had been introduced in January 1931 as part of the rationalization of the Chinese tariff system. It replaced the export duty on native goods—that is, the duty charged on native goods when shipped between two treaty ports within China.[43] While the inspector general of customs, Sir Frederick Maze, held that this tax was anomalous "from the point of view of a consistent tax scheme," since native goods transported between treaty ports would be "under a fiscal disability as compared with native goods when moved from a treaty port to an inland place or *vice versa*," he also stated that the "abolition [of this tax], undoubtedly, [would] come in time."[44]

Instead, in September 1937 the Nationalist government changed the nature and scope of the Interport Duty from "goods [being] transported by steamer or aeroplane between treaty ports, but not on junk-borne or rail-borne goods, nor on goods transported by other routes on land" or "even in the case of steamer-borne goods shipped between a treaty port and an inland place." Because "in the circumstances[,] the burden of taxation [was] not fairly borne by all merchants alike" and "the collection of interport duty also [suffered] considerably," the definition of the Interport Duty was changed so as "invariably [to] be levied on all native goods conveyed between a treaty port and an inland place or solely between inland places, regardless of whether they [were] transported by junks, railways, highways, or steamers." The Interport Duty rates were fixed at 7.5 percent for native goods paying ad valorem

43. SHAC 679/1/26910, IG Circular No. 4158, 31 December 1930; Chen Shiqi, *Zhong-guo jindai haiguanshi*, p. 838.

44. SHAC 679/1/26910, IG Circular No. 4158, 31 December 1930.

duties, and 5 percent for native goods paying specific duties (up from an effective 2 percent based on the 1858 tariff rates, and now based on the 1931 Export Tariff). This change was introduced to "increase the revenue."[45] The regulations defining the interaction of this newly defined tax with other aspects of the Nationalist fiscal regime remained the same—Interport Duty was only to be paid once; it was not to be levied on goods already having paid other national taxes, and it was to be refunded, or credited, against the Export Tax in the case of native goods being exported abroad after paying the Interport Duty. The Maritime Customs was given extra power to collect the new Interport Duty: "When goods liable to interport duty are loaded or discharged at, or pass through, places where there is a Customs establishment, interport duty should invariably be levied by the Customs or Maritime Customs stations[,] as the case may be. The Customs are also authorised to establish additional stations in order to facilitate the collection of interport duty."[46]

These powers, however, had to be used advisedly and also within the budgetary constraints of the wartime Maritime Customs. In the circular accompanying these instructions, Sir Frederick Maze wrote that "duty on goods borne by rail should be levied only at places of loading or discharge" unless there were "exceptional circumstances which [permitted] the Customs to take special action." Similarly, despite the new powers to establish additional collecting stations, "discretion [would] have to be exercised to ensure that the expenditure [would] be justified" because of the "present imperative need for drastic economy."[47] Table 6.3 shows that, while the revised Interport Duty proved an effective fiscal instrument until the end of 1939, its revenue yield fell drastically in 1940 and 1941. Although the nominal figures suggest a recovery of customs revenue in the later years of the war, adjusting the nominal figures for inflation makes it clear that this was not the case; the adjusted figures are given in table 6.4.

45. SHAC 679/1/26919, Ministry of Finance, Guanwu shu Daidian No. 143, "General Rules for Improving the Collection of Interport Duty," Enclosure No. 2, IG Circular No. 5585, 2nd ser., 21 September 1937.

46. SHAC 679/1/26919, "General Rules for Improving the Collection of Interport Duty," Enclosure No. 2, IG Circular No. 5585, 2nd ser., 21 September 1937.

47. SHAC 679/1/26919, IG Circular No. 5585, 2nd ser., 21 September 1937.

Table 6.3.

National government receipts, 1937–45 (in millions of Chinese dollars)

	1937–38[a]	1938[b]	1939	1940	1941	1942	1943	1944	1945
Maritime Customs receipts[c]	$239	$128	$346	$38	$15	$160	$377	$494	$3,321
Wartime Consumption Tax receipts	—	—	—	—	—	$399	$718	$1,838	$304
Total receipts collected by Maritime Customs	$239	$128	$346	$38	$15	$559	$1,095	$2,332	$3,625
Other nonborrowed receipts	$413	$182	$380	$1,545	$1,307	$5,598	$17,514	$38,420	$156,737
Borrowed receipts	$1,451	$871	$2,336	$3,842	$9,570	$20,445	$44,743	142,080	$1,106,076
Total government receipts	$2,103	$1,181	$3,063	$5,425	$10,892	$26,602	$63,352	$182,832	$1,266,438
Total, excluding borrowed receipts	$652	$310	$726	$1,583	$1,322	$6,157	$18,609	$40,752	$160,362
Total Customs receipts as % of total nonborrowed receipts	36.66	41.30	47.66	2.40	1.13	9.08	5.88	5.72	2.26
Price index (June)	1.0 (July)	1.4	2.3	4.9	11	36	132	466	2,167

Sources: Data from Young, *China's Wartime Finance and Inflation*, pp. 332, 358; Bickers, "The American IG," p. 25.

[a] Fiscal year ending 30 June 1938.

[b] Second half of year only.

[c] Including Interport Duty until 1942.

Table 6.4.

National government receipts, 1937–45, adjusted for inflation using July 1937 prices (in millions of Chinese dollars)

	1937–38[a]	1938[b]	1939	1940	1941	1942	1943	1944	1945
Maritime Customs receipts[c]	$239	$91.45	$150.43	$7.76	$1.36	$4.44	$2.86	$1.06	$1.53
Total receipts collected by Maritime Customs	$239	$91.45	$150.43	$7.76	$1.36	$15.53	$8.30	$5.00	$1.67
Other nonborrowed receipts	$413	$130	$165.22	$315.31	$118.82	$155.5	$132.68	$82.45	$72.33
Total government receipts	$2,103	$843.57	$1,331.74	$1,107.14	$990.18	$738.94	$479.94	$392.34	$584.42
Total, excluding borrowed receipts	$652	$221.43	$315.65	$323.06	$120.18	$171.03	$140.98	$87.45	$74.00
Total Customs receipts as % of total nonborrowed receipts	36.66	41.30	47.66	2.40	1.13	9.08	5.88	5.72	2.26
Price index (June)	1.0 (July)	1.4	2.3	4.9	11	36	132	466	2,167

Source: Figures based on data from Young, China's Wartime Finance and Inflation, pp. 332, 358; Bickers, "The American IG," p. 25. See table 6.3.
[a] Fiscal year ending 30 June 1938.
[b] Second half of year only.
[c] Excluding Wartime Consumption Tax.

The Interport Duty was abolished as of 15 April 1942 and replaced by the Wartime Consumption Tax (Zhanshi xiaofeishui).[48] The Wartime Consumption Tax was the reincarnation, under a different name, of an even older form of taxation, the *lijin*, or transit tax (transliterated in older texts as *likin*). *Lijin* had been abolished by the Nationalist government on 1 January 1931 as part of the commitments undertaken by Duan Qirui's government in the Treaty between the Nine Powers relating to the Chinese Customs Tariff, concluded at the 1922 Washington Conference, which led to the restoration of tariff autonomy to China by the treaty powers between 1927 and 1929.[49] Problems arose from the abolition of *lijin*, owing to the nature and form of collection of this tax. A transit tax that was formally introduced to finance military expenditures during the Taiping Rebellion, *lijin* was collected at roadside barriers by members of diverse government agencies.[50] No expertise or skill was necessary to collect *lijin*, unlike Maritime Customs revenue collection; all that was required was military power to enforce payment, if necessary. For this reason, *lijin* was a favorite financing tool of local power holders, and it remained so even after *lijin* collection was officially declared illegal by the Nationalist government.

Recognizing its own inability to enforce the abolition of *lijin*, the Nationalist government in 1930 offered central government subsidies to the provincial governments in an attempt to compensate them for the *lijin* revenue they stood to lose.[51] Despite this attempt to purchase their compliance, local power holders continued to collect *lijin*. The Nationalist government, the Chinese merchant community, and the foreign community in China all associated *lijin* with everything that was wrong with China's fiscal system. By reverting to charging a transit tax, albeit under a different name, the Nationalist government was admitting that it was impossible under the prevailing circumstances to sustain the program of fiscal reform and rationalization that it had

48. SHAC 679/8/143, IG Circular CIS No. 131, 8 May 1942.

49. SHAC 679/1/26910, IG Circular No. 4158, 31 December 1930; Young, *China's Nation-Building Effort*, p. 66; SHAC 679/1/26097, IG Circular No. 3310, 2nd ser., 1 June 1922.

50. Zheng Beijun, *Zhongguo jindai lijin zhidu yanjiu*, pp. 54–57.

51. Mr. E. M. B. Ingram to Mr. A. Henderson, Despatch, 20 January 1931 [F 984/2/10], *BDFA*, vol. 39, p. 52.

advanced during the Nanjing decade. While the revision of the Interport Tax had empowered the Maritime Customs to collect tariffs on
goods transported by all means of transport within Nationalist-held
China, the Wartime Consumption Tax gave the Maritime Customs
even greater revenue-collecting powers. The officiating inspector general, C. H. B. Joly, noted:

> As will be seen from the regulations[,] the introduction of the War-time
> Consumption Tax is, to all intents and purposes, a tax on the consumer.
> It follows therefore that the tax is not only to be levied on goods on [sic]
> movement but is also to be levied at places where the goods are produced
> or consumed. Pending the enforcement of regulations governing the
> registration of factories and payment of tax on existing stocks and goods
> produced, you may, as a temporary measure, concentrate at first on col-
> lecting the tax on all goods moved and consumed locally and gradually
> extend your activities, with the assistance of the Chambers of Commerce
> and Trade Guilds[,] to every city and district if its collection justifies the
> establishment of a Customs Station.[52]

As table 6.3 demonstrates, the Wartime Consumption Tax delivered significant amounts of revenue from 1942 until 1944. In 1942, the
first year in which the Maritime Customs collected the tax, Maritime
Customs' share of nonborrowed government revenue increased to 9.08
percent, from 1.13 percent in 1941, the last full year in which the Maritime Customs collected the revised Interport Duty. This share fell to
just under 6 percent in 1943 and 1944, and the increase in the Wartime
Consumption Tax revenue collected fell behind the increase in the
price index, as is demonstrated in table 6.4. However, the Wartime
Consumption Tax was collected until 25 January 1945.[53] It was abolished for the same reason that had led foreign merchants to complain
so vociferously about lijin—because of its negative impact on trade
within China.

Commenting on the introduction of the Wartime Consumption
Tax, Arthur N. Young, the Nationalist government's chief financial

52. SHAC 679/8/143, IG Circular CIS No. 131, 8 May 1942.
53. SHAC 679/8/158, IG Circular CIS No. 883, 27 February 1945.

adviser, recollected in 1965 that "clearly the method was far from good, and in a memorandum of January 15, 1942, I warned of the danger that such taxes would degenerate into a system of endless barriers to trade and movement, as the old *likin* had." The result of introducing the Wartime Consumption Tax, he said, was "to restore an obstructive system similar to the old *likin* or transit tax, the abolition of which in the early 1930s, though not wholly effective, had been one of the fine accomplishments of the Nationalist Government." For Young, lobbying for the Maritime Customs to be awarded the job of collecting the Wartime Consumption Tax was a way of limiting its potentially damaging effect by giving the responsibility to an institution that had no vested interest in perpetuating it.[54]

Because of its highly intrusive nature, the Wartime Consumption Tax was frequently resented, not only by local power holders who stood to lose revenue by the imposition of a new central government tax but also by consumers.[55] Complaints against this new tax were varied and ranged from procedural issues to complaints of physical mistreatment. In one case reported from Wuzhou in September 1942, a range of complaints was combined to achieve a greater effect with the Inspectorate General of Customs and the Office of Customs Affairs. The complaints were arranged in ascending order of importance, from a procedural mistake to an emotive charge of physical violence against a woman by low-ranking Maritime Customs officials. The Office of Customs Affairs ordered an internal Maritime Customs investigation into the latter charge, which revealed that the woman had been stopped while attempting to walk past a Maritime Customs barrier without having her baggage inspected. The local commissioner of customs denied that the woman had been assaulted by a member of his staff and reported that, when questioned by the local police, the woman had withdrawn her accusation.[56] The attempt to evade taxation by linking a procedural complaint with a highly emotional one had failed.

54. Young, *China's Wartime Finance and Inflation*, p. 36.

55. Bickers, "The Chinese Maritime Customs at War," p. 303.

56. SHAC 679/26090, E. T. Williams, Commissioner, Wuchow, Wuchow No. 4230/CIS No. 74, 25 September 1942.

Besides its intrusive nature, general unpopularity, and negative impact on trade within Nationalist-controlled China, there was another reason why the Wartime Consumption Tax was abolished. Implementing the Nationalist government's instructions on revenue collection brought the Maritime Customs into conflict with other revenue-collecting and antismuggling institutions of the Nationalist government, of which a plethora had sprung up in wartime, particularly after the government's move to Chongqing. In his circular transmitting the Ministry of Finance's original instructions regarding the introduction of the Wartime Consumption Tax, Joly noted that: "As the various Tax Bureaux in the provinces have now been ordered by the Government to abolish all local taxes on the movement of cargo from the date of introduction of the War-time Consumption Tax by the Customs, the action taken by the local authorities in this regard should be reported by despatch in due course."[57]

Anomalies of Wartime Trade

The anomalies of wartime trade affected both tariff revenue and the Maritime Customs' primacy as a revenue-gathering and antismuggling institution. Because legal trade was carried on across enemy lines after 1939, one faces yet another layer of conceptual difficulties when defining the meaning of smuggling in wartime China.[58] Before the beginning of the Second Sino-Japanese War, the distinction between licensed and unlicensed trade was more meaningful than that between trade and smuggling. During the war, however, the Nationalist government's policy added another layer of complexity to the understanding of licensed versus unlicensed trade. From October 1937 until July 1939, the Nationalist government banned any trade with the Japanese-occupied areas of China; anecdotal evidence as well as Maritime Customs statistics suggest that this trade went on, regardless.

57. SHAC 679/8/143, IG Circular CIS No. 131, 8 May 1942.
58. Eastman, "Facets of an Ambivalent Relationship," pp. 276–77.

As stated, by November 1938 the Nationalist government had lost control over seaports that had produced about 80 percent of Maritime Customs revenue. Losing control of the coastal areas, the North China Plain, the Lower Yangzi Delta, and the middle reaches of the Yangzi meant that, besides losing the areas that generated the most customs revenue, the Nationalists also lost control over the areas that encompassed the emerging modern sector of China's national economy as well as key agricultural production areas. Faced with accelerating material depredation in the territory remaining under its control, the Nationalist government in July 1939 declared it would allow the import of all but a list of specifically proscribed commodities, "irrespective of their places of origin"—a lightly veiled reference to the Japanese-occupied areas.[59] In 1942 the number of proscribed commodities was reduced from 168 to 103, an indication of yet further material depredation: "In reply to a query as to whether products of factories and firms in Hongkong and Shanghai—these two places being now occupied by the Japanese—should be treated as enemy goods and prohibited importation into Free China, the Ching-Chi Pu [Jingji Bu; Ministry of Economic Affairs] have notified the Ts'ai-cheng Pu [Caizheng Bu; Ministry of Finance] of their ruling that goods produced by factories and firms in Hongkong, Shanghai, etc., other than those specified by them as enemy goods, should still be allowed importation into Free China in order to help stabilize prices and meet the needs of the military and the general public."[60] The wording of this circular reveals the official motivation on the Nationalist side for permitting legal trade across wartime front lines.

The ambivalence of the Nationalist government's position on trade with Japanese-held areas is well expressed in the following comment by the officiating inspector general about a tariff increase on goods banned from importation into Nationalist-held areas: "It is to be noted that the Government's revision of the duty rates for certain foreign goods on the embargo list does not mean their removal from the embargo list. The new rates are intended to be applicable to the articles concerned only when they are required to pay duty, e.g. seized goods

59. Eastman, "Facets of an Ambivalent Relationship," p. 277.
60. SHAC 679/1/4145, IG Circular CIS No. 82, 26 March 1942.

and goods allowed importation under Special Import Permit."[61] This means that the Nationalist government, in effect, neither banned nor licensed this trade. At the same time, the decision to license trade with Japanese-held areas also created opportunities for Nationalist government officials and military officers to seek their own financial advantage: "The Executive Yuan have received information that Government employees and employees of Government Enterprises have been found engaging privately in trade, in speculation, or in the hoarding of commodities. As such action is bound to affect the price of commodities and to disturb public confidence, the Yuan have ruled that the matter should be investigated and the offenders severely punished."[62] Japan's motivation for allowing this trade to continue was the presumed inflationary effect on the economy of Nationalist-held China. By deliberately overpaying for goods imported from Nationalist-held areas, the Japanese military authorities in occupied China caused "inflation [to be] doubly aggravated by drain of goods from and increased supply of currency in Free China," as the US embassy in Chongqing noted.[63]

Differing estimates exist as to the volume of trade between Nationalist- and Japanese-held areas. In 1940, the Nationalist government estimated the trade to be worth $400 million (about US$21 million), while the US Office of Strategic Services (OSS) estimated a value of approximately $2,280 million (about US$120 million).[64] Also according to OSS estimates, the volume of trade between Nationalist- and Japanese-held areas was even greater in 1941 than it had been in 1940. According to this estimate, 20,000 tons of goods were brought into Nationalist-held China monthly from Hong Kong, Macao, and Guangzhouwan, twice the volume of goods brought into Nationalist-held China by the Burma Road from British India.[65]

61. SHAC 679/1/4145, IG Circular CIS No. 22, 3 February 1942.

62. SHAC 679/1/4145, IG Circular CIS No. 52, 7 March 1942.

63. Chargé in China (Atcheson) to Secretary of State, Chungking, 2 August 1943 [893.5151/953: Telegram], in US Department of State, FRUS, China, 1943, p. 440.

64. Freyn, Free China's New Deal, p. 73; OSS, doc. C: China 2.3-c, "Trade between Occupied China and Free China," 16 June 1942, p. 2 (Office of War Information, Box 397), both in Eastman, "Facets of an Ambivalent Relationship," p. 278.

65. OSS, doc. C: China 2.3-c, "Trade between Occupied China and Free China," p. 1, in Eastman, "Facets of an Ambivalent Relationship," p. 279.

Assessments of Nationalist trade with Japanese-held areas differ according to whether the trade is viewed in economic or in moral terms. With regard to the economic effect of the trade, Eastman states: "In economic terms, it is probable that the Nationalists generally benefited from the inflow of goods. Without the cloth and other consumer goods brought in from the occupied area, life in the interior would have been harsher and perhaps even intolerable. Moreover, to the extent that these goods partially satisfied consumer demands, the trade had a moderating effect on the spiraling inflation."[66] It is interesting to note that Eastman's conclusion regarding the effect on inflation of trade across enemy lines is the exact opposite of that drawn by the US embassy in Chongqing. Still, regardless of its economic effects, trade with the enemy, whether licensed or unlicensed, was anathema to many outside observers, such as the journalist Israel Epstein, who observed that this trade was "not only morally obtuse but strategically nonsense."[67] As Eastman also points out:

> Even if the Nationalists derived economic benefits from the trade, however, these benefits must be weighed against the detrimental effects of the trade on the Chinese war effort. Supplying the enemy with food and with raw materials for their industries was surely a pernicious practice. And the massive involvement of the military appears to have thoroughly corrupted the officers stationed where they could participate in the traffic, which provided them with a personal interest in avoiding conflict with the Japanese. And the corruption and self-serving that were engendered by their commercial involvements weakened the already frail moral fiber of the Chinese army.[68]

In our assessment of this wartime trade, we must beware of unconsciously reflecting a Western, "orientalist" discourse of warfare or indeed the Stilwell-White paradigm itself. That the Chinese Nationalist wartime leadership did things differently from the way they were

66. Eastman, "Facets of an Ambivalent Relationship," p. 283.
67. Israel Epstein quoted in Eastman, "Facets of an Ambivalent Relationship," p. 283.
68. Eastman, "Facets of an Ambivalent Relationship," p. 283.

being done in Washington or London does not necessarily mean that they were wrong. In 1943, Arthur Young recorded in his diary, with no apparent censure, a conversation with Kong Xiangxi in which the latter stated his belief that Chongqing's wartime black market in foreign currencies served a useful purpose in allowing individuals to exchange foreign currencies at a market rate.[69] Moreover, recent studies attest to the existence of trade across enemy lines during, for instance, the British-American War of 1812. In the words of one US military officer: "They do say it is wrong to supply an innimy [sic] and I think so too, . . . but I don't call that man my innimy [sic] who buys what I have to sell and gives such a genteel price for it."[70] There is indeed something to be said for Hubert Freyn's view: "Which side gains and which side loses if Japanese army gasoline find its way, for a consideration, into Chinese hands? or if Japanese cloth is bought to make uniforms for guerrillas or shivering Chinese farmers? or if Shanghai and Hong Kong manufactures are 'smuggled' through the lines in order to fill, in the rear, a gap which local production is unable to close?"[71]

From the Maritime Customs' point of view, trade, both licensed and unlicensed, with the Japanese-held areas played an appreciable part in the service's downfall from being the Nationalist government's preeminent revenue-gathering institution. While the taxation of licensed trade and seizures of unlicensed trade were sources of revenue for the customs service, the complex and continually changing nature of trade with the occupied areas made it increasingly difficult for the service to function effectively, since its virtual monopoly on collecting revenue on and policing foreign trade—again notice the conceptual difficulty: was trade with Japanese-held areas *foreign* trade?—was being challenged by a proliferation of competing agencies under the direct control of the Nationalist government or the military.

During the Second Sino-Japanese War, the Maritime Customs lost its primacy among revenue-policing and antismuggling organizations. The administrative upheavals of the war facilitated the rise of no fewer

69. Arthur N. Young Papers, Box 113, Diaries, 27 November 1943, Hoover Institution Archives.

70. Quoted in Porter, "Friendly Fire," p. 9.

71. Freyn, *Free China's New Deal*, p. 73.

than three central government organizations nominally charged with smuggling suppression but that in fact frequently engaged in trade with the occupied areas themselves. These were the Tax Police (Shui-jing zongtuan), the Smuggling Prevention Bureau (Jisi shu), and the Wartime Goods Transport Management Bureau (Zhanshi huoyun guanli ju). All three organizations were controlled, more or less directly, by the Nationalist Military Secret Service (Juntong), under General Dai Li.[72] The Maritime Customs' conflicts with the Juntong arose not least because the Nationalist government's instructions to the Maritime Customs, such as the following, failed to reflect the Juntong's power in the realm of trade and revenue collection.

> According to the regulations, the Customs are the only organ authorised to carry out inspections to prevent native goods from being sent for the use of the enemy, and . . . it is only at places at which there is no Customs establishment that the Preventive Bureau may enforce the embargo. Seizures made by the Bureau should be handed over to the Customs for disposal according to the latter part of Article 10 of the regulations. If the Bureau [fails] to hand over seizures made by them, you are to report the matter by despatch, with a Chinese version in duplicate.[73]

The conflicts with trade-policing institutions subordinate to the Juntong may well have contributed to an attempt by General Dai in late 1944 to incorporate the Maritime Customs into his network of security agencies and to charge the customs with all cargo supervision, transport, and security duties. L. K. Little, by then the inspector general, "strenuously" resisted this proposal; to his relief, he learned in January 1945 that the Nationalist government had formally decided not to proceed with this proposal.[74]

72. Wakeman, *Spymaster*, pp. 320–29.

73. SHAC 679/1/4145, IG Circular CIS No. 66, 14 March 1942.

74. Lester Knox Little Papers (hereafter cited as Little Papers), Ms Am 1999.2, L. K. Little Personal [on spine], Letters, Memoranda etc. relating to Customs Affairs 1945 [title page], L. K. Little to B. E. F. Hall, IGS No. 52, 9 February 1945, Houghton Library, Harvard University; also cited in Bickers, "The American IG," pp. 25–26.

The Demise of the Maritime Customs

The decline of the Maritime Customs as a revenue-collecting institution of the Nationalist government, although under foreign leadership and with certain measures of administrative independence, was overdetermined in many ways. Early during the Second Sino-Japanese War, the Nationalists lost control of the areas that had yielded the greatest share of Maritime Customs revenue, and wartime duties collected by the Maritime Customs could not make up for that loss. The Maritime Customs also ended up on the losing side of the institutional turf wars within the wartime Nationalist state. But besides fiscal realities, the main reason for its demise was an increasing hostility within the Guomindang toward the Maritime Customs' position during the war.

For the Maritime Customs Service, its institutional survival obscured other responsibilities. Throughout the war, senior foreign staff members argued with the Ministry of Finance and the Office of Customs Affairs about the degree to which Japanese aggression should be accommodated. In this conflict, old patterns came to the fore once again: a Chinese government concerned with the extent of its control found itself confronting foreigners in leading positions within the Maritime Customs who were more concerned with ensuring the survival of the Maritime Customs Service than with following the instructions of the Chinese government. Senior members of the Maritime Customs also began, once more, to articulate didactic visions of China that they held to be superior to the views of the Chinese government. In both these respects Sir Frederick Maze adopted an attitude very similar to that of Sir Francis Aglen, whom he had criticized so stridently when he was attempting to succeed him in 1927. In late 1942, Maze wrote to the nonresident secretary, the Maritime Customs' representative in London, justifying the Maritime Customs' continued operation in the occupied areas until December 1941:

> I pointed out on that occasion that whether we quit or whether we remain in occupied China, the occupying Power, Japan, will in any case secure the revenue; that if we elect to stay and can succeed in preserving the integrity of the Service, a certain prestige will attach to the Govern-

ment as the controlling Authority; that a unified Service would sustain China's credit and be recognized abroad as a security organ; and finally, that the ultimate settlement of the Customs issue when the "China incident" is settled would be facilitated if the Administration can be kept intact and not divided into two sections.[75]

Maze's rhetoric has a fatal similarity to his predecessor's image of the Maritime Customs as a ship that had to be steered through troubled waters.[76] In Aglen's case, the troubled waters represented Chinese politics; in Maze's, they represented the Second Sino-Japanese War. To recall, Aglen's reluctance to see the Maritime Customs become responsible to the Chinese government led to his dismissal in 1927. Now, too, the Nationalist government saw the Maritime Customs' actions from a perspective very different from Maze's. As early as February 1938, Kong Xiangxi, the Nationalist government's minister of finance, wrote to Maze:

The Government attaches very great importance to the maintenance of the integrity of the customs service, which has had such a long and useful history in China, and will continue to do all that it properly can to that end. Maintenance of the mere semblance of integrity, however, does not justify the sacrifice of important principles. At present in Tientsin and elsewhere, according to the information which has now reached me, the customs offices fly the 5-barred flag; collect the tariff duties prescribed by the Japanese puppets; turn over the customs revenues to the Yokohama Specie Bank, from which withdrawal to meet China's obligations for which they are pledged is prevented; and in effect must heed the instructions of the Japanese-controlled puppet regime. No material benefit derives from this state of affairs either to China or to the foreign Governments and their nationals that are interested in the integrity of the customs.[77]

75. SHAC 679/31746, F. W. Maze to J. H. Cubbon, Confidential, 21 December 1942.
76. FO 228/3740/5A/68A 1928, A. H. F. Edwardes to M. Lampson, 28 February 1928, in Atkins, *Informal Empire in Crisis*, pp. 27–28.
77. SHAC 679/1/32747, Dr. H. H. Kung to Sir Frederick Maze, Confidential, 10 February 1938.

Maze's decision to remain in Shanghai and operate the Maritime Customs from the International Settlement, rather than follow the Nationalist government first to Hankou and then to Chongqing, demonstrates the extent to which the Ministry of Finance still had to accept a certain amount of independence on the part of the Maritime Customs. The following passage reveals the Maritime Customs' perspective on the state of affairs:

> At the end of 1941, the Inspector General and the Inspectorate General of Customs were functioning without serious interference in Shanghai. The various Commissioners at the occupied and unoccupied ports and their staffs were still obeying Sir Frederick Maze's orders though, of course, all revenue collected in occupied ports was frozen in the Yokohama Specie Bank, subject to withdrawal only by checks signed by the Commissioner concerned. In November, after long and steadily increasing pressure, the British Commissioner in charge of the Shanghai Customs had to give way to a Japanese Commissioner. The British and American Governments were kept acquainted with the circumstances of this case.[78]

By 1945, the Maritime Customs was in a different position altogether. Maze, whose interests, fortuitously for his career, had coincided with those of the Nationalist government for so long, retired in 1943, when their respective interests had shown themselves to diverge, with a sinecure worth one year's salary as compensation and having secured his pension in hard currency. His immediate successor, Cecil Joly, asked not to have his acting appointment renewed and to be allowed to retire instead, having completed the thirty years of service necessary to qualify for a full service pension. Joly's eventual successor and the last foreign inspector general, L. K. Little, would retire in early 1950, after having secured the foreign employees' pensions.[79]

The Ministry of Finance and the Office of Customs Affairs used Joly's tenure in office, the interregnum between Maze and Little, as an

---

78. SHAC 679/1/31746, R. M. Talbot, "Notes of the Situation of the Chinese Customs in the Unoccupied Areas as Affected by the War," in F. W. Maze to J. H. Cubbon, Confidential, 29 December 1942.

79. Bickers, "The American IG," p. 34.

opportunity to strengthen their hold over the Maritime Customs. The Maritime Customs was subjected to the National Treasury Law, and thus lost its budgetary independence, in 1942.[80] In 1938, when the National Treasury Law was first introduced, the Maritime Customs, still headquartered in Shanghai although its superior authorities were in Chongqing, had argued its way out of being subjected to the law on the grounds that "the very announcement of the Law would involve a shock to China's credit."[81] A. C. E. Braud, the financial secretary in the Inspectorate General, wrote to Sun Siyong, a Maritime Customs staff member in Chongqing who was charged with arguing the Maritime Customs case to the Office of Customs Affairs:

> The average foreign bondholder cannot be expected to understand the detailed and complicated stipulations of the Law. What he is most concerned [with] is that the custodianship of the revenue, which is pledged by agreement for the service of his bonds and coupons, would pass from the Inspector-General of Customs to the Public Treasury. . . . It would . . . be very difficult to rectify the very natural distrust engendered by the breaking off from a long established and lawfully instituted procedure. Thus China's credit, which it is now of paramount importance to preserve, will suffer for something, which, to say the best, serves to satisfy pro forma requirements only! Moreover, as the loan service is now suspended and the quotas therefor [sic] from ports in areas under government control are deposited in special accounts with the Central Bank of China, Chungking, which cannot be drawn on without the Minister's specific authority, the necessity of applying the Law to the Customs at the present juncture does not exist.[82]

In short, according to Braud, "for the Customs[,] application of the Treasury Law [was] unnecessary."[83] This was also the position of Sir Frederick Maze, who regarded the application of the National Treasury

---

80. Ambassador in China (Gauss) to Secretary of State, 20 July 1942 [693.002/1151 Telegram], US Department of State, *FRUS*, China, 1942, pp. 680–82, in Bickers, "The American IG," p. 22.
81. SHAC 679/9/8563, Braud to Sun Si Yung, 17 July 1939.
82. SHAC 679/9/8563, Braud to Sun Si Yung, 17 July 1939.
83. SHAC 679/9/8563, Braud to Sun Si Yung, 17 July 1939.

Law as "impolitic, impractical and dangerous," since it would undermine the bondholders' confidence, encourage local authorities at occupied ports to adopt similar procedures, be inconvenient in administrative terms, and endanger the Maritime Customs' present position.[84] The Maritime Customs' position found support from within the Ministry of Finance; Arthur N. Young, the financial adviser to the minister of finance, considered that "it would be desirable to wait [for] a more favourable opportunity before undertaking to apply this Law to the Customs and Salt Administration."[85] This blatant refusal on the part of the Maritime Customs to be subjected to the same laws as China's other revenue-collecting agencies, despite Maze being on record with a great deal of rhetoric stressing the Maritime Customs' position as a Chinese government agency, seems to have carried the day; the Maritime Customs was exempted from the National Treasury Law. In 1942, however, renewed attempts by the Maritime Customs to uphold the exemption were unsuccessful. By then, customs revenue had dwindled compared with prewar collection levels and the Inspectorate General was located in Chongqing, the Nationalist center of power, no longer beyond the Nationalists' reach in the International Settlement in Shanghai.

Yet another indication that the winds of change were blowing through the Maritime Customs in the war years was the extent to which Chinese was replacing English as the official language in Maritime Customs documents. As Joly noted in 1942 in commenting on an instruction from the Ministry of Finance, the "tendency in the Customs in recent years [had] already been to replace English by Chinese steadily and as rapidly as possible." The reason for the continued use of English within the Maritime Customs was "that a great many of the senior posts [were] still filled by foreign members of staff who, though they [had] studied Chinese, [were] not proficient enough to draft and translate Chinese despatches, etc., with the accuracy that [was] needed to avoid mistakes." Although Joly stated that the "principle involved in the Pu's present instructions [was] one of great importance and should be implemented as far as circumstances permit," he qualified this instruction with the following:

84. SHAC 679/9/8563, "Re: New Treasury Law," n.d.
85. SHAC 679/9/8563, Arthur N. Young, Memorandum, 17 August 1939.

To change suddenly a procedure that has been the outcome of the historical background of the Customs would entail a great deal of reorganization as new equipments, filing and indexing systems, and an extensive supply of new stationery and forms would have to be acquired, and during the process of change, delay and heavy expenditure would be unavoidable. Moreover, as Customs affairs have been disorganized by the seizure by the Japanese of the former Inspectorate in Shanghai and of Customs facilities and staff, the present is especially a difficult time to make a sudden change.[86]

During the war, the Maritime Customs also lost its perceived and actual primacy among the revenue-gathering institutions of the Nationalist government. Between 1929 and 1937, it rested assured in the knowledge that it provided the government with a share of central government revenue that at no point was smaller than 40 percent. Within the provinces where the Nationalist government exercised actual political and military control, the Maritime Customs could also rely on the government's cooperation in reaching accommodations with revenue-gathering institutions seeking to extract revenue within the same territory. This changed after the Inspectorate General relocated to Chongqing. As the share of revenue delivered by the Maritime Customs decreased, so did its clout compared with other revenue-gathering institutions. The roots of this decline are to be found in the period between the outbreak of the war and the removal of the Inspectorate General to Chongqing. The decline was aggravated by a growing "hostility from elements in the Nationalist Government" toward Maritime Customs, partly "inspired by a genuine nationalist agenda which aimed to restore China's sovereign rights," but also the result of "simple bureaucratic competition" and "turf warfare."[87]

After Japan's surrender at the end of the war, the Maritime Customs never recovered its prewar standing among the revenue-collecting agencies of the Nationalist government. Besides the decrease in its relative importance, the Maritime Customs also faced the problem of reintegrating those members of its pre-1941 administration who had

86. SHAC 679/1/4145, IG Circular CIS No. 90, 31 March 1942.
87. Bickers, "The Chinese Maritime Customs at War," p. 301.

served in the customs service of Wang Jingwei's collaborationist government. During the war years, successive inspector generals had stressed the importance of combating corruption among the ranks of the Maritime Customs to avoid giving the Ministry of Finance grounds for further reducing the importance of the service. The Maritime Customs was also keen to stress the decline of administrative and moral standards in the customs service of the collaborationist government in order to stress its own probity by comparison:

> In fact it is now the golden age for dishonest officers in Occupied China whose idea it is that connivance with merchants in smuggling, undervaluation, etc., even though bought with bribery, is far better than honest performance of duties resulting in the flow of money to the enemy's treasury. Corruption reached such proportions in 1944 that the *Shanghai Times* made a vigorous attack on the Customs in its September 1st issue. It was stated in the paper that "corruption has taken the place of integrity, and various methods of extortion, graft, and squeeze are being widely practiced by the outdoor officers, sometimes in collusion with their indoor colleagues at the stations."[88]

The last nail in the coffin of the Maritime Customs' foreign-led and semi-independent status was the fact that employees who were nationals of foreign countries had continued to operate in Japanese-held territories. Initially, those staff members were all to be dismissed from the service.[89] However, when questioned by the Staff Investigation Committee, set up to investigate the behavior of staff members who had remained in occupied China, those accused of collaboration were able to prove that they had been instructed by Sir Frederick Maze to remain within Japanese-held territory to ensure that the Maritime Customs continued to function as an institution. Staff members who were investigated included V. Muling, a Russian émigré, who "was able to produce a letter which Maze wrote to A. Feragen confirming his advice during a meeting at his house in December 1941 that they should

88. SHAC 679/1/32745, Wu Yaoqi to IG of Customs, 26 May 1945, in Little to Yui, 17 July 1945.
89. White, "'A Question of Principle with Political Implications,'" p. 523.

stick to their posts in the interests of the Service and that he would defend their action with the Government."[90] In this letter, Maze stated that he would "defend the action of employees who continue their work without interruption; that it would be advantageous in many respects if those who were in position to do so prosecuted their routine as usual and thus provide[d] for continuity of established practice, and ultimately facilitated a final settlement by helping to avoid more staff disorganization than is absolutely necessary at the present time."[91] In his memoirs, Gustaf Asker, a Dane, mentions receiving even more definite instructions: "Before the communications were broken, however, I had received orders to follow those instructions given by the Customs Inspectorate, which the Japanese had set up in Shanghai, in order to keep the service going."[92]

By the time the Ministry of Finance instructed the Maritime Customs to set up a wartime Inspectorate General of Customs in Chongqing, the association of administrative and technical expertise with foreignness, dominant in earlier discussions about the future of the Maritime Customs Service, had undergone a change. The Maritime Customs had stopped recruiting foreign nationals to the Indoor Staff of the service—the management branch—in 1925. Exceptions for technical experts who could not be recruited from among Chinese nationals had to be approved individually by the Office of Customs Affairs of the Ministry of Finance. The post-1925 consensus between the Maritime Customs, still led by a foreign national and dominated at the senior levels by the last generation of foreign commissioners of customs and inspectorate secretaries, and its superior authorities in the Office of Customs Affairs and the Ministry of Finance, was that the Maritime Customs' expertise would be preserved by the gradual reduction of foreign employees through retirement, while at the same time Chinese employees would acquire the management and technical skills and experience that they did not yet possess. Both Song Ziwen

90. B. E. F. Hall Papers, B. E. F. Hall to Charles Powell, 18 October 1945, Bristol University Customs Collections.

91. Little Papers, Ms Am 1999.2, Sir F. W. Maze to A. Feragen, 13 December 1941, in V. Muling to L. K. Little, 10 September 1945, in L. K. Little to K. T. Ting, 22 September 1945, S/O No. 4, Houghton Library.

92. Asker, "China Memories," p. 42.

and Kong Xiangxi stressed the importance of a gradual process in order to preserve the operation and revenue collection of the Maritime Customs, even in the feverish and excited atmosphere of wartime Chongqing politics.[93]

As Hugh Bradley wrote to L. K. Little in early 1943, the Maritime Customs had become one of the objects of Chongqing factional politics.[94] Defended by Kong and Song as a semi-autonomous institution with a remaining foreign element that was still very influential, the Maritime Customs found itself under attack from other factions of the wartime Nationalist establishment, notably Li Tang, director general of the Office of Customs Affairs from 1943 to 1945 and thus Maze's and then Little's direct superior in the Nationalist hierarchy. Whether the customs service should deal directly with the minister of finance, or go through the director general of the institution charged with the supervision of the Maritime Customs administration in China, was a constant theme of wartime and postwar exchanges.[95] The relationship was not any easier on a personal level. Indeed, Little, for all his professed pro-Chinese feelings (in which respect he felt himself to be very different from Maze), wondered at one point whether what he felt to be Li's excessive observance of administrative protocol might not be explained by the fact that Li had studied in Germany.[96] For Little, preserving the original scheme of removing the remaining foreign element in the Maritime Customs through retirement and replacing them with Chinese nationals was important for two reasons. First, he felt that the expertise of his foreign colleagues was worth preserving and wanted to save the Maritime Customs from further administrative

93. Little Papers, Ms Am 1999.15, L. K. Little to His Excellency C. Gauss, US Ambassador, 7 February 1945, Houghton Library; Lester Knox Little Diaries, 82M-103 (hereafter cited as Little Diaries), 12 August 1943 and 5 April 1945, Houghton Library, Harvard University; Little Papers, Ms Am 1999.2, L. K. Little to His Excellency Dr. T. V. Soong, President of the Executive Yuan, Personal and Private, 23 June 1945, Houghton Library.

94. Little Papers, Ms Am 1999.1, Hugh Bradley to L. K. Little, 11 January 1943, Houghton Library.

95. Little Papers, Ms Am 1999.1, Hugh Bradley, Circular letter to foreign Commissioners of Customs, 1 July 1943, Houghton Library; Little Diaries, 13 January 1945, 8 February 1945, 12 May 1949, Houghton Library.

96. Little Diaries, 9 December 1944, Houghton Library.

upheaval.[97] This suggests that he deliberately ignored the fact that it was because so many foreigners remained in the Maritime Customs that it was vulnerable to attacks from other parts of the Nationalist administration. Little's attitude is easier to understand in light of his concern for the livelihood of his foreign colleagues, the second reason he wanted to preserve the gradual transition within the Maritime Customs.[98] Little retained this attitude until the end of his tenure as inspector general, the final months of which were dominated by discussion of his colleagues' pension arrangements, once the Nationalist government decided to pension off all foreigners remaining in the Maritime Customs in 1950.

The wartime standing of the foreigners working in the Maritime Customs was not helped by the behavior of Sir Frederick Maze, who had been the head of the Maritime Customs for the greatest length of time during the Nationalist period. Maze experienced the end of the war in South Africa. By then, many of his former colleagues, foreign and Chinese, had turned against him. In 1943, just before Maze resigned from the Maritime Customs, Hugh Bradley had written to his colleagues of the officiating inspector general with a heart but no head—referring to C. B. Joly—succeeded by an inspector general who had a head but no heart—Maze having resumed charge briefly on his arrival in Chongqing, after release from Japanese internment.[99] Kong Xiangxi's fit of rage, as reported by Zheng Lai, when confronted with the news that Maze had resumed charge was echoed even by many of Maze's foreign colleagues, who suspected that Maze had traveled to Chongqing chiefly to claim his pension as a one-off payment in hard currency.[100] Maze retired with a pension of £23,000 in 1943, equivalent to £932,800 in 2015 currency when using historical standards of living

97. Little Papers, Ms Am 1999.2, L. K. Little to His Excellency Dr. T. V. Soong, President of the Executive Yuan, Personal and Private, 23 June 1945, Houghton Library.

98. Little Diaries, 30 April 1945, Houghton Library.

99. Little Papers, Ms Am 1999.1, Hugh Bradley, Circular letter to foreign Commissioners of Customs, 1 July 1943, Houghton Library.

100. Little Papers, Ms Am 1999.1, L. K. Little, Aide Memoire, 5 October 1943, and T. R. Banister, Comment on Sir F. W. Maze's letter to Capt. Sabel, 24 August 1943, Houghton Library; Little Diaries, 10 August 1943, Houghton Library.

as an indicator of relative worth. His granduncle, Sir Robert Hart, had left an estate of £13,000 at his death in 1911, equivalent to £1,194,000 in 2015, based on the same methodology.[101] By the standards of his predecessor, Maze's pension was not any more extravagant. The pension matter drew ire from so many of his colleagues because Maze insisted that it be paid in full, in hard currency, before he would authorize the payment of pensions to three of his foreign colleagues. The Maritime Customs found it difficult to raise Maze's £23,000, and one of his three colleagues, T. J. Macauley, died before receiving his pension payments.[102] Once enough hard currency had been found, Maze's payment was made from a secret account that he revealed only after arriving in Chongqing, and that he alone had been able to access in the meantime. The official serving as additional audit secretary insisted that Maze return a down payment of £7,000 that he had previously received, which Maze did, according to Little—between them little love was lost, especially at this stage—but with such bad grace that he refused to speak to the additional audit secretary again before his departure from Chongqing for South Africa.[103]

The impression created by L. K. Little's papers and diaries is that he found himself with a lot of fences to mend on his arrival in Chongqing in the summer of 1943. His papers are dominated by exchanges with the Ministry of Finance, the Office of Customs Affairs, and the Executive Yuan regarding the status of the Maritime Customs. One subject of these exchanges was the intended postwar treatment of neutral nationals who had continued to serve in the Japanese-occupied areas after December 1941. As mentioned, many claimed to have been instructed by Maze to remain in the occupied territories to facilitate the eventual postwar reconstruction of the Maritime Customs. Maze, when asked to comment on this alleged instruction, denied having given it and stated that he had encouraged neutral nationals to decide for themselves whether to remain. This produced a stream of affidavits

101. Calculated using www.measuringworth.com, accessed 30 July 2016.

102. Little Papers, Ms Am 1999.1, W. E. Annett, Audit Secretary (additional), "Confidential Memorandum for Mr. L. K. Little, Inspector General," 28 August 1944, Houghton Library.

103. Little Diaries, "L. K. Little's Diary 1943–1954, NOTES. Identifications and Explanations," in envelope labeled "Introduction by J. K. F. + notes for the diary. MS Storage 175 Box 1," Houghton Library.

and statements to the contrary from Maze's former colleagues; Little eventually recorded in his diary: "Freddie [Maze] is a thoroughgoing Jesuit!"[104] Two years later, writing on the same matter, Little put it even more bluntly: "As usual, he lies."[105] This episode did not raise Maze's stock among either his former superiors in the Ministry of Finance or his former colleagues, foreign and Chinese. Little recorded in his diaries shortly after his arrival in Chongqing that "every man with whom [he had] talked curses Maze, who, they say, came back to Chungking for one purpose only—'to rob the till and run away.'"[106] By October 1943, B. E. F. Hall, then the nonresident secretary, that is, the Maritime Customs' representative in London, noted in a letter to a friend that Maze was "dodging income tax in Durban."[107] Kong Xiangxi's reaction to Maze's reappearance in Chongqing in December 1942 to reclaim his post—Zheng Lai described him as "livid with rage"—was echoed after the war by Zhang Fuyun, who had been appointed to a second term as director general of the Office of Customs Affairs in September 1945; Zhang remarked to Little in early 1946 that "Maze had betrayed the Customs."[108]

When Little was preparing to leave the United States for China in 1943, R. C. P. Rouse, the personal secretary at the Inspectorate General in Chongqing, had written to him that he would "not want any evening clothes" in Chongqing.[109] Some aspects of informal empire remained, though. After Little arrived in Chongqing, he shared his official residence with several of his colleagues, one of whom, being Scottish, attempted to instruct their chef in the preparation of haggis in the weeks leading up to Burns Supper, 1944. No need for such instruction, the chef replied—he had made that dish for the *yangduhui* (羊肚會) before the war.[110] The chef's reference to this "sheep's stomach society" may

104. Little Diaries, 7 December 1943, Houghton Library.
105. Little Diaries, 20 September 1945, Houghton Library.
106. Little Diaries, 10 August 1943, Houghton Library.
107. B. E. F. Hall to Charles Powell, 8 October 1943, B. E. F. Hall Papers, Bristol University Customs Collection.
108. Little Papers, Ms Am 1999.1, L. K. Little, Aide Memoire, 5 October 1943, Houghton Library; Little Diaries, 28 January 1946, Houghton Library.
109. Little Papers, Ms Am 1999.1, R. C. P. Rouse to L. K. Little, 6 May 1943, Houghton Library.
110. Little Diaries, 21 October 1943, Houghton Library.

be taken as meaning Chongqing's prewar expatriate Scottish community. Sadly, we do not know how accurate the chef's knowledge of the preparation of haggis was. Little, otherwise a keen chronicler of what he ate in wartime Chongqing, did not record the result of the chef's prior experience with Scottish cuisine; it is of course possible that, not being Scottish, he was not invited to attend.

Conclusion

As a result of the Japanese occupation, Maritime Customs revenue collapsed, with two consequences. The "imperial retreat" in China's revenue administration, to borrow Edmund Fung's phrase, lost its guarantee of an orderly progression; instead, foreign remnants in the Maritime Customs were speedily dispatched.[111] More importantly, Chinese government revenue collapsed and with it the Nationalist government's fiscal modernization project. Bringing *lijin* back under a different name as the Wartime Consumption Tax, only a few years after its official abolition as part of a program of tax rationalization, represented an acknowledgment of defeat. Furthermore, the Nationalist government's decision to license trade with Japanese-held areas had damaging consequences for China's fiscal system: it created conflicts of interest and allowed competing revenue-collection and trade-policing agencies to mushroom, while failing to establish clear lines of responsibility. Both of these policies led to a loss of political capital, as did the fact that most of the Nationalist government's antismuggling agencies were in fact engaging in smuggling themselves. Not even reviving previously discredited revenue collection methods like the Wartime Consumption Tax could compensate for the Nationalists' loss of control over China's most productive regions at a time of spiraling military expenditures. Because China's economy could not sustain the economic effort of a modern war, the Nationalists had to turn to deficit financing, which caused the onset of hyperinflation. By the end of the Second Sino-Japanese War, the Nationalist government was fiscally bankrupt and politically discredited.

111. Fung, *The Diplomacy of Imperial Retreat*, p. 8.

Nationalist fiscal policy might have recovered some stability, and the Maritime Customs might have gained a reprieve as a foreign-led institution with some—though diminished—administrative independence from the Nationalist hierarchy, had China's external trade recovered quickly in the immediate postwar years. In the absence of such a recovery, the demise of the Maritime Customs as an institution, owing to the Nationalists' loss of control over large parts of its revenue base as well as to growing hostility within the Guomindang toward the Maritime Customs as an institution in the orbit of foreign, mainly British, interests, heralded the collapse of Nationalist fiscal policy and the disintegration of the Nationalists' prewar polity. Fittingly, it was L. K. Little, the last foreign national to serve as inspector general, who provided the epitaph for the Maritime Customs, in a letter he wrote to Sir Frederick Maze when serving as commissioner of customs at Guangzhou. Little quoted the French consul general as having remarked to him in the course of a conversation, "Les douanes? Pouf! Les Chinois? Pouff!! [The Customs? Poof! The Chinese? Poof!]"[112] Little's reaction—"It took all my self-control not to say "Et les français? Pouff!! Pouff!! [And the French? Poof!! Poof!!]"—does him credit in retrospect and was certainly justified in 1935. By 1945, however, the unnamed French diplomat's judgments were true.

112. Maze Papers, SOAS, vol. 10, 1934–35, Little to Maze, 10 February 1935.

Conclusion

I n the final stages of the Second World War, postwar planning was a major preoccupation for all Allied combatant countries. Unlike the end of the war in Europe for the Western allies, though, the precise timing of the end of the Second Sino-Japanese War came as a surprise to large segments of the Chinese Nationalist government. Some postwar planning had begun in Chongqing amid the aerial bombings, long before there was any sign that the Japanese would surrender. The Maritime Customs, for example, proceeded along two different lines: considering what policy it should enforce in the postwar period, and what form the postwar Maritime Customs Service should take as an institution. Thus when the Japanese surrender was suddenly announced on 15 August 1945, the Nationalist government was surprised, but it was not entirely unprepared.

In the rush to return to the eastern seaboard after the departure of the Japanese, every government department had to fight for itself—often against other departments. First, civil servants, including customs employees, had to obtain transportation on military transport aircraft flying east to Nanjing and Shanghai. Contemporary descriptions of the scramble for seats suggest that if there was a central authority allocating passenger space—and it is unclear whether such an authority existed—its instructions were frequently ignored.[1] Second, in the case of the Maritime Customs, once customs officials had secured

1. Little Diaries, 4 September and 20 September 1945, Houghton Library.

transportation and returned to Shanghai, they had to retake possession of the Maritime Customs' property and reassert the service's role in policing trade. Nationalist troops in some instances proved to be every bit as difficult to dislodge as Japanese troops, sometimes more so.[2] That was one reason why the Ministry of Finance preferred to send Chinese employees to head the recovery teams.

Another reason was that the ministry and the Office of Customs Affairs seemed determined to use this opportunity to prevent the appointment of foreign customs commissioners in key ports.[3] In Shanghai, the port that had delivered the single greatest share of tariff revenue before the war, the government attempted to impose a blanket veto on all foreigners. Ding Guitang added the responsibilities of the Shanghai commissioner of customs to those he already held in his position as deputy inspector general, overseeing the recovery of Maritime Customs assets while based in Shanghai. Ding stated several times in semiofficial letters to the inspector general that, in his view, the eventual commissioner would have to be Chinese, so as to gain the greatest possible support for the recovery of the Maritime Customs' authority in Shanghai. When L. K. Little announced his intention to appoint Carl Neprud, an American, as the Shanghai commissioner, Ding protested against the appointment on the grounds that Neprud was not Chinese.[4] With regard to the appointment of a new commissioner of customs in Guangzhou, the Office of Customs Affairs stated very clearly that it would not accept a British national.[5] Thus, in the months following the end of hostilities in summer 1945, it became clear that, even in peacetime, the Maritime Customs would not be a foreign-dominated institution for much longer.

While the foreigners in the Maritime Customs were wondering how long their positions in China would last, the Nationalists continued to be criticized by the Chinese Communist Party for being beholden to their foreign backers. Once again we may turn to Mao

2. Little Papers, Ms. Am 1999.2, K. T. Ting to L. K. Little, 7 November 1945, Houghton Library.

3. Little Diaries, 20 August 1945, Houghton Library.

4. Little Papers, Ms. Am 1999.2, K. T. Ting to L. K. Little, 7 November 1945, Houghton Library.

5. Little Diaries, 13 November 1945, Houghton Library.

Dun's literary creation, the farmer Old Tung Pao, for a portrayal of the Communists' deeply negative attitude toward the Nationalist state. Given the author's affiliation with the Chinese Communist Party and his aim of discrediting the Guomindang, Old Tung Pao does not necessarily represent the broader popular Chinese view. However, Mao Dun sums up the contradiction inherent in the Nationalist state-building project, with its aim of creating a hybrid modernity that was modern, Western, and yet authentically Chinese.

> Five years before, in 1927, someone had told him: The new Kuomintang government says it wants to "throw out" the foreign devils. Old Tung Pao didn't believe it. He heard those propaganda speech-makers the Kuomintang sent when he went into the market town. Though they cried "throw out the foreign devils," they were dressed in Western style clothing. His guess was that they were secretly in league with the foreign devils, that they had been purposely sent to delude the countryfolk! Sure enough, the Kuomintang dropped the slogan not long after, and taxes and prices rose steadily. Old Tung Pao was firmly convinced that all this occurred as part of a government conspiracy with the foreign devils.[6]

Because of its associations with the West, Old Tung Pao does not believe that Nationalist modernity is authentic. Mao Dun singles out Guomindang economic and fiscal policies for particular condemnation. For him, they were an embodiment of the Nationalist government's rapacity, lack of interest in the economic effects of its policies, and absence of patriotic feeling. The last point was also made in an editorial in *Renmin ribao* (People's daily) on 2 July 1946, which criticized the Guomindang for "compromising China's integrity" by appointing foreigners to senior positions in the Maritime Customs in the postwar period.[7]

This critique was attractive to historians, who attempted to explain the collapse of the Nationalist regime and the rise to power of the Chinese Communist Party through the "inherent structural infirmities" of the Nationalists, "a military-authoritarian regime lacking a base in

6. Mao Dun, "Spring Silkworms," in *Spring Silkworms, and Other Stories*, pp. 5–6.
7. Cited in Chang, *Government, Imperialism and Nationalism*, p. 146.

society."[8] Douglas S. Paauw claimed as early as 1952 that the Nationalist government's major fiscal failure had been to wilfully sign over land tax revenue to the provinces and rely instead on the taxation of the modern sector of the Chinese economy.[9] Following Paauw's argument, Lloyd Eastman, in his seminal monograph *The Abortive Revolution*, summarized his indictment of the Guomindang's governance record by saying that "the Nationalists' insouciance in face of the problems of economic development was manifested clearly in the regime's taxation policies, which were both regressive and inelastic."[10] Eastman also argued that the 1935 currency reform was a mistake that led to hyperinflation.[11]

To determine whether these judgments are appropriate, we first have to clarify our understanding of the Nationalist party-state as a political organism. Many negative assessments imply that the Guomindang was a monolithic entity. In 2003, Joseph W. Esherick argued, however, that the Chinese Communist Party, rather than being "an organizational weapon of obedient apparatchiks commanded by the Party Centre," was a "social construct of considerable internal complexity."[12] Viewing the Chinese Communist Party as a "unified, disciplined historical agent," Esherick said, risked ignoring the fact that it was a "multi-layered social construct." To understand its history, historians needed to "deconstruct, not reify" the Communist party-state.[13] Esherick's research also raises more general questions about understanding party-states in modern China, and it makes sense to apply the same understanding to the Nationalists. Like the Chinese Communist Party, the Guomindang is better understood as an internally complex social construct, or a bureaucracy "fragmented into administrative blocks, responding to competing political leaders," in Margherita Zanasi's phrase.[14]

The Chinese Communist Party and its advocates, such as the writer Mao Dun, later the minister of culture of the People's Republic of

8. Eastman, *Seeds of Destruction*, p. 225.

9. Paauw, "Chinese National Expenditures during the Nanking Period," pp. 6–7.

10. Eastman, *The Abortive Revolution*, p. 235.

11. Eastman, *The Abortive Revolution*, p. 235.

12. Esherick, "Ten Theses on the Chinese Revolution," p. 52.

13. Esherick, "Ten Theses on the Chinese Revolution," p. 53.

14. Zanasi, *Saving the Nation*, p. 82.

China, seized on the tension between rejection and acceptance of Western modernity and used it to discredit the Nationalist state-building project. Guomindang tariff policy, besides providing government revenue, was also part of a Nationalist agenda to modernize China's political and administrative system and thus to strengthen Nationalist governance and increase the Guomindang's political legitimacy. This modernization was pursued at both the performative and the substantive levels; modern practices were adopted for the sake of appearing modern, as well as for their perceived utility. The Maritime Customs served the Guomindang as one of several conduits through which to introduce an administrative, technical, and visible Western modernity in China; as a source of revenue to finance technocratic, modernist Nationalist governance; and as a vehicle for projecting the Guomindang's claim to political legitimacy beyond the areas under Nationalist control.

While the Nationalists had sought to construct a hybrid modernity committed to Chinese authenticity but based on Western models, the Communists consciously sought to disprove the inevitability of Western modernity by replacing it with a different model of modernization. Nationalist governance emerged from the Second Sino-Japanese War entirely discredited, and the ultimate defeat of the Nationalist state in the Chinese Civil War (1946–49) brought a dramatic end to the Guomindang's project of creating a modern China on the Chinese mainland. For all the continuities between the Nationalist wartime state and the early People's Republic of China in terms of economic planning and state involvement in the economy more generally, 1949 marked a stark divide in modern Chinese history.

What does this mean for debates about the competence of Nationalist governance? I argue that Nationalist taxation and fiscal policy were successful in terms of revenue extraction and sustainability until the early stages of the Second Sino-Japanese War, when the Nationalists lost control over large parts of the modern economic sector on which their taxation system relied. The strength of the Nationalists' state building in the crucial area of taxation and fiscal policy challenges the contention that the Nationalist government was invariably incompetent, corrupt, and focused on short-term revenue extraction. I do not dispute the negative social impact of Nationalist tariff policy.

Fiscal stability and the ability to meet foreign financial obligations were achieved at the cost of economic and material hardships for large parts of the population. High import tariffs also had a political cost, by stimulating the growth of a secondary economy based on smuggled imported goods.

The earlier success of the Nationalists' tariff policy was predicated on their regaining China's tariff autonomy and achieving control of the Chinese Maritime Customs Service. In a changing foreign-policy environment, regaining tariff autonomy was the Nationalists' first major foreign-policy feat, accomplished in 1929. Furthermore, taking over the Maritime Customs fulfilled a long-standing ambition of Chinese nationalism. The Nationalist takeover of the Maritime Customs is best understood as a process that spanned the Nanjing decade as well as the years of the Second Sino-Japanese War and the Chinese Civil War. Sir Frederick Maze's support for the Nationalists' ambitions regarding the customs service reveals the difficulty of seeing the Maritime Customs as either a tool of imperialism or an ideal case of synarchy. A realistic perspective on the customs service needs to emphasize elements of cooperation while acknowledging that, to some extent, the Maritime Customs remained in the orbit of foreign interests.

The Nationalists' approach of fiscal realism—by which I refer to their decision to tolerate vestiges of informal empire in the revenue-collecting bureaucracy as well as their preference for high import tariffs, which increased central government revenue at the cost of stimulating smuggling—delivered fiscal stability until the beginning of the Second Sino-Japanese War. After the outbreak of war, Guomindang fiscal policy managed to preserve a degree of stability from 1937 until 1940, but the loss of eastern China by 1940 propelled Guomindang fiscal policy into eventual collapse, leading to hyperinflation in the late 1940s; not even the introduction of wartime fiscal instruments could reverse this trend.

The fiscal disintegration of the Nationalist state during the war was one of the chief causes of its loss of political legitimacy. That disintegration was the result of a tax structure that relied to a disproportionately high extent on one particular form of taxation: tariffs. There were good reasons for the Nationalists' reliance on tariff revenue given the fragmented nature of the Nationalist polity and the central government's need to reach a political and financial settlement with provincial governments over which it had no actual control. In relying heavily on indirect taxation and public debt before the beginning of the Second Sino-Japanese War, the Nationalists chose to use rational and legitimate financial tools rather than to revert to requisitions or irregular levies. In the end, however, the Guomindang's experience demonstrates that governments that disproportionately rely on one particular form of tax revenue are more vulnerable—not only fiscally but also politically—than those with diverse types of tax revenue.

Appendix 1: Custom Houses

T he following chart presents a list of the custom houses mentioned in this book, along with the romanization of each name as it appears in customs documents, the name in Chinese characters, the years of the custom house's initial operations, and the years when it operated under Chinese central government jurisdiction. (This is not a comprehensive list of all locations where Maritime Customs custom houses were present.) When Maritime Customs stations were referred to officially by a name other than the place name, that name is also given in parentheses, in the third column.

Pinyin name of custom house (present-day name in parenthesis)[a]	Romanization used in customs documents	Name in characters	Years of operation; period under central government control
Andong	Antung	安東	1907–32; 1947
Beihai	Pakhoi	北海	1877–1941; 1948
Changsha	Changsha	長沙	1904–45
Chongqing	Chungking	重慶	1891–1948
Dalian	Dairen	大連	1907–32; 1946
Fuzhou	Foochow	福州（閩海關）	1861–1948
Gongbeiguan	Lappa	拱北關	1887–1948
Guangzhou	Canton	廣州（粵海關）	1859–1941; 1946–48
Hangzhou	Hangchow	杭州	1896–1941
Hankou	Hankow	漢口（江漢關）	1862–1941; 1946–48
Haěrbin	Harbin	哈爾濱（濱江關）	1907–32
Hunchun	Lungchingtsun	琿春（龍井村）	1910–32
Jiangmen	Kongmoon	江門	1904–41; 1946–48
Jiujiang	Kiukiang	九江	1861–1939
Jiulong	Kowloon	九龍	1887–1941; 1946–1948
Longzhou	Lungkow	龍州	1889–1944; 1948
Mengzi (Kunming)	Mengtsz	蒙自（昆明）	1889–1948
Nanjing	Nanking	南京	1889–1938; 1946–48
Ningbo	Ningpo	寧波（浙海關）	1861–1941; 1946–48
Niuzhuang (Yingkou)	Newchang	牛莊（營口）	1864–1932; 1947
Qingdao (Jiaozhou)	Tsingtao (Kiaochow)	青島（膠州）（膠海關）	1899–1941; 1946–48
Qinhuangdao	Chinwangtao	秦皇島（山海關）	1931–41; 1946–48
Qiongzhou	Kiungchow	瓊州	1876–1941
Sanshui	Samshui	三水	1897–1941

Shanghai	上海（江海關）	1854–1941; 1946–48
Shantou	汕頭（潮海關）	1860–1941; 1946–48
Shashi	沙市	1896–1945
Suzhou	蘇州	1896–1941
Tianjin	天津（津海關）	1861–1941; 1946–48
Wanxian	萬縣	1943–45
Wenzhou	溫州（甌海關）	1877–1948
Wuhu	蕪湖	1877–1937
Wuzhou	梧州	1897–1946
Xiamen	廈門	1862–1941; 1946–48
Yichang	宜昌	1877–1941
Yuezhou (Yueyang)	岳州（岳陽）	1900–1933
Zhenjiang	鎮江	1861–1941
Zhifu (Yantai)	芝罘（煙台）（東海關）	1877–1941

Source: Adapted from Sun Xiufu, *Zhongguo jindai haiguan gaoji zhiguan nianbiao*, pp. 1–2.

[a] The Qingdao Customs House was originally located at Jiaozhou.

Appendix 2: Chinese and Japanese Names

This list provides the Chinese or Japanese characters for romanized names of individuals, places, and other entities as they appear in this volume. English translations are provided where applicable. Note: Where an alternate romanization exists for a person's name, that version appears in parenthesis after the characters.

Chinese Names

Bei Zuyi (貝祖詒; Tsuyee Pei)

Chen Bokang (陳柏康; Chan Pak Hong)

Chen Chi (陳熾)

Chen Hansheng (陳翰笙)

Chen Jingdeng (陳競澄)

Chen Jingkun (陳景琨)

Chen Jitang (陳濟棠)

Chen Xiafei (陳霞飛)

Chengling (城陵)

Dai Li (戴笠)

Ding Guitang (丁贵堂; K. T. Ting)

Duan Qirui (段祺瑞)

Fang Xianting (方顯廷; H. D. Fong)

Feng Yuxiang (馮玉祥)

Fu Bingchang (傅秉常)

Fuguo ce (富國策), "Strategy for enriching the country"

Fuguo yangmin ce (富國養民策), "Strategy to enrich the country and nourish the people"

Funü shenghuo (婦女生活), the journal *Women's Life*

Guan (管)

Guandong (關東)

Guanwu shu (關務署), Office of Customs Affairs in the Ministry of Finance

He Lian (何廉; Franklin Ho)

He Zhihui (河智慧)

Hu Huaishen (胡懷深)

Hu Sheng (胡繩)

Hu Yaoqing (胡耀卿; Hu Yu Ching)

Huang Guojie (黃國傑; Joseph K.C. Huang)

Huang Hanliang (黃漢樑)

Huang Qingxun (黃清潯)

Jia Shiyi (賈士毅)

Jiang Jieshi (蔣介石; Chiang Kai-shek)

Jisi shu (緝私署), Smuggling Prevention Bureau

Juntong (軍統), Nationalist Military Secret Service

Kong Xiangxi (孔祥熙; H.H. Kung)

Li Guiyong (李規庸)

Li Tang (李儻; Li Tong)

Liang Qichao (梁啟超)

Lu Bin (盧斌; Lu Ping)

Lu Xun (魯迅)

Luanxian (灤縣)

Ma Yinchu (馬寅初)

Mao Dun (茅盾)

Pencheng (俸城)

Qian Jiaju (千家駒)

Qianlong (乾隆)

Sanmin zhuyi (三民主義), Three Principles of the People

Shamian (沙面)

Shanghai shangye chuxu yinhang (上海商業儲蓄銀行), Shanghai Commercial Savings Bank

Shantou (汕頭)

Shen Shuyu (瀋叔玉)

Shenbao (申報), Shanghai News

Shijie zhishi (世界知識), the journal World Knowledge

Shiye jihua (實業計劃), Industrialization Plan

Shuijing zongtuan (稅警總團), the Tax Police

Shuiwu chu (稅務處), a board of taxation jointly responsible to the Ministry of Finance and the Ministry of Foreign Affairs

Song Ziwen (宋子文; T.V. Soong)

Sun Siyong (孫思永)

Sun Yat-sen (孫中山; Sun Zhongshan)

Tang'gu (塘沽), a place name; also refers to the Tang'gu Truce

Tangshan (唐山)

Wang Fengzao (汪風藻)

Wang Jingwei (汪精衛)

Wang Wenju (王文舉)

Wei Yuan (魏源)

Wu Chaogui (伍朝樞)

Wu Yaoqi (吳耀祺; Woo Yao-tchi)

Xiaodaohui (小刀會), Small Swords Society

Xue Fucheng (薛福成)

Xujiahui (徐家匯), the Xujiahui Observatory in Shanghai

Xukouzhuang (胥口庄)

Yan Xishan (閻錫山)

Yang Jingnian (楊敬年)

Yang Tingbao (楊廷寶)

Yao Dingxin (姚鼎新)

Yin Rugeng (殷汝耕)

Yonglining (永利寧), name of a chemical plant near Nanjing

Yongsheng (永生), the journal Everlasting Life

Yuan Shikai (袁世凱)

Zhang Fuyun (張福運)

Zhang Xueliang (張學良)

Zhanshi huoyun guanli ju (戰時貨運管理局), Wartime Goods Transport Management Bureau

Zhanshi xiaofeishui (戰時消費稅), the Wartime Consumption Tax

Zheng Lai (鄭萊)

Zheng Youkui (鄭友揆; Cheng Yu-kwei)

Zhongguo haiguan xuehui (中國海關學會), Chinese Maritime Customs Studies Association

Zhou Youbi (周友碧; Yau-Pik Chau)

Zhuankoushui (轉口稅), Interport Duty

Zongli Yamen (總理衙門), agency dealing with the foreign relations of the late Qing state

Japanese Names

Hamaguchi Osachi (濱口雄幸)

Kishimoto Hirokishi (岸本廣吉)

Baron Shidehara Kijūrō (幣原喜重郎)

Shigemitsu Mamoru (重光葵)

Baron Tanaka Giichi (田中義一)

Bibliography

Archival Materials

B. E. F. Hall diary, private collection
Bristol University Customs Collections, Bristol, UK
  B. E. F. Hall Papers
Bundesarchiv, Department R, German Reich Records 1871–1945, Berlin-Lichterfelde
  German Legation Peking/German Legation Nanking/German Embassy Nanking
  (R9208); materials since transferred to the Politisches Archiv des Auswärtigen Amts,
  Berlin
Hoover Institution Archives, Stanford, CA
  Arthur N. Young Papers
Houghton Library, Harvard University, Cambridge, MA
  Lester Knox Little Diaries, 82M-103
  Lester Knox Little Papers, Ms Am 1999
National Archives of the UK, Kew
  Foreign Office [FO]: Political Departments: General Correspondence from 1906–
  1966, FO 371
Queens University Library Special Collections, Queens University, Belfast
  Wright Collection (Official Correspondence), MS 16, hand list, n.d.
School of Oriental and African Studies [SOAS], London
  Sir Frederick Maze Papers, PP MS 2
Second Historical Archives of China [SHAC], Nanjing
  Inspectorate General of Maritime Customs Records, SHAC 679

Government Documents

Butler, Rohan, and J. P. T. Bury, eds. *Documents on British Foreign Policy, 1919–1939*
  [*DBFP*], 2nd ser., vol. 8: *Chinese Questions 1929–1931*. London: Her Majesty's Stationery Office, 1960.

Butler, Rohan, and Douglas Dakin, eds. *Documents on British Foreign Policy, 1919–1939*, 2nd ser., vol. 9: *The Far Eastern Crisis 1931–1932*. London: Her Majesty's Stationery Office, 1965.

Inspectorate General of Customs (Haiguan zongshuiwusi shu 海關總稅務司署). *Code of Customs Regulations and Procedure: Third Edition, Revised and Enlarged (1st July 1937)*. Shanghai: Statistical Department of the Inspectorate General of Customs, 1937.

———. *Decennial Reports on the Trade, Industries, etc., of the Ports Open to Foreign Commerce, and on Conditions and Development of the Treaty Port Provinces; Preceded by "A History of the External Trade of China, 1834–81," Together with a "Synopsis of the External Trade of China, 1882–1931,"* 5th issue: *1922–1931*. 2 vols. Shanghai: Statistical Department of the Inspectorate General of Customs, 1933.

———. *Documents Illustrative of the Origin, Development and Activities of the Chinese Customs Service*. 7 vols. Shanghai: Statistical Department of the Inspectorate General of Customs, 1937–39.

———. *The Trade of China*. Published annually for 1932–1940, 1946. Shanghai: Statistical Department of the Inspectorate General of Customs, 1933–47.

Ministry of Industry. *Statistics of China's Foreign Trade by Ports*. See Shiye bu guoji maoyi ju, ed. *Zuijin sanshisi nian lai Zhongguo tongshang kou'an duiwai maoyi tongji*.

Ministry of Information, Republic of China. *China Handbook, 1937–1945: A Comprehensive Survey of Major Developments in China in Eight Years of War*. New York: Macmillan, 1947.

Rehn, Olli. Letter from Vice President Olli Rehn to ECOFIN (Economic and Financial Affairs Council) Ministers, 13 February 2013, ARES (2013) 185796, http://ec.europa.eu/commission_2010-2014/rehn/documents/cab20130213_en.pdf, accessed 14 October 2014.

Shiye bu guoji maoyi ju 實業部國際貿易局 (Bureau of Foreign Trade, Ministry of Industry), ed. *Zuijin sanshisi nian lai Zhongguo tongshang kou'an duiwai maoyi tongji: Yi, zhongbu* 最近三十四年來中國通商口岸對貿易統計：一，中部 (Statistics of China's foreign trade by ports, 1900–1933, part 1: Central China ports) [cited as Ministry of Industry, *Statistics of China's Foreign Trade by Ports*]. Shanghai: Shangwu yinshuguan, 1935.

Trotter, Ann, ed. *British Documents on Foreign Affairs: Reports and Papers from the Foreign Office Confidential Print, Part 2: From the First to the Second World War,* Series E, Asia, 1914–39 [*BDFA*]. Bethesda, MD: University Publications of America, 1991–1997. See vols. 19, 20, 31, 34, 36, 39, and 44.

US House Budget Committee. "The Path to Prosperity: A Blueprint for American Renewal." Fiscal Year 2013 Budget Resolution prepared by the US House Budget Committee under Chairman Paul Ryan of Wisconsin, http://budget.house.gov/uploaded files/pathtoprosperity2013.pdf, accessed 13 October 2014.

US Department of State. *Foreign Relations of the United States: Diplomatic Papers* [*FRUS*]. Washington, DC: US Government Printing Office, 1956–67. See vols. 1924 (vol. 1), 1925 (vol. 1), 1926 (vol. 1), 1927 (vol. 2), 1928 (vol. 2), 1942 (China), 1943 (China).

Zhongguo Guomindang zhongyang weiyuanhui, dangshi weiyuanhui 中國國民黨中央委員會，黨史委員會(Commission for Party History, Central Committee of the Guomindang), ed. *Xian zongtong Jiang gong sixiang yanlun zongji* 先總統蔣公思想

言論總集 (Complete collection of the ideas, speeches, and writings of the late president Chiang Kai-shek). Taibei, 1985.

Zhongyang dang'anguan, Zhongguo di'er lishi dang'anguan, Jilin sheng shehui kexueyuan 中央档案馆，中国第二历史档案馆，吉林省社会科学院 (Central Committee Archives, Second Historical Archives of China, and Jilin Province Academy of Social Sciences), eds. *Huabei jingji lüeduo* 华北经济掠夺 (Economic aggression in Northern China). Beijing, 2004.

Other Publications

Aitchison, Jean. "The Chinese Maritime Customs Service in the Transition from the Ch'ing to the Nationalist Era: An Examination of the Relationship between a Western-Style Fiscal Institution and the Chinese Government in the Period before the Manchurian Incident." PhD diss., School of Oriental and African Studies, University of London, 1983.

Akita, Shigeru. *Imperialism and Global History*. London: Palgrave Macmillan, 2002.

Ardant, Gabriel. "Financial Policy and Economic Infrastructure of Modern States and Nations." In *The Formation of National States in Western Europe*, edited by Charles Tilly, pp. 164–242. Princeton, NJ: Princeton University Press, 1975.

Asker, Gustaf. "China Memories: Some Memories from 36 Years of Service as an Official in China, Translated from the Swedish by Author's Daughter [*sic*]." Translated by Caroline Asker Newman. Unpublished manuscript. Bristol, UK: Bristol University Customs Collections.

Atkins, Martyn. *Informal Empire in Crisis: The Chinese Customs Succession 1927–1929*. Ithaca, NY: Cornell University East Asia Program, 1995.

Barrett, David P. "The Wang Jingwei Regime, 1940–1945: Continuities and Disjunctures with Nationalist China." In *Chinese Collaboration with Japan, 1932–1945: The Limits of Accommodation*, edited by David P. Barrett and Larry N. Shyu, pp. 102–15. Stanford, CA: Stanford University Press, 2001.

Barrett, David P., and Larry N. Shyu, eds. *Chinese Collaboration with Japan, 1932–1945: The Limits of Accommodation*. Stanford, CA: Stanford University Press, 2001.

Baumler, Alan. "Opium Control versus Opium Suppression: The Origins of the 1935 Six-Year Plan to Eliminate Opium and Drugs." In *Opium Regimes: China, Britain and Japan*, edited by Timothy Brook and Bob Tadashi Wakabayashi, pp. 270–91. Berkeley: University of California Press, 2000.

Bergère, Marie-Claire. *Sun Yat-sen*. Translated by Janet Lloyd. Stanford, CA: Stanford University Press, 1998.

Bian, Morris. "How Crisis Shapes Change: New Perspectives on China's Political Economy during the Sino-Japanese War, 1937–1945." *History Compass* 5, no. 4 (June 2007): 1091–1100.

Bickers, Robert. "The American IG: L. K. Little and the End of the Foreign Inspectorate, 1943–1950." Unpublished manuscript, 2007.

———. *Britain in China: Community, Culture and Colonialism, 1900–1949*. Manchester, UK: Manchester University Press, 1999.

———. "The Chinese Maritime Customs at War, 1941–1945." *Journal of Imperial and Commonwealth History* 36, no. 2 (June 2008): 295–311.

———. *Empire Made Me: An Englishman Adrift in Shanghai*. London: Allen Lane, 2003.

———. "Revisiting the Chinese Maritime Customs Service, 1854–1950." *Journal of Imperial and Commonwealth History* 36, no. 2 (June 2008): 221–26.

———. *The Scramble for China: Foreign Devils in the Qing Empire, 1832–1914*. London: Allen Lane, 2011.

Bisson, T. A. *Japan in China*. New York: Macmillan, 1938.

Bodenhorn, Terry, ed. *Defining Modernity: Guomindang Rhetorics of a New China, 1920–1970*. Ann Arbor: Center for Chinese Studies, University of Michigan, 2002.

Boecking, Felix. "Unmaking the Chinese Nationalist State: Administrative Reform among Fiscal Collapse, 1937–1945." *Modern Asian Studies* 45, no. 2 (2011): 277–301.

Borg, Dorothy. *The U.S. and the Far Eastern Crisis of 1933–1938*. Cambridge, MA: Harvard University Press, 1964.

Brandt, Loren. *Commercialization and Agricultural Development: Central and Eastern China, 1870–1937*. Cambridge: Cambridge University Press, 1989.

Braun, Rudolf. "Taxation, Sociopolitical Structure, and State-Building: Great Britain and Brandenburg-Prussia." In *The Formation of National States in Western Europe*, edited by Charles Tilly, pp. 243–327. Princeton, NJ: Princeton University Press, 1975.

Bray, Francesca. "Agriculture." In *Science and Civilization in China*, vol. 6: *Biology and Biological Technology*, edited by Joseph Needham. Part 2. Cambridge: Cambridge University Press, 1984.

Brewer, John. *The Sinews of Power: War, Money, and the English State, 1688–1783*. London: Unwin Hyman, 1989.

Brodie, Patrick. *Crescent over Cathay: China and ICI, 1898 to 1956*. Hong Kong: Oxford University Press, 1990.

Brook, Timothy. *The Chinese State in Ming Society*. London: Routledge Curzon, 2005.

Brook, Timothy, and Bob Tadashi Wakabayashi, eds. *Opium Regimes: China, Britain and Japan, 1839–1952*. Berkeley: University of California Press, 2000.

Brunero, Donna. *Britain's Imperial Cornerstone in China: The Chinese Maritime Customs Service 1854–1949*. London: Routledge, 2006.

Buck, John Lossing. *Land Utilization in China: A Study of 16,786 Farms in 168 Localities, and 38,256 Families in Twenty-two Provinces in China, 1929–1933*. New York: Paragon, 1964.

Byrne, Eugene. "The Dismissal of Sir Francis Aglen as Inspector-General of the Chinese Maritime Customs Service, 1927." University of Leeds, Department of East Asian Studies, Occasional Papers, No. 30, 1995.

Cain, P. J., and A. G. Hopkins, eds. *British Imperialism 1688–2000*. Harlow, UK: Longman, 2001.

Casalin, Federica. *L'introduzione del pensiero economico occidentale in Cina e il suo impatto sulla formazione del lessico cinese moderno (1818–1898)*. Rome: Edizione Nuova Cultura, 2006.

Chan, Wellington. *Merchants, Mandarins, and Modern Enterprise in Late Ch'ing China*. Cambridge, MA: East Asian Research Center, Harvard University, 1977.

Chang, Chihyun. *Government, Imperialism and Nationalism in China: The Maritime Customs Service and its Chinese Staff.* London: Routledge, 2013.

Chau, Yau-Pik 周友碧 (Zhou Youbi). "The Taxation Reforms of the Chinese National Government in the Decade 1927–1937." PhD diss., University of Chicago, 1945.

Chen Chi 陳熾. *Yong shu* 庸書 (Everyday record).Taibei: Tailian guofeng chubanshe, 1970. (Photoreprint of original 1890 ed.)

Ch'en, Han-sheng. *Agrarian Problems in Southernmost China.* Shanghai: Kelly and Walsh for Lingnan University, 1936.

Ch'en, Jerome. *State Economic Policies of the Ch'ing Government 1840–1895.* New York: Garland, 1980.

Chen Shiqi 陈诗启. *Zhongguo jindai haiguanshi* 中国近代海关史 (History of the modern Chinese customs service). Beijing: Renmin chubanshe, 1997.

Chen Xiafei 陈霞飞, ed. *Zhongguo haiguan midang—Hede, Jin Deng'gan handian huibian* 中国海关密档—赫德，金登干函电汇编 (Confidential archives of the Chinese Maritime Customs—The Hart-Campbell letters and telegrams). Beijing: Zhonghua shuju, 1990.

Chen Xiafei, and Han Rongfang, eds. *Archives of China's Imperial Maritime Customs—Confidential Correspondence between Robert Hart and James Duncan Campbell, 1874–1907.* Beijing: Foreign Languages Press, 1990.

Cheng, Linsun. *Banking in Modern China: Entrepreneurs, Professional Managers, and the Development of Chinese Banks, 1897–1937.* Cambridge: Cambridge University Press, 2003.

Cheng Linsun 程麟荪, ed. *Zhang Fuyun yu jindai Zhongguo haiguan* 张福运与近代中国海关 (Zhang Fuyun and the modern Chinese customs). Shanghai: Shanghai shehui kexueyuan chubanshe, 2007.

———. "Zhang Fuyun yu jindai Zhongguo haiguan xingzheng guanli gaige" 张福运与近代中国海关行政管理改革 (Zhang Fuyun and the administrative reform of the modern Chinese customs) pp. 28-35. In Cheng Linsun, *Zhang Fuyun yu jindai Zhongguo haiguan.* Shanghai: Shanghai shehui kexueyuan chubanshe, 2007.

Cheng, Pei-kai, Michael Lestz, and Jonathan Spence, eds. *The Search for Modern China: A Documentary Collection.* New York: Norton, 1999.

Cheng, Yu-Kwei. *Foreign Trade and Industrial Development of China: An Historical and Integrated Analysis through 1948.* Washington, DC: University Press of Washington, DC, 1956.

Chiang, Kai-shek. *China's Destiny and Chinese Economic Theory.* Translated and edited by Philip Jaffe. New York: Roy Publishers, 1947.

———. *Geming dangyuan banshi de jingshen he fangfa* 革命黨員辦事的精神和方法 (The spirit and methods in which party members ought to undertake matters). 17 August 1925, pp. 172-77. In Zhongguo Guomindang zhongyang weiyuanhui, dangshi weiyuanhui 中國國民黨中央委員會，黨史委員會 (Commission for Party History, Central Committee of the Guomindang), *Xian zongtong Jiang gong sixiang yanlun zongji* 先總統蔣公思想言論總集, vol. 10. Taibei, 1985.

———. Kexue de daoli: Yuanming kexue jingshen yu kexue fangfa 科學的道理－原名科學精神與科學方法 (The truth of science: Originally: Scientific spirit and methods), 28 January 1935, pp. 13-31. In Zhongguo Guomindang zhongyang weiyuanhui, dangshi weiyuanhui 中國國民黨中央委員會，黨史委員會 (Commission for Party History, Central Committee of the Guomindang), *Xian zongtong Jiang gong sixiang yanlun zongji* 先總統蔣公思想言論總集, vol. 13.

Ch'ien, Tuan-sheng. *The Government and Politics of China, 1912–1949*. Stanford, CA: Stanford University Press, 1970.

Clifford, Nicholas R. "Britain, America and the Far East, 1937–1940: A Failure in Co-operation." *Journal of British Studies* 3, no. 1 (Nov. 1963): 137–54.

———. "Sir Frederick Maze and the CMC, 1937–1941." *Journal of Modern History* 37, no. 1 (Mar. 1965): 18–34.

Coble, Parks M., Jr. *Facing Japan: Chinese Politics and Japanese Imperialism, 1931–1937*. Cambridge, MA: Harvard University Press, 1991.

———. *The Shanghai Capitalists and the Nationalist Government, 1927–1937*. Cambridge, MA: Council on East Asian Studies, Harvard University, 1986.

Cochran, Sherman. *Big Business in China: Sino-Foreign Rivalry in the Cigarette Industry, 1890–1930*. Cambridge, MA: Harvard University Press, 1980.

———. *Encountering Chinese Networks: Western, Japanese, and Chinese Corporations in China, 1880–1937*. Berkeley: University of California Press, 2000.

Cochran, Sherman, and Andrew C. K. Hsieh, with Janis Cochran, trans. and eds. *One Day in China: May 21, 1936*. New Haven, CT: Yale University Press, 1983.

Cohen, Paul A. "Reflections on a Watershed Date: The 1949 Divide in Chinese History." In *Twentieth Century China: New Approaches*, edited by Jeffrey N. Wasserstrom, pp. 27–36. London: Routledge, 2003.

Cohen, Paul A., and Merle Goldman, eds. *Fairbank Remembered*. Cambridge, MA: John K. Fairbank Center for East Asian Research, Harvard University, 1992.

Crespo, Horacio. "Trade Regimes and the International Sugar Market, 1850–1980: Protectionism, Subsidies and Regulation." In *From Silver to Cocaine: Latin American Commodity Chains and the Building of the World Economy, 1500–2000*, edited by Stephen Topik, Carlos Marichal, and Zephyr L. Frank, pp. 147–73. Durham, NC: Duke University Press, 2006.

Crisp, Olga. *Studies in the Russian Economy before 1914*. London: Macmillan, 1976.

Dai Yifeng 戴一峰. *Jindai Zhongguo haiguan yu Zhongguo caizheng* 近代中国海关与中国财政 (The modern Chinese customs service and China's fiscal affairs). Xiamen: Xiamen daxue chubanshe, 1993.

Davies, R. W. *Soviet Economic Development from Lenin to Khrushchev*. Cambridge: Cambridge University Press, 1998.

Dikötter, Frank. *The Discourse of Race in Modern China*. London: Hurst, 1992.

———. *Things Modern: Material Culture and Everyday Life in China*. London: Hurst, 2007.

Domes, Jürgen. *Vertagte Revolution: Die Politik der Kuomintang in China, 1923–1937*. Berlin: Walter de Gruyter, 1969.

Drea, Edward. *Japan's Imperial Army: Its Rise and Fall, 1853–1945*. Lawrence: University Press of Kansas, 2009.

Eastman, Lloyd E. *The Abortive Revolution: China under Nationalist Rule, 1927–1937*. Cambridge, MA: Council on East Asian Studies, Harvard University, 1990. First published in 1974.

———. "Facets of an Ambivalent Relationship: Smuggling, Puppets and Atrocities during the War, 1937–1945." In *The Chinese and the Japanese: Essays in Political and Cultural Interactions*, edited by Akira Iriye, pp. 275–303. Princeton, NJ: Princeton University Press, 1980.

———. *Seeds of Destruction: Nationalist China in War and Revolution, 1937–1945*. Stanford, CA: Stanford University Press, 1984.

Eberhard-Bréard, Andrea. "Robert Hart and China's Statistical Revolution." *Modern Asian Studies* 40, no. 3 (2006): 605–29.

Edkins, Joseph, trans. *Fuguo yangmin ce* 富國養民策 (Strategy to enrich the country and nourish the people). Shanghai: Inspectorate General of Customs, 1886.

Epstein, Israel. *The People's War*. London: Victor Gollancz, 1939.

Esherick, Joseph W., ed. *Remaking the Chinese City: Modernity and National Identity, 1900–1950*. Honolulu: University of Hawai'i Press, 2000.

———. "Ten Theses on the Chinese Revolution." In *Twentieth Century China: New Approaches*, edited by Jeffrey N. Wasserstrom, pp. 37–65. London: Routledge, 2003.

Evans, Peter B., Dietrich Rueschemeyer, and Theda Skocpol, eds. *Bringing the State Back In*. Cambridge: Cambridge University Press, 1985.

Fairbank, John K., ed. *The Cambridge History of China*, vol. 12. Cambridge: Cambridge University Press, 1983.

———, ed. *Chinese Thought and Institutions*. Chicago: University of Chicago Press, 1957.

———. "Synarchy under the Treaties." In *Chinese Thought and Institutions*, edited by John K. Fairbank, pp. 204–31. Chicago: University of Chicago Press, 1957.

Fairbank, John K., Katherine Frost Bruner, and Elizabeth MacLeod Matheson, eds. *The I.G. in Peking: Letters of Robert Hart, Chinese Maritime Customs, 1868–1907*, vol. 1. Cambridge, MA: Belknap Press of Harvard University Press, 1975.

Fairbank, John K., and Albert Feuerwerker, eds. *The Cambridge History of China*, vol. 13. Cambridge: Cambridge University Press, 1986.

Farooqui, Amar. *Smuggling as Subversion: Colonialism, Indian Merchants and the Politics of Opium*. New Delhi: New Age Publishers, 1998.

Faure, David. "The Plight of the Farmers: A Study of the Rural Economy of Jiangnan and the Pearl River Delta, 1879–1937." *Modern China* 11, no. 1 (Jan. 1985): 3–37.

———. *The Rural Economy of Pre-Liberation China: Trade Expansion and Peasant Livelihood in Jiangsu and Guangdong, 1870–1937*. Hong Kong: Oxford University Press, 1989.

Fawcett, Henry. *A Manual of Political Economy*. London: Macmillan, 1863.

Fenby, Jonathan. *The Generalissimo: Ch'iang Kai-shek and the China He Lost*. London: Free Press, 2003.

Feuerwerker, Albert. *The Chinese Economy, 1870–1949*. Ann Arbor: Center for Chinese Studies, University of Michigan, 1995.

———. *The Chinese Economy, 1912–1949*. Ann Arbor: Center for Chinese Studies, University of Michigan, 1968.

———. "Economic Trends in China, 1912–1949." In *The Cambridge History of China*, vol. 12, edited by John K. Fairbank, pp. 28–127. Cambridge: Cambridge University Press, 1983.

Fitzgerald, John. *Awakening China: Politics, Culture and Class in the Chinese Revolution*. Stanford, CA: Stanford University Press, 1996.

———. "Increased Disunity: The Politics and Finance of Guangdong Separatism, 1926–1936." *Modern Asian Studies* 24, no. 4 (1990): 745–75.

Floud, Roderick, and Paul Johnson, eds. *The Cambridge Economic History of Modern Britain*, vol. 3: *Structural Change and Growth, 1939–2000*. Cambridge: Cambridge University Press, 2004.

Fong, H. D. (Fang Hsien-t'ing). "The Prospect for China's Industrialization." *Pacific Affairs* 15, no. 1 (Mar. 1942): 44–60.

———. *Reminiscences of a Chinese Economist at 70*. Singapore: South Seas Press, 1975.

Fox, Josephine. "Common Sense in Shanghai: The Shanghai General Chamber of Commerce and Political Legitimacy in Republican China." *History Workshop Journal* 50 (2000): 22–44.

Freyn, Hubert. *Free China's New Deal*. New York: Macmillan, 1943.

Fuess, Harald, ed. *The Japanese Empire in East Asia and Its Postwar Legacy*. Munich: Iudicium, 1998.

Fung, Edmund S. K. *The Diplomacy of Imperial Retreat: Britain's South China Policy, 1924–1931*. Hong Kong: Oxford University Press, 1991.

Gamble, Sidney D. *North China Villages: Social, Political and Economic Activities before 1933*. Berkeley: University of California Press, 1963.

———. *Ting Hsien: A North China Rural Community*. Stanford, CA: Stanford University Press, 1968.

George, Henry. *Progress and Poverty*. London: C. Kegan Paul, 1881.

Gerth, Karl. *China Made: Consumer Culture and the Creation of the Nation*. Cambridge, MA: Harvard University Asia Center, 2003.

———. "Consumption as Resistance: The National Products Movement and Anti-Japanese Boycotts in Modern China," pp. 119–42. In *The Japanese Empire in East Asia and Its Postwar Legacy*, edited by Harald Fuess. Munich: Iudicium, 1998.

Halsey, Stephen R. "Money, Power, and the State: The Origins of the Military-Fiscal State in Modern China." *Journal of the Economic and Social History of the Orient* 56, no. 3 (2013): 392–432.

———. "State Formation and European Imperialism in Late Qing and Republican China: The Development of the Shanghai Region, 1842–1937." PhD diss., University of Chicago, 2007.

Hanson, Haldore. "Smuggler, Soldier and Diplomat." *Pacific Affairs* 9, no. 4 (Dec. 1936): 544–56.

Harley, C. Knick. "Trade, 1870–1939: From Globalisation to Fragmentation." In *The Cambridge Economic History of Modern Britain*, vol. 2: *Economic Maturity, 1860–1939*, edited by Roderick Floud and Paul Johnson, pp. 161–89. Cambridge: Cambridge University Press, 2004.

Harrison, Henrietta. *The Making of the Republican Citizen: Political Ceremonies and Symbols in China, 1911–1929*. Oxford: Oxford University Press, 2000.

He Changling 賀長齡, ed. *Huangchao jingshi wenbian* 皇朝經世文編 (Collected writings on the statecraft of the reigning dynasty), vol. 3. N.p., 1827.

He, Wenkai. *Paths toward the Modern Fiscal State: England, Japan, and China.* Cambridge, MA: Harvard University Press, 2013.

Henderson, W. O. *Friedrich List: Economist and Visionary.* London: Frank Cass, 1983.

Heriot, T. H. P. *The Manufacture of Sugar from the Cane and Beet.* London: Longmans, Green, 1920.

Herndon, Thomas, Michael Ash, and Robert Pollin. "Does High Public Debt Consistently Stifle Economic Growth? A Critique of Reinhart and Rogoff." Political Economy Research Institute, University of Massachusetts Amherst, Working Paper Series, No. 322, 2013.

Hevia, James L. *English Lessons: The Pedagogy of Imperialism in Nineteenth-Century China.* Durham, NC: Duke University Press, 2003.

Hicks, John. *A Theory of Economic History.* Oxford: Clarendon Press, 1969.

Hill, Emily M. *Smokeless Sugar: The Death of a Provincial Bureaucrat and the Construction of China's National Economy.* Vancouver: UBC Press, 2010.

Hobart, Alice Tisdale. *Oil for the Lamps of China.* Indianapolis: Bobbs-Merrill, 1933.

Holtfrerich, Carl-Ludwig. "Government Debt in Economic Thought of the Long 19th Century." School of Business and Economics, Discussion Paper: Economics, Freie Universität Berlin, 2013/14.

Hopkins, A. G., ed. *Globalization in World History.* London: Pimlico, 2002.

Horesh, Niv. "'Many a Long Day': HSBC and Its Note Issue in Republican China, 1912–1935." *Enterprise and Society* 9, no. 1 (2008): 6–43.

Hou, Chi-ming. *Foreign Investment and Economic Development in China, 1840–1937.* Cambridge, MA: Harvard University Press, 1965.

Howlett, Peter. "The War-time Economy, 1939–1945." In *The Cambridge Economic History of Modern Britain,* vol. 3: *Structural Change and Growth, 1939–2000,* edited by Roderick Floud and Paul Johnson, pp. 1–26. Cambridge: Cambridge University Press, 2004.

Hsiao, Liang-lin. *China's Foreign Trade Statistics, 1864–1949.* Cambridge, MA: East Asian Research Center, Harvard University, 1974.

Hsiung, James, and Stephen Levine, eds. *China's Bitter Victory: The War with Japan.* Armonk: M. E. Sharpe, 1992.

Hu, Huaishen. "Foreign Economic Domination in China." *Pacific Affairs* 2, no. 11 (Nov. 1929): 707–14. Translated from *Eastern Miscellany.*

Hu Sheng. *Imperialism and Chinese Politics.* Beijing: Foreign Languages Press, 1981.

Huang, Philip C. C. "'Public Sphere'/ 'Civil Society' in China? The Third Realm between State and Society." *Modern China* 19, no. 2 (Apr. 1993): 216–40.

Huang Qingxun 黃清潯. *Haiguan suiyue: Wode zongshen zhiye* 海關歲月: 我的終身職業 (Years in the Customs: My life's work). Taibei: N.p., 2001.

Huang, Ray. "The Grand Canal during the Ming Dynasty 1368–1644." PhD diss., University of Michigan, 1964.

Inlow, Burke. "Japan's 'Special Trade' in North China, 1935–1937." *Far Eastern Quarterly* 6, no. 2 (Feb. 1947): 139–67.

Iriye, Akira. *After Imperialism: The Search for a New Order in the Pacific 1921–1931.* Cambridge, MA: Harvard University Press, 1965.

———. *The Chinese and the Japanese: Essays in Political and Cultural Interactions.* Princeton, NJ: Princeton University Press, 1980.

———. "Japanese Aggression and China's International Position." In *The Cambridge History of China,* vol. 13, edited by John K. Fairbank and Albert Feuerwerker, pp. 492–546. Cambridge: Cambridge University Press, 1986.

Irwin, Douglas. *Against the Tide: An Intellectual History of Free Trade.* Princeton, NJ: Princeton University Press, 1996.

Jevons, William Stanley. *Political Economy.* London: Macmillan, 1870.

Jia Shiyi 賈士毅. *Guanshui yu guoquan* 關稅與國權 (Tariff autonomy and sovereignty). Shanghai: Shangwu yinshuguan, 1925.

Jindaishi yanjiusuo shehui jingji shi zu 近代史研究所社会经济史组 (Section for Social and Economic History, Institute of Modern History). *Caizheng yu jindai lishi* 财政与近代历史 (Finance and modern history). Taibei: Zhongyang yanjiuyuan jindaishi yanjiusuo, 1999.

Jordan, Donald. *Chinese Boycotts versus Japanese Bombs.* Ann Arbor: University of Michigan Press, 1991.

Keegan, John. *War and Our World: The Reith Lectures 1998.* London: Pimlico, 1998.

Kibata, Yoichi. "Reasserting Imperial Power? Britain and East Asia in the 1930s." In *Gentlemanly Capitalism, Imperialism and Global History,* edited by Shigeru Akita, pp. 169–84. London: Palgrave Macmillan, 2002.

King, Frank H. H. "The Boxer Indemnity: 'Nothing but Bad.'" *Modern Asian Studies* 40, no. 3 (July 2006): 663–89.

———. *A Concise Economic History of Modern China 1840–1961.* New York: Praeger, 1969.

———. *The History of the Hongkong and Shanghai Banking Corporation,* vol. 1: *The Hongkong Bank in Late Imperial China, 1864–1902: On an Even Keel.* Cambridge: Cambridge University Press, 1987.

———. *The History of the Hongkong and Shanghai Banking Corporation,* vol. 3: *The Hongkong Bank between the Wars and the Bank Interned, 1919–1945: Return from Grandeur.* Cambridge: Cambridge University Press, 1988.

King, Paul. *In the Chinese Customs Service: A Personal Record of Forty-Seven Years.* London: T. Fisher Unwin, 1924.

Kirby, William C. "The Chinese War Economy." In *China's Bitter Victory: The War with Japan,* edited by James Hsiung and Stephen Levine, pp. 185–212. Armonk, NY: M. E. Sharpe, 1992.

———. "Continuity and Change in Modern China: Economic Planning on the Mainland and in Taiwan." *Australian Journal of Chinese Affairs,* no. 24 (July 1990): 121–41.

———. "Developmental Aid or Neo-Imperialism? German Industry in China, 1928–1937." In *Die Deutsche Beraterschaft in China, 1927–1938: Militär- Wirtschaft- Aussenpolitik,* edited by Bernd Martin, pp. 201–215. Düsseldorf: Droste, 1981.

———. "Engineering China: Birth of the Developmental State, 1928–1937." In *Becoming Chinese: Passages to Modernity and Beyond,* edited by Wen-hsin Yeh, pp. 137–60. Berkeley: University of California Press, 2000.

———. *Germany and Republican China.* Stanford, CA: Stanford University Press, 1984.

———. "The Internationalization of China: Foreign Relations at Home and Abroad in the Republican Era." *China Quarterly,* no. 150 (June 1997): 433–58.

Kitson, Michael, and Solomos Solomou. *Protectionism and Economic Revival: The British Inter-war Economy.* Cambridge: Cambridge University Press, 1990.

Kong Xiangxi 孔祥熙, "Caizhengbu niju 1934 niandu ji heqi yihou caizheng qingkuang baogao," 财政部拟具1934年度及核期以后财政情况报告 (Draft report on the year 1934 and appraisal of the fiscal situation thereafter), 1 August 1936. In Zhongguo Di'er Lishi Dang'anguan 中国第二历史档案馆 (Second Historical Archives of China), eds. Zhonghua Minguo dang'an ziliao huibian 中华民国史档案资料汇编 (Collection of archival material on Republican history), 第五辑 第一编，财政经济（一）, Part 5/1, Finance and Economics (1). Nanjing: Jiangsi guji chubanshe, n.d.

Kuhn, Philip. *The Origins of the Modern Chinese State.* Stanford, CA: Stanford University Press, 2002.

Ladds, Catherine. *Empire Careers: Working for the Chinese Maritime Customs Service, 1854–1949.* Manchester, UK: Manchester University Press, 2013.

———. "'In the Chinese Customs Service': Foreign Careers in the Customs, 1854–1950." PhD diss., University of Bristol, 2007.

Lee, Bradford A. *Britain and the Sino-Japanese War, 1937–1939: A Study in the Dilemmas of British Decline.* Stanford, CA: Stanford University Press, 1973.

Leonard, Jane Kate, and John R. Watts, eds. *To Achieve Security and Wealth: The Qing Imperial State and the Economy, 1644–1911.* Ithaca, NY: Cornell East Asia Program, 1992.

Levenson, Joseph. *Confucian China and Its Modern Fate,* vol.1: *The Problem of Intellectual Continuity.* Berkeley: University of California Press, 1958.

Li Maosheng 李茂盛. *Kong Xiangxi zhuan* 孔祥熙传 (A biography of Kong Xiangxi). Beijing: Zhongguo guangbo dianshi chubanshe, 1992.

Lian Xinhao 连心豪. *Zhongguo haiguan yu duiwai maoyi* 中国海关与对外贸易 (Chinese customs and foreign trade). Changsha: Yuelu chubanshe, 2004.

Liepman, Heinrich. *Tariff Levels and the Economic Unity of Europe.* London: George Allen & Unwin, 1938.

Liesner, Thelma, ed. *One Hundred Years of Economic Statistics: United Kingdom, United States of America, Australia, Canada, France, Germany, Italy, Japan, Sweden.* London, Economist Publications, 1989.

Lin, Alfred H. Y. "Building and Funding a Warlord Regime: The Experience of Chen Jitang in Guangdong, 1929–1936." *Modern China* 28, no. 2 (Apr. 2002): 177–212.

Lin, Man-houng. *China Upside Down: Currencies, Society, and Ideologies 1808–1856.* Cambridge, MA: Harvard University Asia Center, 2006.

Lin Meili 林美莉. *Kangzhan shiqi de huobi zhanzheng* 抗戰時期的貨幣戰爭 (Currency warfare during the War of Resistance against Japan). Taibei: Guoli Taiwan shifan daxue lishi yanjiusuo, 1996.

———. *Xiyang shuizhi zai jindai Zhongguo de fazhan* 西洋稅制在近代中國的發展 (The development of modern taxation systems in modern China). Taibei: Zhongyang yanjiuyuan jindaishi yanjiusuo, 2006.

Liu, Jung-Chao. *China's Fertilizer Economy.* Chicago: Aldine, 1970.

Liu, Ta-chung. *China's National Income, 1931–1936: An Exploratory Study*. Washington, DC: Brookings Institution, 1946.

Liu, Ta-chung, and Kung-chia Yeh. *The Economy of the Chinese Mainland: National Income and Economic Development, 1933–1959*. Princeton, NJ: Princeton University Press, 1965.

Louis, Wm. Roger. *British Strategy in the Far East, 1919–1939*. Oxford: Clarendon Press, 1971.

———. "Introduction." In *Oxford History of the British Empire*, vol. 4: *The Twentieth Century*, edited by Judith M. Brown and Wm. Roger Louis, pp. 1–46. Oxford: Oxford University Press, 1999.

Lu Xun 魯迅. *Selected Works*. 3rd ed., vols. 3 and 4. Beijing: Foreign Languages Press, 1980.

Lyons, Thomas P. *China Maritime Customs and China's Trade Statistics, 1859–1948*. Trumansburg, NY: Willowcreek, 2003.

Ma Yinchu 馬寅初. *Woguo guanshui wenti* 我國關稅問題 (Our country's tariff problem). Shanghai: Shangwu yinshuguan, 1927.

Maddison, Angus. Statistics on the World Population, GDP, and Per Capita GDP, 1–2008 AD, 2010 version, http://www.ggdc.net/maddison/oriindex.htm

Maier, Charles S. *In Search of Stability: Explorations in Historical Political Economy*. Cambridge: Cambridge University Press, 1987.

Mao Dun. *Spring Silkworms, and Other Stories*. Translated by Sidney Shapiro. 2nd ed. Beijing: Foreign Languages Press, 1979.

Marshall, Jonathan. "Opium and the Politics of Gangsterism in Nationalist China, 1927–1945." *Bulletin of Concerned Asian Scholars* 8, no. 3 (July–Sept. 1976): 19–48.

Martin, Bernd. *Die Deutsche Beraterschaft in China 1927–1938: Militär-Wirtschaft-Aussenpolitik*. Düsseldorf: Droste, 1981.

Martin, W. A. P. *Fuguo ce* 富國策 (Strategy for enriching the country). Translated by Wang Fengzao 汪風藻. Beijing: Tongwen guan, 1880.

Mazumdar, Sucheta. *Sugar and Society in China: Peasants, Technology, and the World Market*. Cambridge, MA: Harvard University Asia Center, 1998.

Mitter, Rana. *China's War with Japan, 1937–1945: The Struggle for Survival*. London: Allen Lane, 2013.

Mommsen, Wolfgang, and Jürgen Osterhammel. *Imperialism and After: Continuities and Discontinuities*. London: German Historical Institute, 1986.

Muhse, Albert C. "Taxation of Foreign and Domestic Goods in China." *Journal of Political Economy* 43, no. 2 (Apr. 1935): 226–45.

Myers, Ramon H. *The Chinese Peasant Economy: Agricultural Development in Hopei and Shantung, 1890–1949*. Cambridge, MA: Harvard University Press, 1970.

———. "The Chinese State during the Nationalist Era." In *The Modern Chinese State*, edited by David Shambaugh, pp. 42–72. Cambridge: Cambridge University Press, 2000.

Nakamura, Takafusa. "Japan's Economic Thrust into North China, 1933–1938: Formation of the North China Development Corporation." Translated by Robert Angel. In *The Chinese and the Japanese: Essays in Political and Cultural Interactions*, edited by Akira Iriye, pp. 220–53. Princeton, NJ: Princeton University Press, 1983.

Nehring, Holger. "The Paradoxes of State-Building: Transnational Expertise and the Income Tax Debates in the United States and Germany, c. 1880–1914." In *Global Debates about Taxation: Political Legitimacy and Transnational History,* edited by Holger Nehring and Florian Schui, pp. 97–115. London: Palgrave Macmillan, 2007.

Nehring, Holger, and Florian Schui. "Introduction: Global Debates about Taxation— Transfers of Ideas, the Challenge of Political Legitimacy and the Paradoxes of State-Building." In *Global Debates about Taxation: Political Legitimacy and Transnational History,* edited by Holger Nehring and Florian Schui, pp. 1–17. London: Palgrave Macmillan, 2007.

Neumann, Franz. *Behemoth: The Structure and Practice of National Socialism.* London: Victor Gollancz, 1942.

Notar, Beth E. "Viewing Currency Chaos: Paper Money for Advertising, Ideology, and Resistance in Republican China." In *Defining Modernity: Guomindang Rhetorics of a New China, 1920–1970,* edited by Terry Bodenhorn, pp. 123–49. Ann Arbor: Center for Chinese Studies, University of Michigan, 2002.

Osterhammel, Jürgen. *Britischer Imperialismus im Fernen Osten: Strukturen der Durchdringung und einheimischer Widerstand auf dem chinesischen Markt 1932–1937.* Bochum: Brockmeyer, 1983.

Paauw, Douglas S. "Chinese National Expenditures in the Nanking Period." *Far Eastern Quarterly* 12, no. 1 (Nov. 1952): 3–26.

———. "The Kuomintang and Economic Stagnation, 1928–1937." *Journal of Asian Studies* 16, no. 2 (Feb. 1957): 213–20.

Perkins, Dwight H. *Agricultural Development in China, 1368–1968.* Chicago: Aldine, 1969.

Pomeranz, Kenneth L. *The Great Divergence: Europe, China, and the Making of the Modern World Economy.* Princeton, NJ: Princeton University Press, 2000.

———. "Issues in the History of Consumption in China: Notes on an Emerging Field." Paper presented at the Fiftieth Anniversary Conference for the Institute of Modern History, Academia Sinica, Taiwan, 2005.

Porter, Bernard. "Friendly Fire." *London Review of Books* 30, no. 4 (21 Feb. 2008): 9–10.

Pratt, John. *War and Politics in China.* London: Jonathan Cape, 1943.

Qing gongye bu ganzhe tangye kexue yanjiusuo, Guangdong sheng nongye kexueyuan 轻工业部甘蔗糖业科学研究所，广东省农业科学院, ed. *Zhongguo ganzhe caipei xue* 中国甘蔗栽培学 (Cutting and preparing China's sugar beet). Beijing: Nongye chubanshe, 1985.

Rawski, Thomas. *Economic Growth in Pre-War China.* Berkeley: University of California Press, 1989.

Rawski, Thomas, and Lillian Li, eds. *Chinese History in Economic Perspective.* Berkeley: University of California Press, 1992.

Reinhardt, Anne. *Navigating Semi-Colonialism: Shipping, Sovereignty, and Nation-Building in China, 1860–1937.* Cambridge, MA: Harvard University Asia Center, forthcoming.

Reinhart, Carmen M., and Kenneth S. Rogoff. "Growth in a Time of Debt." *American Economic Review* 100, no. 2 (2010): 573–78.

———. *This Time It's Different: Eight Centuries of Financial Folly*. Princeton, NJ: Princeton University Press, 2009.

Reisner, John. "Modern Commercial Fertilizers in China." *American Fertilizer* 54 (7 May 1921): 54–57.

Richardson, Philip. *Economic Change in China, c. 1800–1950*. Cambridge: Cambridge University Press, 1999.

Shai, Aron. *Britain and China, 1941–1947: Imperial Momentum*. London: Macmillan, 1984.

———. *Origins of the War in the East: Britain, China and Japan 1937–1939*. London: Croom Helm, 1976.

———. "Was There a Far Eastern Munich?" *Journal of Contemporary History* 9, no. 3 (July 1974): 161–69.

Shambaugh, David, ed. *The Modern Chinese State*. Cambridge: Cambridge University Press, 2000.

Shan Guanchu 单冠初. Zhongguo shoufu guanshui zizhuquan de licheng 中国收复 关税自主权的历程 (China's process of regaining tariff autonomy). Shanghai: Xuelin chubanshe, 2004.

Shanghai haiguanzhi bianji weiyuanhui 上海海关志编辑委员会 (Editorial Commission of the Shanghai Maritime Customs Gazetteer), ed. *Shanghai haiguanzhi* 上海 海关志 (Gazetteer of the Shanghai Maritime Customs). Shanghai: Shanghai shehui kexue chubanshe, 1997.

Sheehan, Brett. *Trust in Troubled Times: Money, Banks and State-Society Relations in Republican Tianjin*. Cambridge, MA: Harvard University Press, 2003.

Shen, T. H. *Agricultural Resources of China*. Ithaca, NY: Cornell University Press, 1951.

Shih, Paul K. T., ed. *The Strenuous Decade: China's Nation-Building Effort, 1927–1937*. Jamaica, NY: St. John's University Press, 1970.

Skinner, G. William. "Marketing and Social Structure in Rural China," Parts 1, 2, and 3. *Journal of Asian Studies* 24, no. 1 (Nov. 1964): 3–44; no. 2 (Feb. 1965): 195–228; no. 3 (May 1965): 363–99.

Slack, Edward. *Opium, State, and Society: China's Narco-Economy and the Guomindang, 1924–1927*. Honolulu: University of Hawai'i Press, 2001.

Soong, T. V. (Song Ziwen). "Opening Address to the National Economic Conference." In *The China Year Book: 1929–1930*, edited by H. G. W. Woodhead. Tianjin: Tientsin Press, 1929.

Spence, Jonathan. *The Search for Modern China*. 2nd ed. New York: Norton, 1999.

Stilwell, General Joseph W. *The Stilwell Papers*. Edited by Theodore H. White. New York: Da Capo, 1991. First published in 1948.

Strauss, Julia. *Strong Institutions in Weak Polities: State Building in Republican China, 1927–1940*. Oxford: Clarendon Press, 1998.

Stross, Randall E. *The Stubborn Earth: American Agriculturalists on Chinese Soil, 1898– 1937*. Berkeley: University of California Press, 1986.

Su, Frank Kai-Ming, and Alvin Barber. "China's Tariff Autonomy: Fact or Myth?" *Far Eastern Survey* 5, no. 12 (3 June 1936): 115–22.

Sun, E-tu Zen. "The Finance Ministry (Hubu) and Its Relationship to the Private Economy in Qing Times." In *To Achieve Security and Wealth: The Qing Imperial State and the Economy, 1644–1911*, edited by Jane Kate Leonard and John R. Watts, pp. 9–20. Ithaca, NY: Cornell East Asia Program, 1992.

Sun Ruoyi 孫若怡. "'Guanshui tebie huiyi' zhong youguan fujiashui ji shuilü wenti zhi taolun" "關稅特別會議"中有關附加稅及稅率問題之討論 (Discussions about the tariff surtax rate during the Beijing Tariff Conference). In *"Haiguan yu jindai lishi" huiyi shouce* "海关与近代历史"会议手册 (Conference manual: "The Maritime Customs and modern Chinese history"), edited by Zhang Sheng 张生 and Jiang Liangqin 姜良芹. Nanjing, 4–7 September 2005. Unpublished manuscript.

Sun Xiufu 孙修福, ed. *Zhongguo jindai haiguan gaoji zhiguan nianbiao* 中国近代海关高级职员年表 (Annual register of high-ranking officials in the modern Chinese Maritime Customs Service). Beijing: Zhongguo haiguan chubanshe, 2004.

Sun Zhongshan 孙中山 (Sun Yat-sen). *The International Development of China*. London: Hutchison, 1928. First published in 1922.

———. *San min chu i: The Three Principles of the People*. Shanghai: China Committee, Institute of Pacific Relations, 1927.

———. *Sanmin zhuyi* 三民主義 (The three principles of the people). N.p.: Zhengzhong shuju, 1946. First published in 1919.

Tagliacozzo, Eric. *Secret Trades, Porous Borders: Smuggling and States along a Southeast Asian Frontier 1865–1919*. New Haven, CT: Yale University Press, 2005.

Tawney, R. H. *Land and Labour in China*. London: George Allen and Unwin, 1934.

Thai, Philip. "Smuggling, State-Building, and Political Economy in Coastal China, 1927–1949." PhD diss., Stanford University, 2013.

Tien, Hung Mao. *Government and Politics in KMT China, 1927–37*. Stanford, CA: Stanford University Press, 1972.

Tilly, Charles, ed. *The Formation of National States in Western Europe*. Princeton, NJ: Princeton University Press, 1975.

———. "War Making and State Making as Organized Crime." In *Bringing the State Back In*, edited by Peter B. Evans, Dietrich Rueschemeyer, and Theda Skocpol, pp. 169–91. Cambridge: Cambridge University Press, 1985.

Tooze, Adam. *Statistics and the German State, 1900–1945: The Making of Modern Economic Knowledge*. Cambridge: Cambridge University Press, 2001.

Topik, Stephen, Carlos Marichal, and Zephyr L. Frank, eds. *From Silver to Cocaine: Latin American Commodity Chains and the Building of the World Economy, 1500–2000*. Durham, NC: Duke University Press, 2006.

Trescott, Paul B. "Economics at China's Nankai University, 1926–1949." Paper presented at the meeting of the History of Economics Society, South Bend, IN, June 1995.

———. *Jingji Xue: The History of the Introduction of Western Economic Ideas into China, 1850–1950*. Hong Kong: Chinese University Press of Hong Kong, 2007.

Trotter, Ann. *Britain and East Asia, 1933–1937*. Cambridge: Cambridge University Press, 1975.

Tuchman, Barbara. *Stilwell and the American Experience in China, 1911–1945*. London: Phoenix, 2001. First published in 1970.

Tyler, W. F. *Pulling Strings in China*. London: Constable, 1929.

van de Ven, Hans. *Breaking with the Past: The Maritime Customs Service and the Global Origins of Modernity in China.* New York: Columbia University Press, 2014.

———. "Military and Financial Reform in the Late Qing and Early Republic." In Jindaishi yanjiusuo shehui jingji shi zu 近代史研究所社会经济史组 (Section for Social and Economic History, Institute of Modern History). *Caizheng yu jindai lishi* 财政与近代历史 (Finance and modern history), pp. 17–103. Taibei: Zhongyang yanjiuyuan jindaishi yanjiusuo, 1999.

———. "The Onrush of Modern Globalization in China." In *Globalization in World History*, edited by A. G. Hopkins, pp. 167–93. London: Pimlico, 2002.

———. "Public Finance and the Rise of Warlordism." *Modern Asian Studies* 30, no. 4 (1996): 829–68.

———. *War and Nationalism in China, 1925–1945.* London: Routledge Curzon, 2003.

Vries, Jan de, and Adrianus Maria van der Woude. *The First Modern Economy: Success, Failure, and Perseverance of the Dutch Economy, 1500–1815.* Cambridge: Cambridge University Press, 1997.

Wagner, Wilhelm. *Die Chinesische Landwirtschaft.* Berlin: Paul Parey, 1926.

Wakeman, Frederick, Jr. "The Civil Society and Public Sphere Debate: Western Reflections on Chinese Political Culture." *Modern China* 19, no. 2 (Apr. 1993): 103–38.

———. *Policing Shanghai, 1927–1937.* Berkeley: University of California Press, 1995.

———. "A Revisionist View of the Nanjing Decade: Confucian Fascism." *China Quarterly*, no. 150 (1997): 395–432.

———. *Spymaster: Dai Li and the Chinese Secret Service.* Berkeley: University of California Press, 2003.

Wang Wenju 王文舉. *Lanyu haiguan sishi nian* 濫竽海關四十年 (Pretending in the Customs for forty years). Taibei: N.p., 1967.

Wang, Yeh-chien. "Secular Trends of Rice Prices in the Yangzi Delta, 1638–1935," pp. 35–68. In *Chinese History in Economic Perspective*, edited by Thomas Rawski and Lillian Li. Berkeley: University of California Press, 1992.

Wang, Y. C. (Yi-chu). *Chinese Intellectuals and the West.* Chapel Hill, NC: University of North Carolina Press, 1966.

Wang, Yuru. "Economic Development in China." In *The Chinese Economy in the Early Twentieth Century: Recent Studies*, edited by Tim Wright, pp. 58–77. Basingstoke, UK: Macmillan, 1992.

Watson, Ernest. *The Principal Articles of Chinese Commerce.* Shanghai: Statistical Department, Inspectorate General of Customs, 1930.

Wasserstrom, Jeffrey N., ed. *Twentieth-Century China: New Approaches.* London: Routledge, 2003.

Watson, Ernest. *The Principal Articles of Chinese Commerce.* Shanghai: Inspectorate General of Customs, 1931.

Wei Yuan 魏源. *Wei Yuan ji* 魏源集 (Collected works of Wei Yuan). Beijing: Zhonghua shuju, 1983.

White, Benjamin G. "'A Question of Principle with Political Implications': Investigating Collaboration in the Chinese Maritime Customs Service, 1945–1946." *Modern Asian Studies* 44, no. 3 (2010): 517–46.

White, Theodore H., and Annalee Jacoby. *Thunder out of China*. New York: Da Capo, 1980. First published in 1946.

Wilbur, C. Martin. *Sun Yat-sen: Frustrated Patriot*. New York: Cambridge University Press, 1976.

Will, Pierre-Etienne, and R. Bin Wong, eds. *Nourish the People: The State Civilian Granary System in China 1650–1850*. Ann Arbor: University of Michigan Center for Chinese Studies, 1991.

Williams, Jim. "Corruption in the Chinese Maritime Customs Service." M.Phil. diss., University of Bristol, 2008.

Woodhead, H. G. W., ed. *The China Year Book*. Vols. *1923, 1929–1930, 1931, 1933, 1938*, and *1939*. Tianjin: Tientsin Press, 1923, 1930; Shanghai: *North-China Daily News and Herald*, 1931, 1933, 1938, 1939.

Wright, Stanley F. *China's Struggle for Tariff Autonomy 1843–1928*. Shanghai: Kelly and Walsh, 1938; reprint, Taibei: Cheng-Wen, 1966. Reprint ed. is cited.

———. *The Collection and Disposal of the Maritime and Native Customs Revenue since the Revolution of 1911*. Shanghai: Statistical Department of the Inspectorate General of Customs, 1927, reprint, Taibei: Cheng-Wen, 1966. Reprint ed. is cited.

Wu Jingping 吴景平. *Song Ziwen pingzhuan* 宋子文评传 (A critical biography of Song Ziwen). Fuzhou: Fujian renmin chubanshe, 1992.

Xu, Guoqi. *China and the Great War: China's Pursuit of a New National Identity and Internationalization*. Cambridge: Cambridge University Press, 2005.

Yeh, Wen-hsin, ed. *Becoming Chinese: Passages to Modernity and Beyond*. Berkeley: University of California Press, 2000.

Young, Arthur N. *China and the Helping Hand, 1937–1945*. Cambridge, MA: Harvard University Press, 1963.

———. *China's Nation-Building Effort, 1927–1937*. Stanford, CA: Hoover Institution Press, 1971.

———. *China's Wartime Finance and Inflation, 1937–1945*. Cambridge, MA: Harvard University Press, 1965.

Zanasi, Margherita. *Saving the Nation: Economic Modernity in Republican China*. Chicago: University of Chicago Press, 2006.

Zelin, Madeline. *The Magistrate's Tael: Rationalizing Fiscal Reform in Eighteenth-Century Ch'ing China*. Berkeley: University of California Press, 1984.

Zhao Fengtian 趙豐田. *Wanqing wushinian jingji sixiang shi* 晚清五十年經濟思想史 (History of fifty years of economic thought during the late Qing). Beiping: Yanjing xueshe chubanshe, 1939.

Zhang, Fuyun. "Chang Fu-yun: Reformer of the Chinese Maritime Customs." Berkeley: University of California Regional Oral History Office, 1987. Unpublished manuscript.

Zhang Sheng 张生, and Jiang Liangqin 姜良芹, eds. *"Haiguan yu jindai lishi" huiyi shouce* "海关与近代历史"会议手册 (Conference manual: "The Maritime Customs and modern Chinese history"). Nanjing, 4–7 September 2005. Unpublished manuscript.

Zhang Youyi 章有义, ed. *Zhongguo jindai nongyeshi ziliao* 中国近代农业史资料

(Materials on the history of modern Chinese agriculture), vol. 3: *1927–1937*. Beijing: Sanlian, 1957.

Zheng Beijun 郑备军. *Zhongguo jindai lijin zhidu yanjiu* 中国近代厘金制度研究 (Research on the transit tax system in modern China). Beijing: Zhongguo caizheng jingji chubanshe, 2004.

Zheng Youkui 鄭友葵. *Woguo guanshui zizhu hou jinkou shuilü bianqian* 我國關稅 自主後進口稅率變遷 (Fluctuations in import tariff rates after our country's resumption of tariff autonomy). Shanghai: Shangwu yinshuguan, 1939.

Zhongguo jindai jingjishi ziliao congkan bianji weiyuanhui 中国近代经济史资料 丛刊编辑委员会, ed. *Zhongguo haiguan yu zhongFa zhanzheng: Diguozhuyi yu Zhongguo haiguan ziliao zongbian zhiyi* 中国海关与中法战争: 帝国主义与中国 海关资料丛编之一 (The Chinese Maritime Customs and the Sino-French War: Imperialism and the Chinese Maritime Customs materials series). Beijing: Zhonghua shuju, 1983.

Zhongguo yinhang zonghang, Zhongguo di'er lishi dang'anguan 中国银行总行，中 国第二历史档案馆, eds. *Zhongguo yinhangshi ziliao huibian* 中国银行史资料汇 编, 上遍 (1929–1949), 三 (Compilation of materials on the history of the Bank of China, Part 1 [1929–1949]). vol. 3. Beijing: Dang'an chubanshe, 1991.

Zhou Zhengqing 周正庆. *Zhongguo tangye de fazhan yu shehui shenghuo yanjiu: 16 shiji zhongye dao 20 shiji 30 niandai* 中国糖业的发展与社会生活研究: 16世纪中叶到 20世纪30年代 (Research on the development of the Chinese sugar industry and social life: From the middle of the sixteenth century until the 1930s). Shanghai: Shanghai guji chubanshe, 2006.

Zhu Boneng 朱博能. "Zhongguo zhi tangye ji qi tongzhi" 中國之糖業及其統制 (China's sugar industry and its control). *Dongfang zazhi* 東方雜誌 33, no. 3 (1 Feb. 1936): 59–65.

Index

Harvard East Asian Monographs
(most recent titles)